P9-DDU-854

SELECTIONS

from

EARLY GREEK PHILOSOPHY

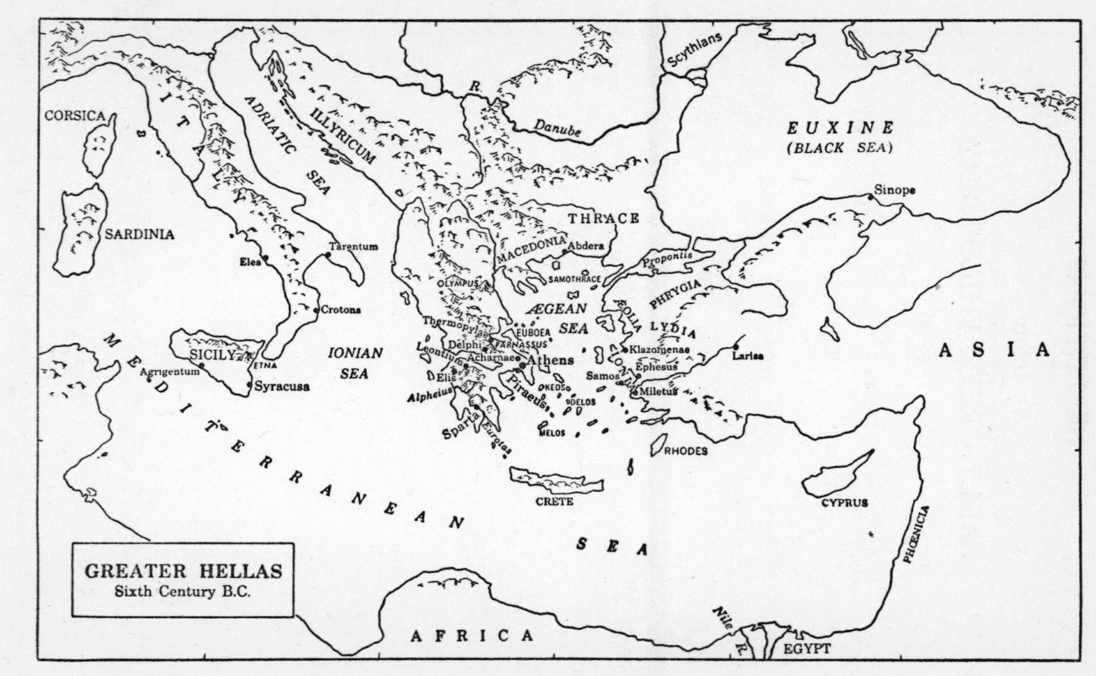

GREATER HELLAS
Sixth Century B.C.

SELECTIONS
from
EARLY GREEK PHILOSOPHY

Edited by

Milton C. Nahm

Bryn Mawr College

Third Edition

APPLETON-CENTURY-CROFTS, INC.

New York

MANUFACTURED IN THE UNITED STATES OF AMERICA

585-10

PREFACE

The fragments of early Greek philosophy contained in this edition throw light upon the religion and culture of the period and upon the development of Greek science, and offer assistance in the explanation of portions of the later philosophy of antiquity. Interesting and valuable as such uses of early Greek philosophy may be, however, it must still be recognized that the ultimate reason for a return to sources lies in the scope and value of the problems raised and in the technique displayed by the early thinkers in attempting the solution to these problems.

In the period from Thales of Miletus to the Atomists, a speculation new to the world was begun and developed. Moreover, most of the problems of philosophy were raised and to them many solutions were offered, to which later philosophers have given more complete expression. For this speculation, beginning, as Aristotle said, "in wonder," set as its primary problem the reduction of the multiplicity of fact to simplicity of explanatory principle. From this central problem, early Greek thought extended its province to include the explanation of sensation and perception, the construction of cosmologies, hypotheses upon morality, evolution and "natural law."

Our purpose in *Selections from Early Greek Philoso-*

phy has been to make available in compact and usable form translations of the source-material of this period from Thales through the Atomists. The inclusion of this speculation in courses in the history of philosophy has presented difficulties which arise not alone because of the importance of the problems treated by the early thinkers but because of the fragmentary state of the source-material itself. The introductions here offered to each collection of sources purport to treat concisely the problems raised and the limitations and value of the solutions offered. Included also are biographical data sufficient to place the man in his time and to give the most important facts known of his life.

No device of editing can overcome the difficulty imposed by the fragmentary state of early Greek philosophy. Nevertheless, the criticism and commentary of the early philosophers offered by Plato, Aristotle, Theophrastus and the doxographical tradition in general are the indispensable data with which the student must begin. In this edition, the commentary is grouped in categories, that is to say, topically, under the headings of cosmology, perception, biology, etc. It is hoped that such an arrangement will assist the student in following the elaboration and application of the philosophical position held by each man. Further to assist the student, the introductions contain references by letter and number to the passages used for explanation and interpretation.

For the translation of Democritus, portions of which have not hitherto been available in English, I am indebted to Dr. Gordon H. Clark of the Department of Philosophy of the University of Pennsylvania. The translations of the other fragments and doxographical material are those of Dr. Arthur Fairbanks, published in *The First Philosophers of Greece.* Permission to use this material and the chapter from *Greek Thinkers* by Theodor Gomperz was given by John Murray and Charles Scribners' Sons. Footnotes indicate the source of translations supplementary to those prepared by Dr. Clark and those appearing in *The First Philosophers of Greece.*

NOTE TO THE THIRD EDITION

In preparing the third edition of *Selections from Early Greek Philosophy* for publication, I have taken the opportunity to bridge a considerable gap in the philosophical materials accessible to the student of Greek thought prior to the *Dialogues* of Plato. The volume now includes, in the fragments of the writings and conversations of the Sophists, as well as in the valuable commentary upon individual thinkers and the philosophical movement as a whole, a considerable subject matter which follows directly in the tradition of speculation which began in Miletus and which, in turn, has become integral to the tradition of western thought. Much of this material, although translated, has remained in scattered and somewhat inaccessible sources; some has remained untranslated. For the more advanced student in philosophy, the Sophists have been available for complete study in Diels' *Die Fragmente der Vorsokratiker;* but even for him it may be of value to observe the problems raised by the principal Sophistic thinkers in relation to the philosophy in which they originated, as well as in relation to that to which it gave rise. For the less advanced student, the presentation of the philosophies of men of such stature as Protagoras and Gorgias will always have a value, and one the more readily discernible, it may be suggested, once the fragments of their thought are withdrawn, so far as is possible, from the overshadowing context of Plato's writings.

The appearance of the new edition at this time owes much to Professor Alister Cameron's interest in the field of early Greek philosophy. Following my suggestion that he translate the Sophists, Professor Cameron, of the Department of Classics at the University of Cincinnati, generously agreed to defer other research projects in order to make translations of Sophistic material not elsewhere available. I should like to express my gratitude to Professor Cameron and to Miss Elizabeth Caskey, who assisted him in the translations.

The scope of Sophistic writings and the range of interest evident in the fragments have made it necessary to omit a considerable portion of the collected material. The selections printed here have been chosen primarily for their intrinsic philosophical worth and, secondarily, for their importance in the history of ideas. Fortunately, even in the case of Sophistic rhetoric, the two values are rarely incompatible. Restrictions of space have led, however, to certain omissions—particularly that of the work of Antiphon the Sophist—which I regret. The omission of the Encyclopaedists is of less consequence, inasmuch as the more important extant theories of men like Hippias are readily accessible in Plato's *Dialogues*.

The map of Greater Hellas which appears in this edition is primarily intended to give the location of centers of philosophical speculation, as well as the birthplaces of the philosophers whose work appears in this book.

I should like to acknowledge the kind permission of the Clarendon Press (Oxford) to include translations from Benjamin Jowett's *The Dialogues of Plato* and *The Works of Aristotle Translated into English,* edited by J. A. Smith and W. D. Ross; and of the President and Fellows of Harvard College to include translations from the following volumes of the Loeb Classical Library: Diogenes Laertius' *Lives of the Eminent Philosophers,* translated by R. D. Hicks; Sextus Empiricus' *Outlines of Pyrrhonism* and *Against the Physicists,* translated by R. D. Hicks; and Philostratus' *The Lives of the Sophists,* translated by Wilmer Cave Wright.

M. C. N.

Bryn Mawr College
May 20, 1947

[illegible] the [illegible] translation of the [illegible] (Kanjur) [illegible] from [illegible] *The Legends of* [illegible] [illegible] translated into English, edited by [illegible] W. D. [illegible] and of the [illegible] and [illegible] in [illegible] and [illegible] from the [illegible] the [illegible] Life of the [illegible] [illegible] [illegible] the [illegible] translated by William Aldis Wright.

M. E. M.

[illegible]

CONTENTS

LIST OF REFERENCES AND ABBREVIATIONS

Aet. *Plac.* *Aetii de placitis reliquae*

Alex. *Meteor.* Alexander of Aphrodisias, *Meteorology*

Aristides *Orationes*

Aristotle *de Anima, de Caelo, de Generatione et Corruptione, Metaphysics, Physics, Rhetoric, de Sophisticis Elenchis*

Diogenes Laertius *Lives and Opinions of Eminent Philosophers*

Dox. *Doxographi Graeci* by Hermann Diels

Epiph. *Haer. Epiphanii varia excerpta*

Eusebius *Praeparatio Evangelica*

Herm. I.G.P. *Hermiae irrisio gentilium philosophorum; in Plat. Phaedrum*

Hipp. *Phil. Hippolyti philosophumena* (also called *Refutatio omnium haeresium*)

Isocr. *Or.* Isocrates' *Orationes*

Philostratus *The Lives of the Sophists*

Plato *Apology, Cratylus, Gorgias, Laws, Meno, Parmenides, Phaedo, Protagoras, Republic, Sophist, Theaatetus*

Plut. Plutarch *de Adult. et Am., de glor. Athen., Solon, Stromateis, Symp. Quaest.*

Sextus Empiricus *Adversus Mathematicos, Outlines of Pyrrhonism*

Simplicius *de Caelo, Commentary on the Physics*

Stobaeos *Florilegium, Eclogae physicae*

Theophrastus *Opera*

INTRODUCTION

INTRODUCTION [1]

All beginnings are obscure, whether owing to their minuteness or their apparent insignificance. Where they do not escape perception, they are liable to elude observation. The sources of history, too, can only be tracked at a foot-pace. They must be followed to their fount, like the current of a stream which springs in a mountain fastness. Such steps or paces are called inferences. They are of two kinds, according as they proceed from causes or from effects. In the second case, we try to infer the existence and the nature of causes from the existence and the nature of effects. Inferences of that type are indispensable, but frequently fallacious. For though every cause, taken by itself, produces the same invariable effect, yet the converse proposition does not by any means hold good. Each effect is not invariably the product of one and the same cause. The condition known as "plurality of causes" plays an important part in the intellectual no less than in the physical universe. The contrary process yields more trustworthy results. It starts from the causes, from the series of great and tangible factors, plainly manifest or readily to be found, which must have influenced the events to be accounted for, and in which the degree of such influence is the sole object of doubt. In the present instance, where we are dealing with the higher intel-

[1] From Theodor Gomperz *Greek Thinkers,* vol. 1, pp. 3–42. Reprinted by permission of John Murray, and Charles Scribner's Sons.

lectual life of a nation, the first place is claimed by its geographical conditions and the peculiar character of its homes.

Hellas is a sea-girt mountain-land. The poverty of her soil corresponds to the narrowness of her river-valleys. And here we find the first clue to some of the essential features of Hellenic evolution proper. It is clear, for instance, that a permanent home and a steady and manifold care and attention were offered to any seeds of civilization which might be deposited in her soil. Her mountain-barriers served her in the office of stone walls, breaking the force of the storm of conquest which sweeps unchecked across the plains. Each hilly canton was a potential seat of culture. Each could develop a separate type of that strongly marked individualism, which was ultimately to prove so favourable to the rich and many-sided civilization of Greece, so fatal to the political concentration of her powers. The country was full of piquant contrasts. Her Arcadia—an inland canton, sunk in torpid provincialism—was matched at the opposite extreme by the extent and curvature of the coast. Her seaboard was larger than Spain's, her mainland smaller than Portugal's. Other conditions, too, fostered this variety of natural gifts. The most diverse trades and professions were practised in the closest proximity. Seamen and shepherds, hunters and husbandmen, flourished side by side, and the fusion of their families produced in later generations a sum of talents and aptitudes complementary to each other. Again, the good fairies who presided at the birth of Greece could have laid no more salutary blessing in her cradle than the "poverty which was ever her familiar friend." It worked powerfully in three ways for the advancement of her civilization. It acted as a spur to compel her to exert all her powers; it served as a further defence against invasion, for the comparatively poor country must have seemed but indifferent booty—a fact noted in connection with Attica by the most philosophical historian of antiquity; and last, and chiefly, it lent a forcible impulse to commerce, navigation, emigration, and the foundation of colonies.

The bays that offer the best harbourage on the Greek peninsula open towards the east, and the islands and islets, with which that region is thickly sown, afford, as it were, a series of stepping-stones to the ancient seats of Asiatic civilization. Greece may be said to look east and south. Her back is turned to the north and west, with their semi-barbaric conditions. Another circumstance of quite exceptional good fortune may be ranged with these natural advantages. There was Greece in her infancy on the one side, and the immemorial civilizations on the other: who was to ply between them? The link was found—as it were by deliberate selection—in those hardy adventurers of the sea, the merchant-people of Phoenicia, a nation politically of no account, but full of daring and eager for gain. Thus it happened that the Greeks acquired the elements of culture from Babylon and Egypt without paying the forfeit of independence. The benefits of this ordinance are obvious. The favoured country enjoyed a steadier rate of progress, a more unbroken evolution, a comparative immunity from the sacrifice of her national resources. And if further proof be required, take the fate of the Celts and Germans, whom Rome enslaved at the moment that she civilized; or take the sad lot of the savage tribes of today, who receive the blessing of civilization at the hands of almighty Europe, and wear it too often as a curse.

Still, the determining influence in the intellectual life of Greece must be sought in her colonial system. Colonies were founded at all times, and under every form of government. The Monarchy, a period of perpetual conflict, frequently witnessed the spectacle of settled inhabitants giving way to immigrating tribes, and seeking a new home beyond the seas. The Oligarchy, which rested entirely on the permanent alliance between noble birth and territorial possession, was often constrained to expel the "pauvre gentilhomme," the type and symbol of disorder, and to furnish him with fresh estates in foreign parts, whither he would speedily be followed by further victims of the incessant party strife. Meantime, the growth of the maritime trade of Greece, the flourishing condition of her industries, and her increasing population, soon made it necessary to establish fixed commercial stations, an uninterrupted supply of raw material, and safe channels for the importation of food. The same outlets were utilized, chiefly under the Democracy, to relieve the indigent poor and to draft off the surplus population. Thus, at an early period, there arose that vast circle of Greek plantations which stretched from the homes of the Cossacks on the Don to the oases of the Sahara, and from the eastern shore of the Black Sea to the coast-line of Spain. Great Greece and Greater Greece,—if the first name belong to the Hellenic portion of Southern Italy, the second might well be given to the sum of these settlements outside. The mere number and diversity of the colonies practically ensured the prospect that any seeds of civilization would happen on suitable soil, and this prospect was widened and brightened to an incalculable degree by the nature of the settlements and the manner of their foundation. Their sites were selected at those points of the coast which offered the best facilities for successful commercial enterprise. The emigrants themselves were chiefly young men of a hardy and courageous disposition, who would bequeath their superior qualities to their numerous issue. Men of duller parts, who lived by rule and rote, were not likely to turn their backs on their homes except under stress of necessity. Again, though a single city-state took the lead in the foundation of each colony, it would frequently be reinforced by a considerable foreign contingent, and this cross-breeding of Hellenic tribes would be further extended by an admixture of non-Hellenic blood, owing to the preponderance of the men over the women among the original emigrants. Thus, every colony served the purpose of experiment. Greek and non-Greek racial elements were mixed in varying proportions, and the test was applied to their resulting powers of resistance and endurance. Local customs, tribal superstitions, and national prejudices swiftly disappeared before the better sense of the settlers. Contact with foreign civilizations, however imperfectly developed, could not but enlarge their mental horizon to a very appreciable degree. The average of capacity rose by leaps and bounds, and the average of intellect was heightened by its constant engagement in new and difficult tasks. Merit counted for more than descent. A man there was a man; good work could command a good wage, and poor work meant a hard bed and indifferent protection. The whole system of economic, political, and social life cried out to be reorganized and reformed, and in these circumstances the force of mere tradition and the reign of unintelligent routine were involved in rapid decline. True, some of the settlements succumbed to the attacks of hostile residents; others, again, were so far outnumbered by the natives that their individuality was gradually absorbed. But from first to last the communication of the colonies with their mother-city and mother-country—a communication fostered by religious ties and frequently strengthened by later arrivals—was sufficiently intimate to preserve in all its parts the reciprocal benefits which proved so eminently fruitful. Greece found in her colonies the great playground of her intellect. There she proved her talents in every variety of circumstances, and there she was able to train them to the height of their latent powers. Her colonial life retained for centuries its fresh and buoyant spirit. The daughter-cities in most respects outstripped their mother in the race. To them can be traced nearly all the great innovations, and the time was to come when they would steep themselves in intellectual pursuits as well, when the riddles of the world and of human life were to find a permanent home and enduring curiosity in their midst.

2. There is a period in Greek history which bears a most striking resemblance to the close of our own Middle Ages, when the repetition of similar causes produced similar effects.

On the threshold of modern Europe stands the era of the great discoverers, and the geographical limits of the Greek horizon at this time were likewise wonderfully extended. On the far east and west of the world, as it was then known, the outline emerged from the mist. Precise and definite knowledge replaced the obscurity of legend. Shortly after 800 B. C., the eastern shore of the Black Sea began to be colonized by Milesians; Sinope was founded in 785, and Trapezunt about thirty years later. Soon after the middle of the same century, Eubœa and Corinth sent out the first Greek settlers to Sicily, where Syracuse was founded in 734 B. C., and before the century's end the ambition and enterprise of Miletus had taken fast foothold at the mouths of the Nile. Three conclusions are involved in the fact of this impulse to expansion. It points to a rapid growth of population on the Greek peninsula and in the older colonies. It presumes a considerable development of Greek industry and commerce; and, finally, it serves to measure the progress in ship-building and in kindred arts. Take navigation, for instance. Where vessels formerly had hugged the shore, and had not ventured in deep waters, now they boldly crossed the sea. The mercantile marine was protected by men-of-war. Seaworthy battleships came into use with raised decks and three rows of oars, the first of them being built for the Samians in 705 B. C. Naval engagements were fought as early as 664 B. C., so that the sea acquired the utmost significance in the civilization of Hellas for the commerce of peace and war. At the same time, the progress of industry was fostered by a notable innovation. A current coinage was created. The "bullocks" of hoary antiquity and the copper "kettles" and "tripods" of a later date successively passed into desuetude, and the precious metals replaced these rougher makeshifts as measures of value and tokens of exchange. Babylonian and Egyptian merchants had long since familiarized the market with silver and gold in the form of bars and rings, and the Babylonians had even introduced the official stamp as a guarantee of standard and weight. A convenient shape was now added to the qualities of worth and durability which make gold and silver the most practical symbols of exchange, and the metals were coined for current use. This invention, borrowed from Lydia about 700 B.C. by the Phocæans of Ionia, conferred remarkable benefits on commerce. It facilitated intercourse and extended its bounds, and its effects may be compared with those of the bill of exchange, introduced in Europe by Jewish and Lombardy merchants at the close of the Middle Ages. Similar, if not greater, in effect was the change in the methods of warfare. The old exclusive service of the cavalry, which had flourished in the dearth of pastoral and corn-land as the privilege of wealthy landowners, was now reinforced by the hoplites, or heavy-armed infantry, who far exceeded the cavalry in numbers. The change was analogous—and its consequences were equal in importance—to that which enabled the armed peasantry of Switzerland to disperse the chivalry of Burgundy and Austria. New orders of the population achieved prosperity and culture, and were filled with a strong sense of self-esteem. A sturdy middle class asserted itself by the side of the old squirearchy, and bore with increasing impatience the yoke of the masterful nobles. But here, as elsewhere, the contradiction between actual conditions of strength and legal dues of prerogative became the cause of civil strife. A battle of classes broke out. It spread to the peasants, where persistent ill-usage and by no means infrequent serfdom had sown the seeds of revolt, and out of the rents and ruins of society there was hatched a brood of usurpers, who partly destroyed and partly set aside the existing order of things. They constructed in its place a form of government which, though commonly short-lived, was not without notable results. The Orthagorides, the Cypselides, the Pisistratides, a Polycrates, and many another, may be compared with the Italian tyrants of the late Middle Ages—the Medici, the Sforza, or the Visconti—precisely as the party feuds of the one epoch recall in the other the conflict between the lords and the guilds. The obscure origin and questionable title of these newly founded dynasties were discreetly veiled in the glitter of warlike undertakings, of alliances with foreign potentates, public works on a lavish scale, splendid buildings, and munificent benefactions, combined with an enhanced regard for the safety of the national sanctuaries and for the encouragement of the fine arts. But we must look deeper for the most lasting result of this *entr'acte* in history. It tranquillized party feeling; it overthrew the rule of the nobles without breaking the foundations of social welfare; it poured new wine in the old vessels, revealing unsuspected possibilities in the extant forms of the constitution. The "tyranny" served as a bridge to the system of democracy, first in a moderate, and at last in its fully developed shape.

Meantime, the stream of intellectual culture found broader and deeper channels. The ballads of the heroes, which had been sung for centuries in the halls of Ionian nobles to the accompaniment of the lyre, slowly fell into desuetude. New forms of poetry began to emerge, and with them, in some instances, the poet's personality emerged from the material of his song. Subjective poetry came into existence, as was bound to happen, when, as now, men escaped in ever-increasing numbers from the groove of hereditary conventions. The State was involved in change and vicissitude, society was governed by uncertain conditions, and individual life accordingly acquired a more adventurous complexion. Men's talents would be more sharply defined, their independent activity stimulated, their self-reliance encouraged. In civic and party business a man would play his own part, advising and blaming as counsellor or critic, and boldly giving vent among his fellows to his sentiments of expectation or disappointment, his joy, his sorrow, his anger, and his scorn. He became a unit in society, self-made for the most part, and entirely self-dependent, and would deem his private concerns of sufficient importance to display them in the light of publicity. He poured out his heart to his fellow-citizens, making them the arbiters in his love-suits and law-suits, and appealing to their sympathy in the injuries he suffered, the successes he achieved, the pleasures he enjoyed. A new spirit, too, was breathed in the older poetical forms. Myth and legend were refashioned by the masters of choric song in differing, if not in contradictory, modes. The didactic poets still aimed at system, order, and harmony in their treatment of the material, but side by side with those endeavours a manifold diversity was to be remarked, and a licence in criticism, expressing itself in a prejudice or preference in respect to this or that hero or heroine of holy tradition. Thus, the neutral tints of the background were ever more and more relieved by strong, self-conscious figures standing out from the uniform mass. Habits of free-will and feeling were created, and with them there grew the faculty of independent thought, which was constantly engaged and exercised in wider fields of speculation.

3. The Greeks were naturally keen-sighted. The faithful representation of sensible objects and occurrences constitutes one of the chief charms of the Homeric poems, and the imitation of figures and gestures by a hand that waxed in cunning now began to succeed to the arts of language and speech. Greece became the apprentice of older civilized countries, turning to Egypt above all for the paramount example of artistic instinct, natural joy, and engaging humour. But even in the limited sphere of the observation of men's ways and manners, fresh material was constantly collected. As travelling grew easier, its occasions would be multiplied. Not merely the merchant, ever intent on new gain, but the fugitive murderer, the exiled loser in the civil strife, the restless emigrant wandering on the face of the earth, the adventurer whose spear was at the service of the highest bidder, who would eat the bread of an Assyrian monarch today and tomorrow would pour down his burning throat the barley-water of Egypt, who was equally at home in the fruit-laden valley of the Euphrates and in the sands of the Nubian desert,—all of these would add to the sum of knowledge about places, peoples, and mankind. The frequent meeting or regular congregation in certain centres of Greeks of all cities and tribes served the purpose of huge reservoirs, in which the observations of individuals and the reports they made to their fellow-townsmen were collected and stored. The shrine of the oracle at Delphi was a chief example of the first, while the second condition was fulfilled by the recurring festi-

vals of the Games, among which those at Olympia held the foremost rank. The sanctuary at Delphi, sacred to Pythian Apollo, was situated in the shadow of steep, beetling crags. Thither would come, and there would meet, an endless line of pilgrims from all parts of Greece and her colonies—private citizens, representatives of whole states, and, since the middle of the seventh century at least, occasional envoys from foreign courts. They all came to consult the god; but the answers they received were mostly the result of the priest's ingenious manipulation of the stock of useful knowledge deposited by former clients. And few indeed can have departed from that romantic mountain glen without finding their imagination quickened and their experience augmented by contact with their companions on the road. The Games which we have mentioned were celebrated in the broad river-valley of the Alpheius, and the attractiveness of that brilliant spectacle increased with each generation. The programme was constantly extended by the inclusion of new kinds of competitions, and the spectators, who at first were drawn merely from the surrounding country, gradually began to arrive—as is shown by the winners' lists, extant since 776 B.C.—from all points in the circumference of the wide Hellenic world. Nor would their intercourse be confined to the exchange of news and information. Men would take one another's measure; opinions would be freely canvassed; the merits of the different institutions in that land of many subdivisions—their customs, habits, and beliefs—would form topics of general discussion. Comparison engendered judgment, and judgment brought reflection in its train to bear on the causes of the differences and on the permanent element in change. It induced, that is to say, an inquiry for the common canons which obtained in the commerce and dogma of daily life. The observation of common things, growing keener and richer by experience, led to comparative discussion and estimation, and, finally, to reflective criticism. Many a proud stream was nourished by that source. To it we refer sententious poetry, the invention of types of human character, and the proverbial wisdom which thoughtful citizens and philosophic statesmen have sown broadcast in the world.

The art of writing, the main vehicle for the exchange of thought, helped to distribute the fresh acquisitions of knowledge. Writing, it is true, was no novelty in Greece. When we read in the Homeric poems of the intimate intercourse with Phœnicia, we readily conceive that the sharp-witted Greek would have borrowed that wonderful aid to the preservation and communication of thought from the Canaanitish dealers, for the customer must often have surprised the merchant making entries in his account-book. Nay, the art of writing would appear to have been familiar, to some of the Greeks at least, even before that date. It is no more possible that the syllabic writing on the recently discovered Cypric monuments, with its awkward and clumsy devices, could have been later than the use of the simple Semitic letters, than that the invention of the battle-axe could have followed that of the musket. All that was wanted was a convenient and easily fashioned material. The want took some time to supply. The remedy was not found till soon after 660 B.C., when Greek trade with Egypt under Psammetich I. received a notable impulse. Then a writing-material of a kind which can hardly be improved was afforded by the pulp of the papyrus shrub, split into slender and flexible strips. From city to city, from land to land, from century to century, the sheets of written symbols now began to fly. The circulation of thought was accelerated, the commerce of intellect enlarged, and the continuity of culture guaranteed, in a degree which can well-nigh be compared with that which marked the invention of the printing-press at the dawn of modern history. To the oral delivery of poems, designed to captivate the hearer, there was presently to be added their silent appeal to the solitary enjoyment of the reader, who could weigh, compare, and discriminate to the top of his critical bent. Yet a little while, and literary communication was to break the last of its bonds, and the beginnings of prose composition were to supersede the era of metric language.

4. The west coast of Asia Minor is the cradle of the intellectual civilization of Greece. Its line stretches from north to south, but the heart of the movement must be sought in the country enclosing the centre of the line, and in the adjacent islands. There nature poured her gifts with lavish profusion, and those on whom they fell belonged to the Ionian tribe, at all times the most talented among Hellenes. The birthplace of the Ionians is obscure. We know that their blood was mixed with elements from central Greece, if, indeed, they were not a mere product of such fusion, and their diverse origin is doubtless mainly accountable for the complexity of their natural gifts. At least, it was not till they were settled in their new Asiatic home that their individuality reached its full powers. As bold seafarers and energetic traders, they enjoyed every benefit of the keen and ferti-

lizing influence to be derived from intercourse with foreign nations in a more advanced state of civilization. They had the further advantage of intermarrying with other fine races, such as the Carians and Phœnicians, a fact which indisputably increased their original diversity of talent. The Ionians were the furthest removed of all Greeks from that fatal stagnation to which dwellers in isolated countries succumb so readily. It must be added that they lacked the sense of security which friendly mountain-barriers and an infertile soil bestow. The proximity of civilized nations, highly developed and united in a State, was as prejudicial to the political independence of the Ionians as it was beneficial to their intellectual progress. The yoke of foreign dominion which was laid on one part of the people, the compulsory exile in which another part was driven, the slow but sure corrosion of its manhood by the inroad of Oriental luxury,—these were among the consequences of the devastating attacks by barbarians from Cimmeria, followed by the victories of the Lydians and Persians. The net result of this cross-series of good influences and bad was the rapid rise and swift decline of a period of prosperity. The ripe fruit fell all too soon, and the seeds it dropped were borne by fugitives from the foreigner's yoke, who would return now and again to the safe protection of Attica's fertile soil.

The evolution we have been describing took its course in but a few centuries; its splendid results included the full bloom of heroic minstrelsy, the triumph of the new forms of verse we have mentioned as the heirs of epic poetry, and, lastly, the rise of scientific pursuits and philosophical speculation. New answers were given to the eternal question of mankind— What is the meaning of self, God, and the world?—and these new answers gradually replaced or reshaped the former acceptations of religious belief.

5. Greek religion is a vessel which has been replenished from the treasury of enlightened minds. Poets and artists have combined to idealize its gods as types of perfect beauty. Still, its ultimate springs are those from which mankind has derived an infinite variety of figures and forms, partly beautiful and wholesome, partly hurtful and ugly.

Human thought follows twin channels. It obeys the law of likeness, and it obeys the law of contiguity. While similar ideas suggest one another, yet the same result is evolved by ideas which occur simultaneously or in immediate succession. An absent friend, for instance, may be recalled to our thoughts not merely by the sight of his portrait; the rooms in which he dwelt, the tools which he handled, serve the purpose just as well. These laws are summarily known as the laws of the association of ideas, and the conception of natural phenomena, which may be called the personification of nature, is directly and inevitably due to their action. Whenever the savage perceives a motion or some other effect, which, whether by its rarity or by its intimate connection with his interests, strikes his mind strongly enough to set his associative faculties at work, he will infallibly conclude that the occurrence is the outcome of an exercise of will. The reason is extremely simple. A savage or civilized man perceives the connection of will-power with movement—or, indeed, with effects of any kind—every day and hour of his life; and no other combination whatever enters in his direct experience.

Observation of other living beings continually strengthens the association which springs from this inner experience. Indeed, effects of all kinds and the deliberate exercise of will-power are connected so frequently in our mind that where one of the two is found we confidently look for the other. This expectation has been gradually confined to narrower limits by the operation of experiences of a different order, chief of which may be mentioned the gradual dominion which man has usurped over nature. But in instances where the associative force of ideas is strengthened by powerful passions, or where it is insufficiently checked by experience of an opposite tendency, or, again, where it is reinforced by the second principle of association, which would here be expressed by a likeness between an unintentional and an intentional event, in such instances our expectation breaks all bounds, and reduces the civilized man, for moments at least, to the level of the primitive savage. These are cases in which we are enabled to test the truth of that explanation by a kind of experiment. Take the view of the savage, for example. A watch, or a gun, or any other unfamiliar mechanism, he regards as a living being. But in our own instance, we are not thrown back on such primitive conceptions. We do not unconditionally refer lightning and thunder, plague and volcano, to the activity of such beings. Nevertheless, there are moments when even a scientific man admits the thought of outside purpose and power, even though he be unable to assign a definite form of the power whose intervention he believes in. Among such occasions may be counted any exceptional windfall, or any unparalleled misfortune, especially when the obvious causes of the event happen not to be in adequate proportion to the effect that is produced. Even a trivial effect may afford an illustration of our argument when the conditions of its origin—as in the dispensations of the gambling-table—defy all human calculation. Such inarticulate thoughts stand wholly apart from the religious beliefs held at this date by civilized mankind. It is not merely that the unbeliever is affected by them; the man of orthodox creed is frequently quite unable to bring the suggestions that flash across his mind into harmony with the dogmas that he has formed for himself or accepted from others as to the government of the world and the nature of its ruler. This Puck of superstition, from whose visitation no man is completely exempt, is the wan and spectral image of that mighty and universal generating power whence is derived an endless host of phantoms of all shapes and colours.

A second step towards the formation of religion follows imperceptibly on the first. We have marked the assumption that an effect is due to an exercise of will. Next comes the observation that a series of frequently recurring effects is to be referred to one and the same natural object. Thus natural objects would be regarded as the animate and volitional authors of such processes, and human instinct and inclination, human passion and design, were ascribed to them in their capacity of exercising an effective will-power after the human pattern. Wonder and admiration were paid to them, and according as their operations were useful and wholesome, or the reverse, they were regarded with love or fear. The great objects of nature exert a very considerable influence over human life, and it was chiefly in such cases that man would feel himself impelled to win their favour, to confirm their good will, and to turn their possible hostility to an auspicious disposition. He would endeavour to persuade the heaven to send fertilizing rain on earth instead of destructive storm; he would try to induce the sun to impart a gentle warmth instead of a scorching heat; he would implore the flood not to sweep away his dwelling, but to bear his frail craft uninjured on its mighty stream. He would seek to mollify the powers that govern his existence by petitions, thanksgivings, and offerings—means he found so efficacious in the instance of his earthly masters. He would invoke their gracious protection, he would thank them for their benefactions in the past, and he would supplicate for their forgiveness when he feared to have incurred their displeasure. In a word, he would employ both prayer and sacrifice in the forms suggested by his limited experience. He would possess a religion and a cult.

Hosts of spirits and demons, not wholly disembodied, and yet not wholly material, speedily range themselves in line with these objects of worship, which we may call natural fetishes. Savage man, unacquainted as he was with the finer distinctions of scientific thought, was led to believe in these beings by a triple set of inferences. The first was drawn from real or apparent observations of the outer world; the second from the inner or moral life; and the third depended on observations taken at the transition from life to death in the human and animal creation.

The smell of a flower teaches the primitive man that

there are objects not the less real because they evade his sight and touch. The wind, whose material nature he can but partially understand, makes him acquainted with objects that can be felt, but not seen. Shadows, that contain the outline of an object without its material resistance, and still more the coloured images reflected in a sheet of water, bring astonishment and confusion to the mind of primitive man. In both instances he is aware of something precisely resembling the material object, which yet mocks his endeavour to seize it and touch it. Dream-pictures serve but to increase his confusion. He perceived them, he thought, with all his senses at once; they stood in bodily shape before his eyes, and still in the morning the doors of his hut were as firmly closed as overnight. Men and beasts, plants, stones, and tools of all kinds, stood indisputably before him, plainly perceptible to sight, hearing, and touch, and yet in many instances there could actually have been no room for them in the limited accommodation of his dwelling. Thus he is driven to the conclusion that, like perfumes and winds, shadows and reflections, they were the souls of things. Occasionally it happens that the visions of sleep require and demand a different sort of explanation. The dreamer is not always receiving visits from the souls of other persons or things. Frequently he believes himself to be traversing long distances, and conversing with his friends in far-off homes. Hence he concludes that something—his own soul or one of his souls, the belief in a plurality of souls being both natural and common,—has temporarily left his body. He is subject to the same experiences with the same train of inferences in the state which we have learnt to call hallucination. The irregular life led by primitive man, with its long fastings and sudden excesses, rendered him as liable to such attacks as to heavy and exciting dreams. Those souls or essences of things must be taken as standing in the closest relation with the things themselves, which are affected by whatever affects their souls. In popular belief it is still a bad omen to tread on a man's shadow, and in one of the tribes of South Africa the crocodile is believed to get a man in its power if it merely snaps at the reflection of the man which is thrown on the water from the bank. So the doings and sufferings of persons in dreams is of the gravest import to the living originals.

But popular belief endows the soul with far greater power and with practical independence by a second series of considerations, depending, not on the observations of sense, but on those of the processes of will. So long as the inner life of primitive man moves in a uniform and even groove, he has little cause to reflect on the seat and origin of his will and endeavour. It is when the blood begins to surge in his veins, when he glows and thrills with emotion, that his beating heart teaches him of its own accord how that region of his body is the theatre of occurrences which he is impelled to explain to himself by the light of his own perception and of the analogies already at his disposal. Hitherto he has been accustomed to connect each particular effect with a particular Being; and the more violent and sudden the change, the less he will be able to rid himself of the impression that some Being of the kind is stirring and ruling in his own breast. There are moments when he is seized by an overpowering passion. Rage, for instance, fills his heart and drives him to a deed of bloodshed that he may presently bitterly repent. Or, again, in the very act of committing it, a sudden impulse makes him hold his hand; and it is in moments such as these that he is overcome by an irresistible belief in one or more Beings, within him or without him, who drive him to action or restrain him from the act. Man's belief in the soul reaches its most effective point in the circumstances which accompany the extinction of the individual life. It is once more the cases of sudden change which make the deepest impression on the observer, and give the lead to his reflection. If dying were always a gradual decay and a final folding of the hands to sleep, or if the dead man were always changed beyond recognition, the inferences drawn from the cessation of life might have taken a different form. Frequently, however, no outward changes disturb the features of the dead. Death comes as a sudden transition from complete vigour to complete silence, and the spectator asks himself to what causes is due this dread and terrifying transformation. Something, he says in answer to himself, has departed from the dead man that lent him life and movement. A cessation of powers and qualities which a moment ago were in evidence is taken literally as a departure and as a separation in space. The warm breath, so mysterious in its origin, which the living body always exhaled, has been extinguished, and the reflection is obvious that the source of the arrested processes of life has perished simultaneously with the breath. Violent deaths, when life seems to leave the body with blood pouring from the wound, awaken sometimes a belief that life itself is borne on that crimson stream. A second theory is to be remarked among some other peoples. The reflection in the pupil of the eye which vanishes at the approach of death is there regarded as the source of the processes of life and animation. But these attributes, after all, are most commonly ascribed to the warm breath or steam which proceeds from within the living organism, and by far the most of the words which are used in different languages to signify "soul" and "spirit" express that primary meaning. We saw in both explanations of the visions of sleep that the soul was supposed to be separable from the body. Their temporary separation accounts for states of unconsciousness, catalepsy, and ecstasy, just as the explanation of pathological conditions of all kinds, such as madness, convulsions, and the like, may best be sought in the entry of a foreign soul into the body. The instance of demonic possession is a case in point. The difference is that the separation of the two elements in death is regarded as enduring and final.

We see, then, that the breath is regarded as an independent being, but there is no ground to assume that when it has left the body it must perish as well. On the contrary, the picture of the beloved dead is an unfading possession; his soul, in other words, hovers round us. And how—so primitive man asked himself—should it be otherwise? The soul is plainly impelled to haunt as long as it can the old familiar places, and to linger about the objects which it cared for and loved. The last doubt on this question is dispelled by the frequent visitation of the image of the departed in the dreams of survivors in the night-time.

Two results ensue from the assumption of independent souls or spirits outliving their connection with the human and maybe the animal body. In the first place, it gave rise to a second class of objects of worship parallel to the natural fetishes. Secondly, it supplied a pattern on which imagination could mould a series of other Beings, which either existed independently or temporarily occupied a visible habitation. There was no lack of urgent motives for the adoption of this creed, and for such operations of the fancy on the part of primitive man. He was governed by outward circumstances in a hardly conceivable degree. His desire to enlighten the darkness that surrounded him at every step was only matched by his inability to give it practical satisfaction. Sickness and health, famine and plenty, success and failure in the chase, in sport, and in war, followed one another in bewildering succession. Savage man naturally wished to recognize the agents of his fortune, and to influence them on his own behalf, but his powerlessness to fulfil that longing in any rational manner was stronger than the wish itself. A maximum of curiosity in each individual was combined with a minimum of collective knowledge. Fancy was set in motion on every side with hardly a noticeable exception in order to span that gulf, and it is difficult to form an approximate conception of the amount of imagination at play. For the protective roof which civilization has built over man is at the same time a party-wall interposed between him and nature. The objects of natural worship were indefinitely extended. Forest and field, bush and fountain, were filled with them. But the needs of primitive man outgrew their rate of increase; he could not but observe that his weal and woe, his success and misfortune, were not invariably connected with objects perceptible to sense. He observed a sudden scarcity where game had formerly been abundant; he found himself all at once no match for the foe he had frequently routed; he felt a paralysis creep through his limbs, or a mist obstruct his consciousness, and in none of these instances could he blame any visible being. He seized on any outward circumstance which gave a momentary direction to his bewildered thought as an infallible guide. He would assume a close and definite connection between occurrences that happened in fortuitous coincidence or succession. If an unknown animal, for instance, were suddenly to burst from the thicket at a time when a pestilence was raging, he would straightway worship it and implore its good graces as the author of the plague; and through all this uncertainty primitive man never ceased anxiously to look for the agents of his good luck and ill. His longing for help and salvation remained insatiable throughout. Presently he turned for aid to those who had watched over him in life, and addressed his prayers to the spirits of his departed kinsfolk, parents and forefathers. The worship of ancestors was started, and with it went the supplication of spirits not confined to natural objects, but associated in thought with the ordinances and occurrences of life. Spirits were assumed with powers of protection and mischief. We are thus presented with three classes of objects of worship, overlapping one another at various points. They began to react on one another, and to pass into one another's spheres.

The legendary figure of some remote ancestor, the forefather of a whole tribe or race, would be ranked on a footing of equality with the great natural fetishes. It might happen, indeed, that just as a nation or an illustrious tribe would regard and worship the sun or the sky as the author of its existence, so this legendary forefather would be identified with one of those fetishes. Nor need it arouse our surprise that objects of nature or art should come to be looked on as the homes of ancestral or other spirits, and as such should receive a form of worship and be ranked as secondary fetishes. They would owe these honours not so much to any palpable influence they exercised as to their strangeness, their unaccustomed shape or colour, or their accidental connection with the memory of some important event. Finally, it is obvious that spirits or demons, originally confined to no fixed abode, would be confused at times with a natural fetish through their similarity in name or qualities, and would at last be merged with it in a single being. It is wholly illegitimate to infer from occurrences of this more or less isolated character that any of the three great classes of objects of worship, natural fetishes or independent spirits, for example, is foreign to the original belief of the people, or of later and adventitious derivation. As well might one conclude from the proved worship of animals, as such, or from the deification of men, which has been frequently observed, and which still obtains through the great Hindu civilization, that these are the sole or even the chief sources of religious belief. It is always difficult and often hopeless to attempt to follow the details of such a process of transformation, and to sift the nucleus of a religion from its gradual accretions. But the fact that such transformation took place, and that the course of religious development was thereby deeply affected, is a truth which may be stated without reserve. At this point, however, it will be well to return to the more modest path from which we have digressed.

6. The gods of Greece assembled in Olympus round the throne of Zeus, hearkening the song of Apollo and the Muses, sipping nectar from golden goblets, involved in adventures of war and love—we cannot but perceive how little they resemble the earliest and roughest products of religious imagination. They are severed by a yawning gulf which it would seem to be impossible to bridge over. Nevertheless, the appearance is fallacious. The exact observer will remark a vast number of links and stepping-stones, till he will hardly venture to distinguish between the beginning of the one series of beings and the end of the others; above all, between the end of natural fetish and the beginning of the anthropomorphic god. Comparative philology tells us that Zeus, the chief of the gods of Olympus, was originally no other than the sky itself. Hence he was said to rain, to hurl the lightnings, and to gather the clouds. Homer himself still entitles the Earth-goddess "broad-bosomed" or "broad-wayed" indifferently, and thus shifts, like the colours of the chameleon, between two quite contrary conceptions. When Earth is represented by an old theological poet as giving birth to high mountains and to the starry heaven that it may wholly encompass her, or when Earth as the bride of Heaven is represented as the mother of deep-eddying Ocean, and Ocean again with Tethys as engendering the rivers, we are plainly standing with both feet in the realm of the pure worship of nature. Presently, however, we are confronted with a different set of stories. Fair-flowing Xanthus is represented by Homer as subject to a wrathful mood; Achilles fills his bed with dead men; he is sorely pressed by the flames ignited by Hephæstus, smith of the gods; he is in danger of de-

feat; he stays his course in order to escape from the conflagration; and he implores Hera the white-armed, the woman-like consort of the king of the gods, to help him to resist the savage onslaught of her son. In all these instances we are surely conscious of two fundamentally different kinds of religious imagination, of two strata, as it were, which a volcanic eruption has thrown into hopeless confusion.

The following reply may be attempted to the question why Greek religion, like that of countless other peoples, has undergone this transformation. It was an intrinsic tendency of the associative faculty, which led to the personification of nature, to lend more and more of a human character to the objects of worship. First came the connection in thought between movements or effects and the impulses of the human will. Next volition was connected with the whole range of human emotion; and, finally, the range of human emotion was associated in thought with the external form of man and the sum of the conditions of human life. This development took a slow course. It was delayed by man himself, who, on the confines of savagery, knowing no law but that of need, and harassed as he was by real and imaginary dangers, was not yet sufficiently in conceit with himself to form these supreme powers in his own mean and ignoble image. Still, the gradual beginnings of civilization tended to level the differences and to reduce the distance between the heights and the depths. No people, we may conjecture, ever yet came to regard the great powers of nature as savages living on roots and berries in a state of semi-starvation. But a tribe with an abundance of rich hunting-grounds might conceive a heavenly huntsman such as the Germanic Wotan, or, like the farmers of ancient India, would figure the god of heaven and his clouds as a shepherd with his flock. And this tendency was notably strengthened by the auspicious circumstances of external life, which awoke the desire for clearness, distinctness, and a logical sequence of ideas. It is now the exception, and no longer the rule, to meet with such vague, indefinite, and contradictory conceptions as that of a sensitive stream, or of a river brought to birth by generation. We may not be able to assert conclusively whether the worship of ancestors or of fetishes was the earlier in time, but we can assert that, old as demonism may have been, it must have been extended by the division of labour and the growing diversity of life. Fresh demons had to be created to meet the multiplicity of human business and experience. But these independent spirits offer less opposition to the personifying faculty than objects of natural worship, and they presently formed the model on which the last-named were moulded. Demons, like souls, were conceived as entering human bodies. Our remarks about demonic possession will recur in this connection, and the process which nothing prevented and many conditions assisted was speedily adapted to the case of natural fetishes. Spirits and gods whose habitation is confined to external things, which they use as their instruments, now replace or accompany the volitional and conscious objects of nature. Thus the god and the external thing are no longer completely identified. They merely stand in the relation of tenant and abode. The god becomes more independent of the destiny of the object he inhabits; his sphere of activity is no longer confined to it, but he obtains an allowance of free action.

The graceful feminine figures which the Greeks worshipped as nymphs afford an instructive example of this transformation. Homer's hymn to Aphrodite takes cognizance of dryads who share in the dance of the Immortals and sport with Hermes and the fauns under the shadows of the rocks. But the pines and the high-branching oaks they inhabit are something more than their mere dwelling-place. These beings are but half divine; they are born, they grow, and they die together with the abodes they haunt. Other nymphs are exempt from that fate. They dwell in water-brooks, meadows, and groves, but they are numbered with the Immortals, and they are not missing from the great council of the gods when Zeus gathers them in his gleaming halls. We may draw the following conclusion. There was a time when the tree itself was personified and worshipped. Next came a period when the spirit of its life was regarded as an independent being, separable from it, but closely bound up with its destiny. Finally, this last bond was severed as well; the divine being was liberated, as it were, and hovered indestructibly over the perishable object of its care. This final and decisive step put polytheism in the place of fetishism. Traces of the era of fetishes linger about but a few of the great unique objects of nature, such as the earth, the stars, and the legendary Oceanus. And even in these instances fresh figures were created under the influence of the new thought to accompany the older deities, barely touched as they were by the finger of anthropomorphism. A further development may here be remarked. These natural spirits, released from their external objects, were set an appointed task just as certain independent deities presided over whole categories of occupation. They were appointed to wood or garden, to the fountain, the wind, and so forth, and became what has appropriately been termed "class-gods." This transformation was assisted, apart from the influence of demonism, by the progressive perception of the intrinsic likeness in whole series of beings. Man's generalizing powers found here their earliest satisfaction, and his artistic and inventive faculties were provided with inexhaustible material in the contemplation of the free action of the gods.

The Greeks were furnished in a pre-eminent degree with the conditions requisite for the progress of personification, and for the idealization of the divine powers which depended on it. The demand for clearness and distinctness may have been a birthright of the Greeks; it was obviously strengthened by the bright air and brilliant sky enjoyed through the greater part of Hellas, by the sharp outline of its hills, by its wide and yet circumscribed horizon. The Greek sense of beauty was constantly fed on landscapes combining in the smallest compass all the loveliest elements of nature. Green pastures and snowy peaks, dusky pine-woods and smiling meadows, wide prospects over land and sea, fascinated the eye at every turn. And the inventive spirit which was later to display itself in the rich and teeming inheritance of Greek poetry and art must surely have seized on the first material at its disposal, and therein have spent the powers which were denied expression elsewhere.

It is difficult to follow the course of this evolution in detail, and our difficulty is enhanced by the character of the literary monuments that have reached us. It was a cherished belief of former generations that Homer's poems were produced in the infancy of Greece. Schliemann's spade has destroyed this illusion. A notable degree of material civilization clearly distinguished the eastern portions of Greece—the islands, and the shore of Asia Minor—soon after 1500 B.C. The conditions of human life depicted by the Homeric poems are the result of a comparatively long development contaminated by Egypt and the East. When we recall the splendid banqueting-halls, with their plates of beaten metals, their blue glazed friezes on a gleaming alabaster ground, their ceilings artistically carved, and their drinking-cups of embossed gold, we look in vain for traces of primitive man in the princes and nobles whose Round Table was the theme of the Homeric poems. Their passions, it is true, were still uncontrolled. Otherwise the insatiable wrath of Achilles or Meleager would never have become a favourite subject for poetic description. We recall the period in which the Niebelungenlied was composed, when the original and untamed force of passionate sensibility fell on an era of foreign manners and imported refinement of taste. But we find no trace in these heroes of the timidity and awe with which the almighty forces of nature were regarded by primitive man. The gods were fashioned by the nobles after the pattern of their own existence, as they acquired more and more self-esteem, more and more security, in the stress of life. Olympus became a mirror of heroic experience, and its gorgeous and frequently tumultuous features were faithfully reproduced. Gods and men approached each other with a familiarity never since repeated. Men wore no little of divine dignity; the gods took no mean share of human weakness. The virtues ascribed to the gods were the virtues dearest to those warriors—qualities of valour and pride, and steadfastness in friendship and hate. Gods, like men, were affected by strong individual motives; the obligation of duty was almost always a matter of personal loyalty, and in the Iliad at least they but rarely appear as the champions of abstract justice. To their worshippers who lavished precious gifts on them, to the cities that dedicated splendid temples to them, to the tribes and races which traditionally enjoyed their favour, they lent their faithful protection with a loyalty as resolute as it was untiring. They were but little restrained by any scruples of morality; nay, their special favourites were endowed by them with talents for perjury and theft. They seldom paused to consider the rights or wrongs of the matter to which they devoted their assistance, else how could some of the gods have been found on the side of the Greeks, while others with equal interest and trouble supported the Trojan cause? How, again, could Poseidon in the Odyssey have persecuted patient Ulysses with inexhaustible hate, while Athene proved herself in every danger his trusty counsellor and shield? Their obedience was solely due to the god of heaven, chief of the gods, and more often than not they obeyed him with reluctance, and used every artifice of deceit and guile to evade the obligation of his command. Moreover, the heavenly overlord resembled his earthly prototype in that his power did not rest on the immovable foundation of law. He found himself frequently obliged to extort the fulfilment of his orders by the employment of threats, and even by violent maltreatment. There was a single peremptory exception to the chaos induced by the acts and passions of the Immortals. Moira, or Fate, was supreme over gods and men alike, and in her worship we recognize the faint and earliest perception of the operation of law throughout the range of experience. Thus the oldest monuments of the Greek intellect that have reached us show us the gods in as human a form as is compatible with reverent worship, and instances indeed could be found where that last limit was transgressed. Take, for example, the love-story of Ares and Aphrodite; it stirred the Phæacians to ribald mirth, and it evinces a worldliness in religious conception which, like the exclusive cult of beauty of the Cinquecento, could hardly have spread over wide classes of the population without seriously affecting the heart of religious belief. The majesty of the ancient Greek religion is not to be found in the confines of the courtly epic, where the joys of the world and the flesh and the frank deliciousness of life disperse the gloomier aspects of belief, and clothe them, so to speak, with their brilliance. The exceptional occurrences that seem to contradict this view will be found to be its clearest illustration.

Homeric man believed himself to be constantly and universally surrounded by gods and dependent on them. He attributed his good luck and ill, his successful spear-thrust or his enemy's escape, to the friendship or hostility of a demon. Every cunning plan, every sound device, was credited to divine inspiration, and every act of infatuated blindness was ascribed to the same cause.

It was the aim of all his endeavours to win the favour of the Immortals and to avert their wrath. But despite this dependence, and despite the occurrence, in the Iliad especially, with its shifting battle-scenes, of situations fraught with dire peril, it is to be noted that man himself, the costliest of human possessions, is never offered as a sacrifice to the gods. The religion of the Greeks, like that of most other peoples, was familiar with human sacrifices; but though it survives till the full light of historic times, it is completely missing from the picture of civilization displayed by the Homeric poems. Or rather, the abominable custom is mentioned therein on one single occasion, as the exception which proves the rule. At the splendid obsequies devised by Achilles in honour of Patroclus, the well-beloved, we are told that, besides innumerable sheep and oxen, besides four horses and two favourite hounds, twelve Trojan youths were first slaughtered and then burnt with the body of his dead friend. This complete consumption of the offering by fire is proved by more recent ritual evidence to have been the ceremony in vogue among worshippers of the infernal deities. The blood of the slaughtered beasts and men is first suffered to trickle over the corpse, and the soul is supposed to be present and to be refreshed and honoured by the gifts it receives. Achilles performs by this act a solemn obligation to the dead, and narrates it to the soul, when it appears to him by night, and again at the funeral itself. But, strangely enough, the description of this revolting deed has none of that sensuous breadth and detail which we correctly call the epic style, and find so characteristic of Homer. Rather the poet glides, as it were, with deliberate haste over the horrible story. He and his audience seem to shrink from it; it is the legacy of a world of thought and feeling from which the vitality has departed, and this impression is strengthened by other and kindred observations. Except for this single instance, hardly any trace whatsoever is found in the Homeric poems of the whole series of rites connected with and dependent on the belief in the protracted existence of powerful beings rising with spectral influence from the grave, and constantly demanding fresh tokens of propitiation. There are no sacrifices to the dead, whether bloody or bloodless, there is no purification for homicide, no worship of souls or ancestors. The souls, it is true, survive the bodies, but they are well-nigh exclusively confined to the far infernal realms of death, where they wander as "powerless heads," vagrant shadows, and bloodless ghosts, of no efficacy and of little account. It was quite different in later times, and, as we learn from trustworthy discoveries and equally trustworthy conclusions, in earlier times too. We may appropriately dwell on this point, which is of great importance to the history of the belief in souls and to religious history in general.

7. The sacrifice of prisoners or slaves is a funeral custom of remote antiquity, and one which is widely spread in our own times. The Scythians, when they buried their king, used to strangle one of his concubines and five of his slaves—the cook, the cup-bearer, the chamberlain, the groom, and the doorkeeper—and these, together with his favourite horses, and with a quantity of costly vessels, of golden goblets and so forth, would be committed to the royal grave. After the lapse of a year, fifty more chosen slaves were strangled, set upon

as many slaughtered horses, and stationed round the tomb like a guard of honour.

Many pages and chapters might be filled with the enumeration of similar customs, from which the Hindu suttee is also derived. Naturally they show a long course of gradations, varying from the savage and barbarous to the tender and refined. Human sacrifices were followed by animal sacrifices, and these in their turn by drink sacrifices and other bloodless offerings. Aeschylus and Sophocles represent Agamemnon's tomb in Mycenae as the recipient of libations of milk, locks of hair, and garlands of flowers. But newly discovered tombs of the kings in that city, dating from hoary antiquity, show traces of sacrificial offerings of a far more substantial kind. Bones of animals, and human remains too, were found there, besides innumerable most costly weapons, drinking-cups, and other vessels. Taking these objects in connection with the altars discovered in the vaulted tomb at Orchomenus in Bœotia, we may infer that the souls of the dead enjoyed adoration and worship in the proper sense of the word. The cult of ancestors and souls has been in almost universal vogue. It is still as widely spread among the most debased savages in all regions of the earth as among the highly civilized Chinese, in whose state-religion it plays the most important part. It takes precedence, too, in the beliefs of nations of Aryan descent. The Romans observed it no less than the Greeks, and the "Manes" of ancient Rome were the "pitaras" of the Hindus. The extinction of a family at Athens was regarded as ominous, inasmuch as its ancestors would be deprived of the honours that were due to them. The whole population of Greece, and the communities of which it was composed in a series, as it were, of concentric circles, addressed their prayers to real or imaginary forefathers. And so imperious was this need that professional brotherhoods or guilds would invent a common ancestor, should they otherwise not possess one. The custom was bound up with the origins of state and society, which were originally ranked as merely extended family groups. But our immediate interest is confined to the deepest root of this custom—the belief in the protracted existence of the soul as a powerful being with enduring influence on the success and failure of its living descendants. We have already discussed the source of this belief, and we shall later be occupied with the changes that it underwent. At present we have to dispel a misunderstanding which might darken our historical insight.

The souls depicted by Homer have dwindled to pale and ineffectual shadows. Their worship, and the customs that arise from it, are practically obsolete in his poems, but it would be erroneous to conclude from these facts that the evidence from comparative ethnology should be neglected, or that the oldest form of this part of the Greek religion is preserved in epic poetry. The discoveries dating from the period of civilization which is now called the Mycenæan have shattered the last foundation of every possible doubt. The causes that induced this change in religious ideas can only be arrived at by conjecture. It plainly depended, not merely on temporal, but also on local conditions, and at first, at least, it was probably confined to certain classes of the population. At the period of which we are speaking the custom of burning the dead body prevailed, and the consequent belief obtained, and was clearly expressed by Homer, that the consuming flames finally severed body from soul, and consigned the soul to the realm of shadows. In connection with the development of Greek religion, considerable influence has been attached to this custom and its results. Of hardly secondary account may be reckoned the local separation of colonists from their ancestral tombs, and from the seats of worship appertaining to them in the mother-country. But of greater importance than all was the joy in life and the world, so repellent to melancholy and gloom, which pervades the Homeric poems. It shrank from the sinister and the spectral with the same invincible optimism that banished the ugly and the grotesque from its purview. Nor was it only the shades of the dead that had to recede into the background. Spectral godheads such as Hecate, horrible spirits such as the Titans with their hundred arms and fifty heads, coarse and revolting myths such as that of the emasculation of Uranus, were similarly compelled to give way to the instinct of joy; and monsters of the type of the round-eyed Cyclops were treated in a more playful humour. Two alternative inferences present themselves. We may either regard the gradual growth of the sense of beauty and the rise in the standard of life dependent on the progress of material civilization as the chief factor of development; or we may ascribe to the people who invented philosophy and natural science the possession, even in those early times, of the elements of rationalistic enlightenment. In other words, is the change in the soul-idea which confronts us in Homer to be attributed in the first instance to the lightness or to the brightness of the Ionian genius? This question does not yet admit of a definite answer. We owe the possibility of its discussion to the brilliant intellectual and analytical powers of a contemporary student in these fields.

8. The personification of Nature must, then, primarily be thanked for the inexhaustible material it supplied to the play, first of imagination and next of imagination heightened to art. But it must further be recognized as having been the earliest to satisfy the curiosity of man, and his craving for light in the deep darkness in the midst of which we live and breathe. The "why" and "wherefore" of sensible phenomena are questions that cannot be avoided, and the spontaneous presumption that everything which happens is due to the impulse of volitional beings—a presumption springing from the unlimited dominion of the association of ideas—affords, it must be admitted, a sort of answer in itself. It is a kind of philosophy of nature, capable of infinite extension in proportion to the increase of the number of phenomena observed, and to the more and more clearly defined shapes of the powers of nature, regarded as living beings. Primitive man is not merely a poet, believing in the truth of his inventions; he is, in his way, a kind of investigator as well. The mass of answers which he gives to the questions continually pressing on him is gradually composed to an all-embracing weft, and the threads thereof are myths. As evidence of this, we may instance the popular legends of all times and countries with their remarkable points of likeness and their no less striking points of difference. The two greatest heavenly bodies figure in almost every nation as a related pair, whether in the relation of husband and wife

or of sister and brother. Numberless myths represent the phases of the moon as the wandering of the lunar goddess, and the occasional eclipses of sun and moon as the consequences, partly of domestic strife, partly of the hostile attacks of dragons and monsters. The Semite, for example, explained the weakness of the sun in winter by the story of Samson's—the sun-god's—bewitchment by the seductive goddess of the night, who robbed him of his shining hair; as soon as his long locks, the sunbeams, in which his strength resided, were cut off, it was an easy task to blind him. The ancient Indian regarded the clouds as cows—as soon as they were milked the fruitful rain poured down; if the quickening moisture were long delayed, the drought was ascribed to evil spirits who had stolen the herds and hidden them in rocky caves, and Indra, the god of heaven, had to descend on the storm-wind to free them from their bondage, and rescue them from the robbers. The dreadful spectacle afforded to the gaze of primitive man by a mountain emitting flames would forthwith seem to him the work of a demon dwelling in the bowels of the earth. Many tribes would content themselves with this explanation, but one or another would presently ask why it was that so mighty a spirit should be confined in infernal darkness. The answer would suggest itself spontaneously, that he had been vanquished in conflict with a yet more powerful being. Thus Typhon and Enceladus were looked on by the Greeks as the vanquished opponents of the great god of heaven, bearing the heavy penalty of their crime. Or take the instance of the earth, from whose womb came forth a constant procession of fruits. How natural it was to represent her as a woman impregnated by the heaven above her, who sent down his life-giving rain. This world-wide myth has been turned to various forms. The Maoris and Chinese, the Phœnicians and Greeks, would ask why husband and wife were kept so far apart from each other, instead of dwelling in the intimate relations of a conjugal pair. The inhabitants of New Zealand replied with the story that the offspring of Rangi (heaven) and Papa (earth) had no room to live as long as their parents were united. So at last they made up their minds to relieve themselves from the pressure and the darkness, and one of them—the mighty god and father of the forests—succeeded, after many vain attempts on the part of his brethren, in sundering their parents by force. But the love of heaven and earth survived their separation. Passionate sighs, which men call mist, still rise to heaven from the breast of mother-earth, and tears still trickle from the eyes of the sad god of heaven, and are called by men drops of dew. This ingenious and highly poetical myth of the Maoris gives the key to a similar but far coarser legend which obtained in Greece, and of which merely fragments have come down to us. Hesiod tells us that the earth was cramped and oppressed by her teeming burden of children, of which heaven was the father. But heaven, adds the poet, would not suffer them to come to birth, but thrust them back in their mother's womb. Panting from her labours, she devises a cunning scheme, and confides its execution to one of her sons. Cronos whets his sickle and mutilates Uranus his father, so that he is debarred from further procreation, and Gaia is released thenceforward from her husband's embraces, and is enabled, we may add, to find room for the offspring with whom she is teeming.

We may mark at this point the following conclusion. The process of personification was not confined to mere objects, but was extended to forces, states, and qualities. Night, darkness, death, sleep, love, appetite, infatuation, were all looked on by the Greeks as individual beings more or less successfully personified. Some are completely embodied, others stand out from the background of their content as imperfectly as a bas-relief. The relations existing between these forces or states are explained by analogies from human or animal life. Likeness, for instance, figures as relationship, death and sleep are twin brothers; consecution figures as generation, so that day is the offspring of night, or night of day indifferently. All groups of like nature appear as tribes, kindred, or families, and traces of this process of thought are to be found in our language to this day. Finally, the habit of explaining an enduring condition or the recurring incidents of the world by mythical fictions led to the attempt to solve the great riddles of human life and fate in a similar manner. The Greek in this dark hour of pessimism would ask why the evils of life were so much in excess of its blessings, and the question immediately suggested a second one—Who and what brought evil in the world? And his answer mainly resembles that of the modern Frenchman, the sum of whose researches into the source of innumerable transgressions was contained in the words "cherchez la femme." But the ancient Greek cast his indictment of the weaker and fairer sex in the form of a single charge.

He relates that Zeus, with the help of the rest of the gods, in order to punish Prometheus for his theft of fire and the consequent arrogance of mankind, created a woman adorned with all the graces as the mother of the female race, and sent her down to the earth. At another time the Greek, still groping for enlightenment on this subject, accused curiosity or the thirst for knowledge as the root of all evil. If the gods, he said, had endowed us with every blessing, and had locked up all evils in a box, and had straightly warned us not to open it, human—and chiefly woman's—curiosity would have set at nought the divine prohibition. Both myths are merged in one: Pandora, the woman, as her name implies, adorned with every seductive gift, is the woman, stung by curiosity, who lifts the lid of the fateful box and lets its perilous contents escape. Once more we are astounded at the similarity of mythical invention obtaining among the most diverse peoples, and one almost involuntarily recalls the allied Hebraic story of Eve—the mother of all life—and the ominous consequences of her sinful curiosity.

9. The multiplicity of myths and the crowd of deities must at last have proved a weariness and a stumbling-block to the orthodox Greek. Legends clustered like weeds in a pathless and primeval forest, obstructed by ever-fresh undergrowth. The thinning axe was wanted, and a hand was presently found to wield it with thew and sinew. A peasant's vigour and a peasant's shrewdness accomplished the arduous task, and we reach in him the earliest didactic poet of the Occident. Hesiod of Ascra, in Bœotia, flourished in the eighth century B. C. He sprang from a soil where the air was less bright

than in the rest of Greece, and man's heart was less light in his breast. His intellect was clear but clumsy; he was versed in the management of house and field, and was not a stranger to lawsuits. His imaginative powers were of comparatively restricted range, and his disposition was yet more unyielding. A Roman among Greeks, the author of "Works and Days" was distinguished by sober sensibilities, by a strict love of order, and by the parsimonious thrift of a good business man trained in the manufacture of smooth account-books, averse from any hint of contradiction, and shy of all superfluity. It is in this spirit, so to speak, that he took an inventory of Olympus, fitting each of the Immortals in the framework of his system by the genealogical clamps. He pruned the luxuriance of epic poetry, reviving the immemorial but dimly understood traditions extant among the lower orders of Greece without respect to their claims to beauty. Thus his theogony comprised a complete and comprehensive picture, with but rare gleams of true poetry and hardly a breath of the genuine joy of life. The names of Homer and Hesiod were coupled in remote antiquity as the twin authors of Greek religion. But they stand, in point of fact, in strong contrast. The unchecked imagination of Ionian poets, which made light of the contradictions and diversities of legend, differed as widely from the home-keeping, methodical wisdom of the Bœotian peasant as the brilliant *insouciance* of their noble audience from the gloomy spirit of the meek hinds and farmers for whom Hesiod's poems were composed.

The "Theogony" is at once a cosmogony; the "Origin of the Gods" included the origin of the world. We are chiefly concerned with the last named of these pairs, and may let the poet speak for himself. At the beginning, he tells us, there was Chaos: then come Gaia, the broad-bosomed earth, and next, Eros, loveliest of the gods, who compels the senses of mortals and immortals alike, and melts the strength of their limbs. Chaos engendered Darkness and Black Night, and Air and Day—Æther and Hemera—sprang from their union. Gaia first created of her own accord the starry heaven, the high mountains, and Pontus, the sea; then, as the bride of Uranus, she brought forth Oceanus, the stream that encompasses the earth, and a long series of children, some of them mighty monsters, and others of an almost allegorical description, besides the gods of the lightning called Cyclopes, and Tethys, the great goddess of the sea. From the marriage of Ocean and Tethys sprang fountains and the streams. The sun-god, the moon-goddess, and the Dawn were born to two other children of Heaven and Earth. Dawn is united to her cousin Astræus, god of the stars, and the Winds, the Morning-star, and the rest of the luminaries were born of that marriage.

Part of this exposition is so puerile in its simplicity, that hardly a word of comment is required. "The greater is the author of the less": Hence the mountains were born of the Earth; mighty Oceanus and the smaller streams and rivers stood in the relation of father and sons; the little Morning-star was the son of the wide-spreading Dawn, and the rest of the stars were clearly to be set down as his brothers. It is less obvious why the Day should have sprung from the Night, for the opposite theory would have been equally admissible, and an old Indian hymn-writer actually poses the question whether Day or Night was created first. Still, Hesiod's opinion may perhaps be called the more natural. Darkness appears to us as a permanent state requiring no explanation; light, at each manifestation, is due to a special event, whether it be the rise of the sun, the lightning of the storm-cloud, or the ignition of a flame by human hand. So far, then, we have merely had to deal with the earliest reflections of thoughtful and bewildered man. These tell their own story, but a more attentive examination is required when we come to the most important part of Hesiod's work, where he discusses the origin of the world.

The brief and arid character of this exposition is the first point that we notice, and it arouses our astonishment. The stage-bell rings, as it were, and Chaos, Gaia, and Eros appear as the curtain rises. No hint is vouchsafed as to the reason of their appearance. A bare "but then" connects the origin of Earth with the origin of Chaos. Not a single syllable of explanation is given of the When and How of this process, whether Earth was born of Chaos or not, and what were the aids to birth; and the same unbroken silence is preserved on the promotion of the Love-god to the prominent part which he fills. Of course one may say, the principle of love or generation must have entered the world before any procreation could take place. But why should the didactic poet drop it without a word, why should he never refer to that function of Eros at all, and why should he rather disguise it, as we plainly perceive to be the fact? Various epithets are here predicated of the Love-god, and in a later passage he is given a place next to Himeros—craving—in the train of Aphrodite. But none of these allusions recalls in the remotest degree the mighty, vitalizing creative Being who alone is appropriate in this connection, and whom we shall meet later on in other cosmogonic experiments, where the origin and function of Eros come to adequate expression. One thing is as clear as noonday. A wide gulf is fixed between the summary and superficial methods of Hesiod's inquiry into origins and the devotion of those who applied the whole force of their immature philosophy to the solution of the great enigma. Hesiod's system is a mere husk of thought which must once have been filled with life. It has survived the loss of its contents, just as the shell survives the shell-fish. We seem to be gazing at a *hortus siccus* of conceptions, the growth and development of which we are no longer able to watch. Inference has to take the place of direct observation, and a start must be made at the terms the poet used, presumably with but partial comprehension. These terms will help us to construct the process of thought of which they are the dead deposit. We shall be assisted herein by the consideration of kindred phenomena, not merely in Greece, but in other countries as well. We have already briefly described the nature of Eros, and may now proceed to discuss the meaning of Chaos.

Chaos resembles empty space as closely as the inexact thought of primitive man approximates to the speculative conceptions of advanced philosophers. Primitive man endeavours to imagine the primordial condition of things, in all its striking contrast to the world as he knows it. The earth, and all that is therein, and the dome of the sky were not extant. All that remained was a something stretching from the topmost heights to the uttermost depths, and continuing immeasurably on either side the hollow emptiness interposed between the Heaven and the Earth. The Babylonians called it *apsu,* "the abyss," or *tiamat,* "the deep." The Scandinavians knew it as *ginnunga gap,* "the yawning gap," a term of which the first word belongs to the same root as the Greek *Chaos.* This gaping void, this abysmal deep, was conceived as obscure and dark simply because—in accordance with the principles of this system—none of the sources of light had as yet been put in action. For the same reason, the observer confined his imagination to the depths rather than the heights of Chaos, height and light being hardly distinguishable in his mind. Chaos filled the whole space known to or even suspected by primitive man. Earth and her complement—the dome of heaven with its luminaries—sufficed for his knowledge and his thought; even his vague and aspiring curiosity was content to flutter in those limits. His intellect stopped short at the idea of the distance between heaven and earth stretching into the infinite. The two other dimensions of space troubled him scarcely at all, and whether he believed in their finite or infinite extension it would be equally futile to inquire.

Thus Hesiod's inventory included not merely the simple popular legends but also the oldest attempts at speculation. These last, indeed, are presented in so rough and incomplete a guise that his sparse allusions can only acquaint us with the existence of such attempts at his time, and with their barest and most general outline. We shall have to trust to later accounts to discover their contents more accurately, though our knowledge at the best can only be approximate. Then, too, we shall have occasion to examine the standard of thought to which such experiments belong. Meantime, our survey of Hesiod would be incomplete without a reference to one side of his scheme which also bears a more speculative character. Many of the beings he presents to us, and interweaves in his genealogies, show little or nothing of the vivid personification which marks the figures of simple popular belief. "Lying Speeches," for instance, would hardly impress any one at first sight as individual personages. Yet they are found with "Toilsome Labour," "Tearful Pains," "Battles," and "Carnage" in the enumeration of the offspring of Eris, or Strife. The experience is repeated in the instance of the children of Night. These do not merely include mythical figures of a comparatively life-like kind, such as Eris herself, Sleep, Death, the Moiræ, or goddesses of Fate, and so forth, but also blank, spectral personifications, such as "Deceit" and "Ruinous Old Age." "Deceit's" title to that place would appear to rest on its habit of avoiding the light; Old Age is promoted to it on no other ground than that every untoward and unwelcome event seems appropriate to the region of darkness and gloom, very much in the same way as we ourselves speak of "gloomy thoughts" and "black cares." No one can exactly determine Hesiod's debt to his predecessors either here or elsewhere; but it is fair to believe that in such purely speculative excursions he was trusting to his own imagination.

INTRODUCTORY

[1.] Diogenes Laertius, *Lives* 1.12. But Pythagoras was the first person who invented the term Philosophy, and who called himself a philosopher; for he said that no man ought to be called wise, but only God. For formerly what is now called philosophy was called wisdom and they who professed it were called wise men, as being endowed with great acuteness and accuracy of mind; but now he who embraces wisdom is called a philosopher.

[2.] Aristotle, *Metaphysics* A 2.982. But that the science under investigation is not a science employed in producing, is evident from the case of those who formed systems of philosophy in the earliest ages. For from wonder, men, both now and at first, began to philosophize, having felt astonishment originally at the problems which were more superficial; then, by degrees, in this way having advanced onwards, and, in process of time, having started difficulties about more important subjects,—as, for example, respecting the behavior of the moon, and the phenomena of the sun and stars, and respecting the generation of the universe. But he who labors under perplexity and wonder thinks that he is involved in ignorance.— Wherefore, if, for the avoidance of ignorance, men from time to time have been induced to form systems of philosophy, it is manifest that they went in pursuit of scientific knowledge for the sake of understanding it, and not on account of any utility that it might possess. (Compare *Physics*, B.2.194 b 23)

[3.] Diogenes Laertius, *Lives* 1.13. Now these were they who were accounted wise men: Thales, Solon, Periander, Cleobolus, Chilon, Bias, Pittacus.

THE MILESIANS

ARISTOTLE, preparing for the exposition of his own philosophy, presents in the first book of the *Metaphysics* a critical history of preceding thought. "Wonder," he says (*Introductory,* 2), caused the first speculations. Superior to the phrase "lover of wisdom" (*Introductory,* 1), the Aristotelian terminology carries implications wide enough for early Greek philosophy. Learning had been acquired and knowledge gathered before the origin of philosophy in Miletus: Hesiod had arranged an hierarchy of gods; Homer had aided in establishing the gods of Olympus. To the Milesians, Thales, Anaximander and Anaximenes, the primary question is not merely, "What do we know?" but "How do we know and what evidence do we have to corroborate the explanation offered?" Knowledge, evidence and application, however, are not sought as Aristotle continues, "on account of any utility" but for the "sake of understanding."

More specifically, the interrogatory, "how?" is applied to the problem that persists from the time of Thales through the time of Aristotle: "Wonder" is directed to the reduction of the change and multiplicity of the phenomenal world to a unity of explanatory principle. As the problem is first approached, the unifying principle is interpreted in terms of a fundamental "world-substance" or "world-stuff" which, by its transformations, produces the observed origin and destruction, change and recurrence, process and stability in the world. The adequacy of the principle to explain the world is not, however, the sole criterion applied by early Greek philosophy. The new speculation demands that the principle adopted must not be involved in direct conflict with any other principle unless a satisfactory explanation of the relation of the two principles is offered (*vide* on Anaximander, Aristotle, *Phys.*).

Thales is the first of the Milesians of whom we have record who set for himself the problem of explaining the universe by one principle or "world-stuff" that maintains its identity throughout change. Tradition has attributed to Thales a many-sided genius. One of the Seven Wise Men, he is at once a lawgiver and politician who offers a plan for the confederation of the Hellenic states; civil engineer, diverting the course of the Halys river; mathematician, introducing certain propositions in geometry from Egypt and applying his knowledge to the measurement of the pyramids and to the calculation of the distances of ships at sea; and astronomer, accredited with the prediction of a solar eclipse that occurred on May 28, 585 B. C.

Thales selects a natural substance, water, as the principle of explanation for change and transformation. Aristotle explains the selection (*Metaphysics*) by the suggestion that moisture is essential to the origin of life, and consequently, to growth and change. It is possible that Thales, with the Greek predilection for thinking in concrete, image-making fashion, proceeded from the imagined transformation of earth into dews, mists and springs to the more sophisticated view that water is suitable for selection as the primary substance because it undergoes transformation into gaseous and solid states in the forms of steam and ice. Such an explanation would involve temperature changes as a further explanatory factor, and it is perhaps possible that Thales was aware of the general problem involved, since Aristotle (*de Anima*) suggests that Thales regarded the soul as the source of movement and cites as an example Thales' belief in the power of the lodestone to move iron.

Thales' selection of water as the substance that explains change satisfies the requirement that the substance be able to assume various states. Difficulties remain, however, some of which are perceived by the Milesians themselves. Anaximander, son of Praxiades, "associate of Thales," attempts to meet one of the deficiencies in Thales' theory. Of Anaximander's life, we know little more than that he was sixty-four years of age in 547 B.C., that he constructed a map, probably for use in trade routes in the Black Sea, and that he conducted a colony to Appollonia, where a statue was erected in his honour.

The problem presented by Thales' theory to Anaximander may be stated simply: Granted that water may be selected to explain change because of the variety of forms or states it assumes in the world we experience, would not the pre-eminence of this substance, or, indeed, of any similar natural substance like air or fire destroy the rest? If, for example, water be selected, ordinary experience demonstrates that its moistness is destructive of the heat of fire (Aristotle, *Phys.*). The clarity with which Anaximander saw the difficulty is indicated in the one remaining fragment of his work (Simplicius,

Phys.), involving the germ of the Platonic theory of justice as "minding one's own business" and of not encroaching upon another's task. To avoid this difficulty, Anaximander identifies the fundamental substance with no one of the natural substances, earth, air, fire or water. He selects, rather, the "infinite," a mixture, which may be thought of as a boundless stock from which all things come and to which all things return. The infinite is timeless and in motion. It surrounds all the worlds (Hipp. *Phil.*) and since it is not identical with any natural substance, the conflict of contraries will not cause its destruction and "becoming" or change may continue eternally. As a consequence of the eternal motion of the "infinite," substances are separated off. The first separated are heat and cold (b. Plut.). On Zeller's view, these combine to give the moist, which in turn gives rise to air, fire and water. This view is supported by Alexander's explanation of the origin of the sea as the remainder of the original moisture (b. *Meteor*), and is consistent with Anaximander's view (b. Aet.) that life began in moisture and followed a course of evolution (c). Burnet suggests that of the opposites, heat and cold, heat makes its empirical appearance as fire, while cold is differentiated into air and earth.

The abstract "infinite" is abandoned by the third member of the Milesian school, Anaximenes. The son of Eurystratos and an associate of Anaximander, Anaximenes lived until *ca.* 525 B. C. Anaximenes selects air as the fundamental substance persisting through change. The volatility of air and its seeming inexhaustibility apparently lead to this choice (a). One important consequence of Anaximenes' adoption of air as the primary substance is to be seen in his reinterpretation of Thales' theory that soul is diffused throughout the universe. Anaximenes identifies air and breath and sees in this substance the basis for life and change in living beings. Drawing upon the microcosm for his analogy, Anaximenes interprets the macrocosm as a living, breathing organism in which, by inference, change and movement occur because of the presence of breath (a. Aet.).

Thales suggests that soul is the source of motion. Anaximander offers motion and separation as the cause of the variation of objects in the world. Anaximenes improves upon the views of his fellow-Milesians by offering an ordered sequence of change and by submitting for examination a specific process by which the varied states of objects in the world of experience could have been produced from air. Air, we are told, assumes different states through a process of rarefaction and condensation (a. Simplicius, *Phys.*). Rarefied air is fire. As air is condensed more and more it is, in order, wind, water, earth and stones. No explanation is given of the means by which the process begins but with the theory of rarefaction and condensation, Milesian philosophy has advanced far. In the first place, Anaximenes' hypothesis is one suitable for experimental verification. Secondly, it offers a possibility for reducing to quantitative differences such intangible qualitative differentiations as hardness, softness, etc. Once this step has been taken, the way is prepared for the experimental assumption of the Atomists that an adequate explanation of phenomena may be obtained by the determination of the ratio between the amount of matter and the extent of the space it occupies.

Milesian cosmology may be regarded as an application of the theory of substance to the universe and its general character is dominated by Thales' theory that the earth is a disc floating on water. Anaximenes, for example, adopts the general hypothesis of a flat earth but tells us that it floats on air. From Anaximenes' description of the motion of the stars as similar to the motion of a cap turning upon the head and with the added hypothesis that the stars disappear behind high places, we infer that the Milesian universe was one terminated by the surface of earth and the vault of heaven. Anaximander elaborates the theory with important consequences for later cosmology. The earth is a cylinder, with flat ends, one of which is our habitat. The cylinder swings unattached in the middle of the universe, maintained in this position by its equidistance from the boundaries of the world and by its heaviness, since in the motion of the infinite, heavy objects move towards the centre. This obviates the necessity for the hypothesis of the earth floating on any substance. Out of the original differentiation of hot and moist from the infinite come earth and air as a core, surrounded by a circle of fire. This circle, broken into three hoops or rings, is surrounded by air. Through apertures in the air that surrounds it, fire shines forth as the stars, sun and moon. In Anaximander's cosmos, the earth is the centre of a cosmic eddy and is enclosed within circles or "cartwheels." The hypothesis of circles is adopted and elaborated by the Pythagoreans.

THE MILESIAN SCHOOL

Aristotle, *Metaphysics* 1.3; 983 b 7. Now the majority of those who first formed systems of philosophy consider those that subsist in a form of matter to be alone the principles of all things; for wherefrom all entities arise, and wherefrom they are corrupted,—ultimately the substance, indeed, remaining permanent, but in its passive states undergoing a change,—this they assert to be an element, and this a first principle of all things. And for this reason they are of the opinion that nothing is either generated or annihilated, since this primary entity always persists.

[A.] Thales

Plutarch, *Solon* 3. And in general, it would seem that Thales was the only wise man of the time who carried his speculations beyond the realm of the practical; the rest (i. e. of the Wise Men) got the name of wisdom from their excellence as statesmen.

Diogenes Laertius, 1.23. He (Thales) seems by some accounts to have been the first to study astronomy, the first to predict eclipses of the sun and to fix the solstices.

Aristotle, *Metaphysics* 1.3; 983 b 18. As to the quantity and form of this first principle, there is a difference of opinion; but Thales, the founder of this sort of philosophy, says that it is water (accordingly he declares that the earth rests on water), getting the idea, I suppose, because he saw that the nourishment of all things is moist, and that warmth itself is generated from moisture and persists in it (for that from which all things spring is the first principle of them); and getting the idea also from the fact that the germs of all beings are of a moist nature, while water is the first principle of the nature of what is moist. And there are some who think that the ancients, and they who lived long before the present generation, and the first students of the gods, had a similar idea in regard to nature; for in their poems Okeanos and Tethys were the parents of generation, and that by which the gods swore was water,—the poets themselves called it Styx; for that which is most ancient is most highly esteemed, and that which is most highly esteemed, is an object to swear by. Whether there is any such ancient and early opinion concerning nature would be an obscure question; but Thales is

said to have expressed this opinion in regard to the first cause.
Aristotle, *de Caelo* 2.13; 294 a 28. Some say that the earth rests on water. We have ascertained that the oldest statement of this character is the one accredited to Thales the Milesian, to the effect that it rests on water, floating like a piece of wood or something else of that sort.
Aristotle, *de Anima* 1.2; 405 a 19. And Thales, according to what is related of him, seems to have regarded the soul as something endowed with the power of motion, if indeed he said that the lodestone has a soul because it moves iron. 1.5; 411 a 7. Some say that soul is diffused throughout the whole universe; and it may have been this which led Thales to think that all things are full of gods.

[B.] Anaximander

[a] Simplicius, *Phys.* 6 r; 24, 26 (from Theophrastus, *Dox.* 476) Among those who say that the first principle is one and movable and infinite, is Anaximander of Miletus, son of Praxiades, pupil and successor of Thales. He said that the first principle and element of all things is infinite, and he was the first to apply this word to the first principle; and he says that it is neither water nor any other one of the things called elements, but the infinite is something of a different nature, from which came all the heavens and the worlds in them.
Hipp., *Phil.* 6; *Dox.* 559. And this (first principle) is eternal and does not grow old, and it surrounds all the worlds.
Simplicius, *Phys.* 6 r. And from what source things arise, to that they return of necessity when they are destroyed; for they suffer punishment and make reparation to one another for their injustice according to the order of time, as he says in somewhat poetical language.
Hipp., *loc. cit.* Besides this, motion is eternal, and as a result of it the origin of the worlds was brought about.
Simplicius, *op. cit.* Evidently when he sees the four elements changing into one another, he does not deem it right to make any one of these the underlying substance (substratum), but something else besides them. And he does not think that

things come into being by change in the nature of the element, but by the separation of the opposites which the eternal motion causes.

Simplicius, *Phys.* 32 r; 150, 20. There is another method, according to which they do not attribute change to matter itself, nor do they suppose that generation takes place by a transformation of the underlying substance, but by separation; for the opposites existing in the substance which is infinite matter are separated, according to Anaximander, who was the earliest thinker to call the underlying substance the first principle. And the opposites are heat and cold, dry and moist, and the rest.

Aristotle, *Phys.* 3.5; 204 b 22. But it is not possible that infinite matter is one and simple; either, as some say, that it is something different from the elements, from which they are generated, or that it is absolutely one. For there are some who make the infinite of this character, but they do not consider it to be air or water, in order that other things may not be destroyed by the infinite; for these are mutually antagonistic to one another, inasmuch as air is cold, water is moist, and fire hot; if one of these were infinite, the rest would be at once destroyed. Accordingly, they say that the infinite is something different from these elements, namely, that from which they come.

[b] Simplicius, *Phys.* 5. Those who assumed innumerable worlds, e. g., Anaximander, Leukippos, Democritus, and, at a later date, Epicurus, held that they came into being and passed away *ad infinitum,* some always coming into being and others passing away.

Plut., *Strom.* 2. *Dox.* 579. Anaximander says that at the beginning of this world something productive of heat and cold from the eternal was separated therefrom, and a sort of sphere of this flame surrounded the air about the earth, as bark surrounds a tree; then this sphere was broken into parts and defined into distinct circles, and thus arose the sun and the moon and the stars.

Alexander, *Meteor.* 91 r. *Dox.* 494. Some of the physicists say that the sea is what is left of the first moisture; for when the region about the earth was moist, the upper part of the moisture was evaporated by the sun, and from it came the winds and the revolutions of the sun and moon, since these made their revolutions by reason of the vapours and exhalations, and revolved in those regions where they found an abundance of them. What is left of this moisture in the hollow places is the sea; so it diminishes in quantity, being evaporated gradually by the sun, and finally it will be completely dried up. Theophrastus says that Anaximander and Diogenes were of this opinion.

Plut., *Strom.* 2. *Dox.* 579. Anaximander says that the earth is a cylinder in form, and that its depth is one-third of its breadth.

Hipp., *Phil.* 6. *Dox.* 559. The earth is a heavenly body, controlled by no other power, and keeping its position because it is the same distance from all things; the form of it is curved, cylindrical like a stone column; it has two faces, one of these is the ground beneath our feet, and the other is opposite to it.

Hipp., *Phil.* 6. The stars are a wheel (circle) of fire, separated from the fire about the world, and surrounded by air. There are certain breathing-holes like the holes of a flute through which we see the stars; so that when the holes are stopped up, there are eclipses. The moon is sometimes full and sometimes in other phases as these holes are stopped up or open. The circle of the sun is twenty-seven times that of the moon, and the sun is higher than the moon, but the circles of the fixed stars are lower.

Aet. 2, 13; 342. The stars are wheel-shaped masses of air, full of fire, breathing out flames from pores in different parts. 15; 345. Anaximandros (*et al.*): The sun has the highest position of all, the moon is next in order, and beneath it are the fixed stars and the planets. 16; 345. The stars are carried on by the circles and the spheres in which each one moves. 20; 348. The circle of the sun is twenty-eight times as large as the earth, like a chariot wheel, having a hollow centre and this full of fire, shining in every part, and sending out fire through a narrow opening like the air from a flute. 21; 351. The sun is equal in size to the earth, but the circle from which it sends forth its exhalations, and by which it is borne through the heavens, is twenty-seven times as large as the earth. 24; 354. An eclipse takes place when the outlet for the fiery exhalations is closed. 25; 355. The circle of the moon is nineteen times as large as the earth, and like the circle of the sun is full of fire; and eclipses are due to the revolutions of the wheel; for it is like a chariot wheel, hollow inside, and the centre of it is full of fire, but there is only one exit for the fire. 28; 358. The moon shines by its own light. 29; 359. The moon is eclipsed when the hole in the wheel is stopped. Aet. 3, 3; 367. Anaximandros said that lightning is due to wind; for when it is surrounded and pressed together by a thick cloud and so driven out by reason of its lightness and rarefaction, then the breaking makes a noise, while the separation makes a rift of brightness in the darkness of the cloud.

[c] Hipp., *Phil.* 6. Animals came into being through vapours raised by the sun. Man, however, came into being from another animal, namely the fish, for at first he was like a fish.

Aet., v. 19. Anaximander said that the first animals were generated in the moisture, and were covered with a prickly skin; and as they grew older, they became drier, and after the skin broke off from them, they lived for a little while.

Plut., *Strom.* 2. *Dox.* 579. Anaximander says that at the beginning man was generated from all sorts of animals, since all the rest can quickly get food for themselves, but man alone requires careful feeding for a long time; such a being at the beginning could not have preserved his existence.

[C.] Anaximenes

[a] Simpl., *Phys.* 6 r. *Dox.* 476. Theophrastus. Anaximenes of Miletus, son of Eurystratos, a companion of Anaximander, agrees with him that the essential nature of things is one and infinite, but he regards it as not indeterminate but rather determinate, and calls it air.

Hipp., *Phil.* 7. *Dox.* 560. Infinite air is the first principle, from which arise the things that have come and are coming into existence, and the things that will be, and gods and divine beings, while other things are produced from these.

Aet., *Plac.* 1.3. *Dox.* 278. As our soul which is air, he says, holds us together, so wind (i. e. breath) and air encompass the whole world.

Hipp., *op. cit.* And the form of air is as follows: When it is of a very even consistency, it is imperceptible to vision, but it becomes visible as the result of cold or heat or moisture, or when it is moved. It is always in motion; for things would not change as they do unless it were in motion.

Simplicius, *Phys. op. cit.* Air differs in rarity and in density as the nature of things is different.

[b] Hipp., *op. cit.* When air is dilated so as to be rarer, it becomes fire; while winds, on the other hand, are condensed air. Cloud is formed from air by compression (felting); and water when it is compressed farther, and earth and finally stones as it is more condensed.

Plut., *Strom.* 3. *Dox.* 579. By compression of the air the earth is formed, and it is very broad; accordingly he says that it rests on air.

Hipp., *Phil.* 7. *Dox.* 560. Similarly, the sun and the moon and all the rest of the stars, being fiery bodies, are supported on the air by their breadth. And stars are made of earth, since exhalations arise from this, and these being attenuated become fire, and of this fire when it is raised to the heaven the stars are constituted. There are also bodies of an earthy nature in the place occupied by the stars, and carried along with them in their motion. He says that the stars do not move under the earth, as others have supposed, but around the earth, just as a cap is moved about the head. And the sun is hidden not by going underneath the earth, but because it is covered by some of the higher parts of the earth, and because of its greater distance from us. The stars do not give forth heat, because they are so far away. Winds are produced when the air that has been rarefied is set in motion; and when it comes together and is yet further condensed, clouds are produced, and so it changes into water. And hail is formed when the water descending from the clouds is frozen; and snow, when these being yet more filled with moisture become frozen;— And a rainbow is produced when the sun's rays fall upon thick condensed air.

Aet., 3.10; *Dox.* 377. The form of the earth is like a table. Aet. 2, 1; 327. Anaximenes *et al.:* Infinite worlds exist in the infinite in every cycle. 4; 331. The world is perishable. 11; 339. The sky is the revolving vault most distant from the earth. 14; 344. The stars are fixed like nailheads in the crystalline (vault). 19; 347. The stars shine for none of these reasons, but solely by the light of the sun. 22; 352. The sun is broad [like a leaf]. 23; 352. The stars revolve, being pushed by condensed resisting air.

THE PYTHAGOREANS

In the philosophy of Pythagoras, two aspects are dominant. These aspects, the religious or moral and the formal or mathematical, may be said to have been coordinated in the Pythagorean insistence upon the superiority of man's intellectual nature over his sensual nature and in the supposition that the best life was one devoted to mental discipline.

Of Pythagoras' life little is known, but the presence of Milesian elements in his thought gives credibility to the tradition that he was a disciple of Anaximenes. A native of Samos, Pythagoras migrated from Greece to Croton, in southern Italy, *ca.* 532 B.C. and there established his school. The development of Pythagorean philosophy in the hands of the followers was so varied that the group may be termed a school only in the sense that one man, the founder, stimulated an interest in one or the other of the aspects that dominated his own thought. Pythagoras, himself, was a religious teacher and a mathematician of native gifts. To him are attributed the first cosmology in which the earth is a planet rather than the centre of the universe, the discovery of the Pythagorean theorem, and the formulation of the theory of harmony. Continued persecutions of the Pythagoreans in Croton forced Pythagoras to flee to Mesopontum, where his death occurred *ca.* 495 B.C. His most renowned disciples were Alcmaeon of Croton, Hippasus of Mesopontum, and Philolaus of Croton.

Pythagoreanism, as a religious or ethical school, is most deeply influenced by the tenets and ritual of the cult of Orpheus. Perhaps the most important factor in the teaching of the cult of Orpheus was purification, by which man could recover the godlike character he once had. In this, Orphism is reminiscent of the teachings of the cult of Dionysus, in which the preoccupation with man's immortality owed its origin to the myth of Dionysus' capture by the Titans. In the myth, Dionysus was killed and eaten by his captors who were, in turn, destroyed by Zeus' thunderbolts. From the ashes of the Titans, containing as they did part of the divine Dionysus, man was created. Orphism, retaining the conception of the fallen god, added the theory of the transmigration of the soul. Every human soul, pre-existing with the gods, must occupy a human body and upon the conduct of the human being depended the future state of the soul, in that the soul returned to the gods or was punished for its sins by a return to the earth. For the Orphic, good conduct consisted largely in the observance of the stringent rules of life, including prohibitions upon particular kinds of food and in participation in the mysteries or sacred pantomimes. Pythagoreanism incorporated much of Orphism in its teachings, including the belief in immortality and in metempsychosis (a. Hipp. *Phil.* and d.) and an observance of many rules of conduct (e). The sacrifice of animals was prohibited and the ritual was directed towards the end of demonstrating the superiority of the intellectual over the sensual life, rather than to the mere performance of fixed ceremonies.

In his mathematical philosophy, Pythagoras adopted

number as the principle essential to an explanation of the universe. Perceiving "many qualities of numbers in bodies perceived by sense" (a. Aristotle, *Met.* xiii), the founder and his disciples generalized their observations into a philosophy.

It seems probable that the beginnings of their explanations are to be found, as Aristotle suggests (*loc. cit.*) in Pythagoras' discovery of the relationship of concord in music to number. By experimentation with the lengthening and shortening of a vibrating string, the concordant intervals of the scale could be reduced to the numerical ratios of 1:1, 4:3, 3:2, and 2:1. These ratios, in turn, when reduced to their lowest common denominator, can be represented by the numbers 6, 8, 9, 12. Since these numbers, in turn, form a ratio in which means and extremes are equal, limit or form or unity is said by the Pythagoreans to have been brought into a concord of tones by the union of disparate or contrary elements. The simplicity and exactness with which such a concord could be expressed had a wide influence upon Greek formal or mathematical theories of beauty, particularly upon the Platonic aesthetic.

In the Pythagorean application of the theory of concord in music, *harmonia,* which originally signified the octave or a musical scale, comes to mean a system of relations and eventually the plan, scheme or system which things compose. As such, it is likewise the form or ratio as contrasted to the matter. In these meanings, *harmonia* is applied by the Pythagoreans to sciences as varied as medicine and cosmology. Medicine, on Pythagorean grounds, must have as its end the proper restoration of the complex harmony of the body, a harmony disturbed by illness. The soul is considered to be a harmony or attunement of the body, a theory to which Plato and Aristotle offer objections (d).

There is also a *harmonia* of the cosmos. The Pythagorean construction of the universe is fundamentally influenced by the Milesians and, in particular, by the teaching of Anaximander. Corresponding to the infinite of Anaximander or the boundless air of Anaximenes is the dark, a substance unlimited, cold and dense. As a Pythagorean addition, there is also light, which is limited and formed. By attraction, portions of the dark are drawn to the limited, as if the universe were breathing, and these portions are given form or limit (b. Aristotle, *Phys.*). As a consequence of the "breaths" of the universe, the astronomical system is evolved. Ten heavenly bodies revolve from west to east around the central fire. Between the central fire and earth, a planet moving as do other heavenly bodies, is counter-earth. Counter-earth, according to Aristotle (b. *de Caelo*), is included merely to construct a universe with ten heavenly bodies, as ten was considered to be a sacred number. The earth always presents the same side to the central fire and to counter-earth and we see neither of them. Earth receives light and heat from the sun, which shines by reflected light from the central fire. In the cosmos, after earth and in succession towards the limit of the universe, are the moon, the sun, the five planets, Mercury, Venus, Mars, Jupiter and Saturn. At the limit of the cosmos is the sphere of the fixed stars.

The Pythagorean cosmology derives from that of Anaximander. Certain suggestions in the Milesian's hypothesis indicate the method by which *harmonia* was introduced into the Pythagorean system. Anaximander thought that the movement of the infinite produced wheels of fire and he adopted as a unit of measurement of the universe the radius of the earth. The wheel of the stars was nine times the size of the earth, that of the moon eighteen times that of the earth, that of the sun twenty-seven times the earth's size, from which it may be seen that the cosmology is based upon an arithmetical progression. Adopting the method, the Pythagoreans assume that the heavenly bodies move at distances from the central fire corresponding to the intervals of the octave. Since all moving bodies produce sound, the Pythagoreans, thinking perhaps of the speed of revolution of the bodies around the central fire or perhaps of the distance by which the bodies were separated from the central fire, assumed that a *harmonia* existed, with the resultant "music of the spheres" (b). The theory reveals at once a difficulty in the Pythagorean employment of hypotheses, since the *harmonia* could not relate to the original ten heavenly bodies, as the theory was based either upon seven sounds, if the harmonic system of the heptachord is adopted, or upon eight sounds, if the harmonic system of the octochord is adopted.

The conception of the limited and the unlimited is based upon a similar arbitrary method of definition. All numbers are divided into odd and even. Since odd and even are the components of numbers and numbers are the essence of and material of things in the world, things will likewise be odd or even. The next identification is that of odd with limited and of even with the unlimited (a. Aristotle, *Met.* i.). The reason for this identification is apparent if it be remembered that the Pythagorean number system was exhibited spatially, numbers being represented by dots or pebbles as demarcations of figures. The addition of odd numbers to one will give squares, e.g. $1+3=4$ or 2^2; $1+3+5=9$ or 3^2; similarly, odd numbers added to a square give other squares, e.g. $1^2+3=2^2$; $2^2+5=3^2$; $3^2+7=4^2$. On the other hand, beginning with the even number 2, the addition of even numbers will give the series, 2, 6, 12, 20, called by the Pythagoreans "oblong," owing to their spatial representation in the set figure. Similarly, the addition of odd and even numbers give triangular numbers, 1, 3, 6, 10, etc., as in the *tetraktys*. Odd numbers give squares and other numbers give figures varying indefinitely in shape. Having identified odd and even with limited and unlimited, the world is assumed by the Pythagoreans to be constructed of conflicting components. All things will be combinations of the limited and the unlimited, reconciled by *harmonia* (a. Aristotle, *Met.* 1.5, where the ten pairs of opposites are given).

Proceeding further, the Pythagoreans apply their theory to earth, air, fire and water. Beginning with the identification of one with the point, two with the line, three with the plane and four with the solid, they formally identify the cube with earth, the tetrahedron with fire, etc. (c. Herm.).

The brilliant discovery of the application of ratios and number to music results eventually in definition. The conception of ratio or form as contrasted with matter is applied to physical things in addition to its application to geometrical relations. The strength of Pythagoreanism consists in its reduction of multiple phenomena to formal ratios. Its weakness is the arbitrary application to phenomena of ratios and numbers which are not strictly applicable or are applicable only by altering the phenomena. Counter-earth, added to make the heavenly bodies add to ten, is an example but there are many others. Justice for example, is identified with four or with nine, since if one multiplies two by two or three by three and then takes the square root of the result "equals are returned to equals," a term synonymous with Pythagorean justice. For all of its weaknesses, however, Pythagoreanism pointed the way to and the necessity for definition and exerted perhaps its most important influence upon the Platonic theory of ideas.

The Pythagoreans

[a] Heraclitus, *Fr. 17.* Pythagoras, son of Mnesarchos, prosecuted scientific investigations beyond all other men, and making a selection of these writings, he made a wisdom of his own—

Aristotle, *Metaphysics* xii.6; 1080 b 16. The Pythagoreans say that there is but one number, the mathematical, but things of sense are not separated from this, for they are composed of it; indeed, they construct the whole heaven out of numbers, but not out of unit numbers, for they assume that the unities have quantity; but how the first 1 was constructed so as to have quantity (magnitude), they seem at a loss to say.

Aristotle, *Metaphysics* xiii.3; 1090 a 20. But the Pythagoreans, because they see many qualities of numbers in bodies perceived by sense, regard objects as numbers, not as separate numbers, but as derived numbers. And why? Because the qualities of numbers exist in a musical scale (*harmonia*), in the heavens and in many other things.

Aristotle, *Metaphysics* i.5; 985 b 23–986 b 8. With these and before them (Anaxagoras, Empedokles, Atomists) those called Pythagoreans applying themselves to the sciences, first developed them; and being brought up in them they thought that the first principles of these (*i. e.* numbers) were the first principles of all things. And since of these (sciences) numbers are by nature the first, in numbers rather than in fire and earth and water they thought they saw many likenesses to things that are and that are coming to be, as, for instance, justice is such a property of numbers, and soul and mind are such a property, and another is opportunity, and of other things one may say the same of each one.

And further, discerning in numbers the conditions and reasons of harmonies also; since, moreover, other things seemed to be like numbers in their entire nature, and numbers were the first of every nature, they assumed that the elements of numbers were the elements of all things, and that the whole heavens were harmony and number. And whatever characteristics in numbers and harmonies they could show were in agreement with the properties of the heavens and its parts and with its whole arrangement, these they collected and adapted; and if there chanced to be any gap anywhere, they eagerly sought that the whole system might be connected with these (stray phenomena). To give an example of my meaning: inasmuch as ten seemed to be the perfect number and to embrace the whole nature of numbers, they asserted that the number of bodies moving through the heavens were ten, and when only nine were visible, for the reason just stated they postulated the counter-earth as the tenth. We have given a more definite account of these thinkers in other parts of our writings. But we have referred to them here with this purpose in view, that we might ascertain from them what they asserted as the first principles and in what manner they came upon the causes that have been enumerated. They certainly seem to consider number as the first principle and as it were the matter in things and in their conditions and states; and the odd and the even are elements of number, and of these the former is limited, the latter unlimited, and unity is the product of both of them, for it is both odd and even, and number arises from unity, and the whole heaven, as has been said, is numbers.

A different party in this same school say that the first principles are ten, named according to the following table:

limited and unlimited, even and odd, one and many, right and left, male and female, rest and motion, straight and crooked, light and darkness, good and bad, square and oblong. After this manner Alkmaeon of Kroton seems to have conceived them, and either he received this doctrine from them or they from him; for Alkmaeon arrived at maturity when Pythagoras was an old man, and his teachings resembled theirs. For he says that most human affairs are twofold, not meaning opposites reached by definition, as did the former party, but opposites by chance—as, for example, white-black, sweet-bitter, good-bad, small-great. This philosopher let fall his opinions indefinitely about the rest, but the Pythagoreans declared the number of the opposites and what they were. From both one may learn this much, that opposites are the first principles of things; but from the latter he may learn the number of these, and what they are. But how it is possible to bring them into relation with the causes of which we have spoken if they have not clearly worked out; but they seem to range their elements under the category of matter, for they say that being is compounded and formed from them, and that they inhere in it.

ARISTOTLE, *Metaphysics* i.8; 989 b 32–990 a 32. Those, however, who carry on their investigation with reference to all things, and divide things into what are perceived and what are not perceived by sense, evidently examine both classes, so one must delay a little longer over what they say. They speak correctly and incorrectly in reference to the questions now before us. Now those who are called Pythagoreans use principles and elements yet stranger than those of the physicists, in that they do not take them from the sphere of sense, for mathematical objects are without motion, except in the case of astronomy. Still, they discourse about everything in nature and study it; they construct the heaven, they observe what happens in its parts and their states and motions; they apply to these their first principles and causes, as though they agreed entirely with the other physicists that being is only what is perceptible and what that which is called heaven includes. But their causes and first principles, they say, are such as to lead up to the higher parts of reality, and are in harmony with this rather than with the doctrines of nature. In what manner motion will take place when limited and unlimited, odd and even, are the only underlying realities, they do not say; nor how it is possible for genesis and destruction to take place without motion and change, or for the heavenly bodies to revolve.

Farther, if one grant to them that greatness arises from these principles, or if this could be proved, nevertheless, how will it be that some bodies are light and some heavy? For their postulates and statements apply no more to mathematical objects than to things of sense; accordingly they have said nothing at all about fire or earth or any such objects, because I think they have no distinctive doctrine about things of sense. Farther, how is it necessary to assume that number and states of number are the causes of what is in the heavens and what is taking place there from the beginning and now, and that there is no other number than that out of which the world is composed? For when opinion and opportune time are at a certain point in the heavens, and a little farther up or down are injustice and judgment or a mixture of them, and they bring forward as proof that each one of these is number, and the result then is that at this place there is already a multitude of compounded quantities because those states of number have each their place—is this number in heaven the same which it is necessary to assume that each of these things is, or is it something different? Plato says it is different; still, he thinks that both these things and the causes of them are numbers; but the one class are ideal causes, and the others are sense causes.

Hipp., *Phil.* 2. *Dox.* 555. There is a second philosophy not far distant from the same time, of which Pythagoras, whom some call a Samian, was the first representative. And this they call the Italian philosophy because Pythagoras fled the rule of Polykrates over the Samians and settled in a city of Italy where he spent his life. The successive leaders of this sect shared the same spirit. And he in his studies of nature mingled astronomy and geometry and music <and arithmetic>. And thus he asserted that god is a monad, and examining the nature of number with especial care, he said that the universe produces melody and is put together with harmony, and he first proved the motion of the seven stars to be rhythm and melody. And in wonder at the structure of the universe, he decreed that at first his disciples should be silent, as it were mystae who were coming into the order of the all; then when he thought they had sufficient education in the principles of truth, and had sought wisdom sufficiently in regard to stars and and in regard to nature, he pronounced them pure and then bade them speak. He separated his disciples into two groups, and called one esoteric, and the other exoteric. To the former he entrusted the more perfect sciences, to the latter the more moderate. And he dealt with magic, as they say, and himself discovered the art of physiognomy. Postulating both numbers and measures he was wont to say that the first principle of arithmetic embraced philosophy by combination, after the following manner:

Number is the first principle, a thing which is undefined, incomprehensible, having in itself all numbers which could reach infinity in amount. And the first principle of numbers is in substance the first monad, which is a male monad, begetting as a father all other numbers. Secondly the dyad is a female number, and the same is called by the arithmeticians even. Thirdly the triad is male number; this the arithmeticians have been wont to call odd. Finally the tetrad is a female number, and the same is called even because it is female.

All numbers, then, taken by classes are fours (for number is undefined in reference to class), of which is composed the perfect number, the decad. For the series, one two three and four, becomes ten, if its own name is kept in its essence by each of the numbers. Pythagoras said that this sacred tetraktys is "the spring having the roots of ever-flowing nature" in itself, and from this numbers have their first principle. For the eleven and the twelve and the rest derive from the ten the first principle of their being. The four parts of the decad, this perfect number, are called number, monad, power, and cube. And the interweavings and minglings of these in the origin of growth are what naturally completes nascent number; for when a power is multiplied upon itself, it is the power of a power; and when a power is multiplied on a cube, it is the power of a cube; and when a cube is multiplied on a cube, the cube of a cube; thus all numbers, from which arises the genesis of what arises, are seven:—number, monad, power, cube, power of a power, power of a cube, cube of a cube.

He said that the soul is immortal, and that it changes from one body to another; so he was wont to say that he himself had been born before the Trojan war as Aethalides, and at the time of the Trojan war as Euphorbos, and after that as Hermotimos of Samos, then as Pyrrhos of Delos, fifth as Pythagoras. And Diodoros of Eretria and Aristoxenos the musician say that Pythagoras had come into Zaratas of Chaldaea; and he set forth that in his view there were from the beginning two causes of things, father and mother; and the father is light and the mother darkness; and the parts of light are warm, dry, light, swift; and of darkness are cold, moist, heavy, slow; and of these all the universe is composed, of male and female. And he says that the universe exists in accordance with musical harmony, so the sun also makes an harmonious period. And concerning the things that arise from the earth and the universe they say that Zaratas spoke as follows: There are two divinities, one of the heavens and the other of the earth; the one of the earth produces things from the earth, and it is water; and the divinity of the heavens is fire with a portion of air, warm, and cold; wherefore he says that none of these things will destroy or even pollute the soul, for these are the essence of all things. And it is said that Zaratas forbade men to eat beans because he said that at the beginning and composition of all things when the earth was still a whole, the bean arose. And he says that the proof of this is that if one chews a bean to a pulp and exposes it to the sun for a certain time (for the sun will affect it quickly), it gives out the odour of human seed. And he says that there is another and clearer proof: if when a bean is in flower we were to take the bean and its flower, and putting it into a pitcher moisten it and then bury it in the earth, and after a few days dig it up again, we should see in the first place that it had the form of a womb, and examining it closely we should find the head of a child growing with it.

He perished in a conflagration with his disciples in Kroton in Italy. And it was the custom when one became a disciple for him to burn his property and to leave his money under a seal with Pythagoras, and he remained in silence sometimes three years, sometimes five years, and studied. And immediately on being released from this he mingled with the others and continued a disciple and made his home with them; otherwise he took his money and was sent off. The esoteric class were called Pythagoreans, and the others Pythagoristae. And those of the disciples who escaped the conflagration were Lysis and Archippos and Zalmoxis the slave of Pythagoras, who is said to have taught the Pythagorean philosophy to the Druids among the Celts. It is said that Pythagoras learned numbers and measures from the Egyptians; astonished at the wisdom of the priests, which was deserving of belief and full of fancies and difficult to buy, he imitated it and himself also taught his disciples to be silent, and obliged the student to remain quietly in rooms underneath the earth.

Aristotle, *Metaphysics* xiv, 1092 b 10. Once more, it has in no sense been determined in which way numbers are the causes of substances and of being—whether (1) as limits (as points are of spatial magnitudes). This is how Eurytus decided what was the number of what (e. g. of man or of horse), viz. by imitating the figures of living things with pebbles, as some people bring numbers into the forms of triangle and square.

[b] Aristotle, *Physics* iv.6; 213 b 22. And the Pythagoreans say that there is a void, and that it enters into the heaven itself from the infinite air, as though it (the heaven) were breathing; and this void defines the natures of things, inasmuch as it is a certain separation and definition of things that lie together; and this is true first in the case of numbers, for the void defines the nature of these.

Aristotle, *de Caelo* 2.13; 293 a 19. These (the Pythagoreans) say that fire is at the centre and that the earth is one of the stars, and that moving in a circle about the centre it produces night and day. And they assume yet another earth opposite this which they call counter-earth, not seeking reasons and causes for phenomena, but stretching phenomena to meet certain assumptions and opinions of theirs and attempting to arrange them in a system.—And farther the Pythagoreans say that the most authoritative part of the All stands guard, because it is specially fitting that it should, and this part is the centre; and this place that the fire occupies, they called the guard of Zeus, as it is called simply the centre, that is, the centre of space and the centre of matter and of nature.

Aristotle, *de Caelo* ii.9; 290 b 15. Some think it necessary that noise should arise when so great bodies are in motion, since sound does arise from bodies among us which are not so large and do not move so swiftly; and from the sun and moon and from the stars in so great number, and of so great size, moving so swiftly, there must necessarily arise a sound inconceivably great. Assuming these things and that the swiftness has the principle of harmony by reason of the intervals, they say that the sound of the stars moving on in a circle becomes musical. And since it seems unreasonable that we also do not hear this sound, they say that the reason for this is that the noise exists in the very nature of things, so as not to be distinguishable from the opposite silence; for the distinction of sound and silence lies in their contrast with each other, so that as blacksmiths think there is no difference between them because they are accustomed to the sound, so the same things happen to men. ii.9; 291 a 7. What occasions the difficulty and makes the Pythagoreans say that there is a harmony of the bodies as they move, is a proof. For whatever things move themselves make a sound and noise; but whatever things are fastened in what moves or exist in it as the parts in a ship, cannot make a noise, nor yet does the ship if it moves in a river.

[c] Aet., *Plac.* ii.6; *Dox.* 334. Pythagoras: The universe is made from five solid figures, which are called also mathematical; of these he says that earth has arisen from the cube, fire from the pyramid, air from the octahedron, and water from the icosahedron, and the sphere of the all from the dodecahedron.

Herm., *I.G.P.* 16; *Dox.* 655. The monad is the first principle of all things. From its forms and from numbers the elements arose. And he declared that the number and form and measure of each of these is somehow as follows: Fire is composed of twenty-four right-angled triangles, surrounded by four equilaterals. And each equilateral consists of six right-angled triangles, whence they compare it to a pyramid. Air is composed of forty-eight triangles, surrounded by eight equilaterals. And it is compared to the octahedron, which is surrounded by eight equilateral triangles, each of which is separated into six right-angled triangles so as to become forty-eight in all. And water is composed of one hundred and twenty triangles, surrounded by twenty equilaterals, and it is compared to the icosahedron, which is composed of one hundred and twenty equilateral triangles. And aether is composed of twelve equilateral pentagons and is like a dodecahedron. And earth is composed of forty-eight triangles, and is surrounded by six equilateral pentagons, and it is like a cube. For the cube is surrounded by six tetragons, each of which is separated into eight triangles, so that they become in all forty-eight.

[d] PLATO, *Phaedo* 86 b 7–c 5. Our body being, as it were, strung together by the warm and the cold, the dry and the moist, and things of that sort, our soul is a sort of temperament and attunement of these, when they are mingled with one another well and in due proportion. If, then, our soul is an attunement, it is clear that, when the body has been relaxed or strung up out of measure by diseases and other ills, the soul must necessarily perish at once. cf. Aristotle, *de Anima* Bk. 1 ch. 4. This theory regards the soul as a sort of harmony. Harmony, say its advocates, is a mixture and combination of opposites. The body, too, is composed of opposites. Although it is true that harmony is a sort of relation in mixed parts or a combination of parts, we maintain that it is impossible for the soul to be either of these. Again, although motion is not an attribute of harmony, yet almost all of the philosophers who hold the theory of harmony, I may say, ascribe motion to the soul. Another objection is that it is more fitting to apply the term harmony to conditions of health or to bodily qualities in general than to the soul.

This becomes most evident when one attempts to describe the effects and functions of the soul in terms of harmony; for it is difficult to find any correspondence between them. Now, if we have two sorts of harmony in mind when we use this term, viz. harmony in the primary sense, which means such composition of magnitudes in objects possessing motion and position that they fuse together and admit nothing further that is homogeneous, and in the secondary sense, a ratio in mixed elements,—we still object that in neither sense does harmony apply to the soul. The composition of the parts of the body can be readily examined. There are manifold combinations of the parts, which may be effected in many ways. Of what parts, then, is reason a combination and how is the combination effected? And I raise the same question regarding the sensitive and appetitive soul.

AET., *Plac.* iv.7; *Dox.* 392. The soul is imperishable.

EPIPH., *Haer.* iii.8; *Dox.* 390. And Pythagoras said that the soul goes at death into other animals.

[e] ARISTOTLE, *Eth. Nic.* ii.5; 1106 b 29. The evil partakes of the nature of the unlimited, the good of the limited, as the Pythagoreans conjectured. v.8; 1132 b 21. Reciprocity seems to some to be absolutely just, as the Pythagoreans say; for these defined the just as that which is reciprocal to another.

EPIPH., *Haer.* iii.8; *Dox.* 390. Pythagoras was wont to say that wise men ought not to sacrifice animals to gods, nor yet to eat what had life, or beans, nor drink wine.

HERACLITUS

LATENT in Thales' philosophy is the assumption that the various manifestations of the underlying substance that maintains its identity through change are related to changes in temperature. There is, moreover, in the theory of rarefaction and condensation held by Anaximenes an increasing emphasis upon the means by which the change or alteration is brought about. Heraclitus, who based his philosophy upon Milesian principles, takes fire, the source of heat, as the substance underlying all change. It is, however, rather upon the "how," upon the cosmic process by which fire is transformed, that he concentrates his theory of evidence.

Heraclitus, who died between the years 478 and 470 B.C., was a native of Ephesus, on the coast of Asia Minor. Descended from the royal line of his native city, it is probable that Heraclitus held temporal and religious powers commensurate with his rank. The priestly duties must have retained a considerable importance even after the rise of democracy had restricted royalty's temporal activities. However, it seems probable, from the attacks by Heraclitus upon the mysteries and the sacrifices (Frs. 124–130), that he renounced the priestly privileges. The bitterness of his attack contributed to his reputation as the "weeping philosopher" and the habit of mind inculcated by concentration upon spiritual matters gave to his writings a mystical and esoteric character that resulted in the reference of antiquity to the author as "the dark." No less critical than his view of priestly practices is his evaluation of his predecessors in philosophy (Frs. 16–17) and of his countrymen (Fr. 114).

As has been indicated, the point of departure in Heracliteanism is Milesian. Fire, an infinite mass of substance, uncreated and eternal, is identical with the universe (Fr. 20). Empirical observation, the method so thoroughly adopted by the Milesians, reveals characteristics of the flame that are important for Heraclitus' general theory. Fire, in its combination of movement in flickering and its apparent identity and permanence, and in its consumption of fuel and its giving off of ash and smoke, would appear to be an adequate manifestation of the principle or substance maintaining its identity despite transformation. But the process itself and the order of the change and transformation cause Heraclitus to move beyond his predecessors. Fire, in the sun, is condensed into water. This, in turn, is condensed half into earth, half into smoke, "fiery storm-cloud" or waterspout. This portion of the process, Heraclitus calls the "downward movement" or the "downward way." The "upward movement" or the "upward way" begins with the liquefaction of earth into sea and proceeds through the transformation of the sea into stormcloud or vapour and, ultimately, into fire. The sun is a concave bowl in which the vapours from the sea are gathered and burned and it is here that the process is completed (Frs. 21, 22, 23, 25, 69 and b. Diogenes Laertius). The purely Milesian beginnings of explanation in Heraclitus' theory are clearly present in the theory of process, for it is obvious that he regards as explained what may be referred to common experience. The "upward movement," for example, reverts to the use of images and pictorial thinking, in that the transformation of earth into water would fit into the common supposition that springs rising from the earth or streams flowing from the mountainside, represent a change of earth to water. Unity in the system referred to is the type of explanation under which the image is subsumed.

More important, Heraclitus conceives the "upward movement" and the "downward movement" to be identical in nature and simultaneous in process (Fr. 69). For, while there is transformation of fire into water and water into earth and while the contraries are destructive of each other (Fr. 25), the two processes balance each other. There is, then, "measure." For example, for each portion of water transformed into earth, in the "downward movement," there is an equal transformation of earth into water in the "upward movement." Just as in fire there is an equilibrium of the fuel consumed and the ash and smoke given off, with the maintenance of a steady flame, so in the universe there is equilibrium or balance maintained by the "tension" of the opposing transformations. It follows, therefore, that balance or equilibrium or rhythm is essential. Although such balance may be delayed, as, for instance, during the summer when fire is dominant, the balance eventually must be even (Fr. 29). Heraclitus' balance is analogous to the physical law of the conservation of matter. For the reason that the balance must be maintained by the eternal motion of the process and by the tension or conflict with the opposing movement upward and downward, Heraclitus insists that strife is essential to harmony or balance. When, therefore, he applies his principles to the world at large, strife is considered to be the father of all things (Frs. 43, 44, 46). This view is consistently held with reference to the objects about us: The harp or lyre is what it is because of the equilibrium produced by the tension of strings working against the strength of the frame; the bow is what it is because of a similar conflict or tension of the two opposing forces produced by the hands pulling simultaneously away from and towards the bowman; the river is what it is because the filling compensates the emptying, for if one overbalances, the river no longer exists as such but becomes, in the one case, a lake, in the other, a dry channel (Frs. 41, 42, 45; cf. 50, 52, 57, 58 and 67).

Reality, it is clear, is like the stream or the fire, in constant motion and flux. "All things are flowing," including the percipient being (Fr. 81). Implicit in Heraclitus' theory is what later philosophy developed into "natural law" for it is clear that if all is in change and flux, the one exception to the generalization will be the law of change itself. In a sense, Heraclitus interprets his system in this way, for the law is apart from perceptual things and is identified with *logos* or wisdom (Frs. 4, 16, 18, 19). Nevertheless, it is equally clear that for him the law is always exemplified in concrete things. Heraclitus does not suppose the process to be one of illusion. Change is real and the concrete exemplifications of the process of change indicate that the law and its example are for him one and the same. Heraclitus is thinking in concrete images which have not yet passed into the abstract symbols or ideas of later thought. It must be remembered that even in Aristotle the process of reasoning begins with signs and pictures, later to be abstracted and later to produce the universal.

Wisdom is at once the unity of all things, the measure and the harmony, but it is pure fire as well. With reservations, it is Zeus (Fr. 19). However, not only is it the universal substance, the source from which things come but it is the principle that directs the universe: "The primitive essence forms all things out of itself, by its own power, according to the law in it" (Zeller).

Fire or wisdom is, in this secondary sense, regarded in a manner analogous to mind. Again, it is probable that this analogy is based upon simple empirical observation, upon the assumption that consciousness in animal life is associated with warmth, since at death the body is cold. This assumption is borne out in Heraclitus' theories concerning man, considered as a microcosm. Man, as part of the cosmos, is dependent for life and consciousness upon the fire of the universe. Subject to the constant flux and change of the earth, water and fire which compose him, man breathes in the rational and conscious fire from without (c. Sextus Empiricus). During sleep, the apertures of sense through which consciousness enters in the form of fire are closed and contact with fire is lost. At such times, the exhalations from water cause the fire to burn low. The balance must be restored, as it must be restored in the macrocosm. If the measure or balance is not restored, death results through the destruction of the fire by water. Heraclitus offers rules by which the balance may be maintained or improved (cf. Fr. 68), the most important being the dicta forbidding drink (Frs. 72–76).

Heraclitus

[a] *The Fragments*

1. Not on my authority, but on that of truth, it is wise for you to accept the fact that all things are one.

2. This truth, though it always exists, men do not understand, as well before they hear it as when they hear it for the first time. For although all things happen in accordance with this truth, men seem unskilled indeed when they make trial of words and matters such as I am setting forth, in my effort to discriminate each thing according to its nature, and to tell what its state is. But other men fail to notice what they do when awake, in the same manner that they forget what they do when asleep.

3. Those who hear without the power to understand are like deaf men; the proverb holds true of them—"Present, they are absent."

4. Eyes and ears are bad witnesses for men, since their souls lack understanding.

5. Most men do not understand such things as they are wont to meet with; nor by learning do they come to know them, though they think they do.

6. They know not how to listen, nor how to speak.

7. If you do not hope, you will not find that which is not hoped for; since it is difficult to discover and impossible to attain.

8. Seekers for gold dig much earth, and find little gold.

9. Controversy.

10. Nature loves to hide.

11. The Lord [whose is the oracle] at Delphi neither speaks nor conceals, but gives a sign.

12. And the Sibyl with raving mouth, uttering words solemn, unadorned, and unsweetened, reaches with her voice a thousand years because of the god in her.

13. What can be seen, heard, and learned, this I prize.

14. (For this is characteristic of the present age, when, inasmuch as all lands and seas may be crossed by man, it would no longer be fitting to depend on the witness of poets and mythographers, as our ancestors generally did), "bringing

forth untrustworthy witnesses to confirm disputed points," in the words of Herakleitos.

15. Eyes are more exact witnesses than ears.

16. Much learning does not teach one to have understanding; else it would have taught Hesiod, and Pythagoras, and again Xenophanes, and Hekataios.

17. Pythagoras, son of Mnesarchos, prosecuted investigations more than any other man, and [selecting these treatises] he made a wisdom of his own—much learning and bad art.

18. No one of all whose discourses I have heard has arrived at this result: the recognition that wisdom is apart from all other things.

19. Wisdom is one thing: [to understand the intelligence by which all things are steered through all things]; it is willing and it is unwilling to be called by the name Zeus.

20. This order, the same for all things, no one of gods or men has made, but it always was, and is, and ever shall be, an ever-living fire, kindling according to fixed measure, and extinguished according to fixed measure.

21. The transformations of fire are, first of all, sea; and of the sea one half is earth, and the other half is lightning flash.

22. All things are exchanged for fire, and fire for all things; as wares are exchanged for gold, and gold for wares.

23. (The earth) is poured out as sea, and measures the same amount as existed before it became earth.

24. Want and satiety.

25. Fire lives in the death of air, and air lives in the death of fire; water lives in the death of earth, earth in that of water.

26. Fire coming upon all things will test them, and lay hold of them.

27. How could one escape the notice of that which never sets?

28. The thunderbolt directs the course of all things.

29. The sun will not overstep his bounds; if he does, the Erinnyes, allies of justice, will find him out.

30. The limit of the evening and the morning is the Bear; and opposite the Bear is the boundary of bright Zeus.

31. If there were no sun, it would be night.

32. The sun is new every day.

33. (Herakleitos and Demokritos bear witness that Thales was an astronomer, and predicted eclipses, etc.)

34. The seasons bring all things.

35. Hesiod is the teacher of most men; they suppose that his knowledge was very extensive, when in fact he did not know night and day, for they are one.

36. God is day and night, winter and summer, war and peace, satiety and hunger; but he assumes different forms, just as when incense is mingled with incense; everyone gives him the name he pleases.

37. If all things should become smoke, then perception would be by the nostrils.

38. Souls smell in Hades.

39. Cool things become warm, the warm grows cool; the wet dries, the parched becomes wet.

40. It scatters and brings together; it approaches and departs.

41–42. You could not step twice in the same rivers; for other and yet other waters are ever flowing on.

43. Herakleitos blamed Homer for saying: Would that strife might perish from among gods and men! For then, said he, all things would pass away.

44. War is father of all and king of all; and some he made gods and some men, some slaves and some free.

45. Men do not understand how that which draws apart agrees with itself; harmony lies in the bending back, as for instance of the bow and of the lyre.

46. Opposition unites. From what draws apart results the most beautiful harmony. All things take place by strife.

47. Hidden harmony is better than manifest.

48. Let us not make rash conjectures about the greatest things.

49. Men who desire wisdom must be learners of very many things.

50. For woolcarders the straight and the crooked path is one and the same.

51. Asses would rather have refuse than gold.

52. The sea is the purest and the foulest water; it is drinkable

and healthful for fishes; but for men it is unfit to drink and hurtful.

53–54. Swine like to wash in the mire; barnyard fowls in the dust.

55. Every beast is tended by blows.

56. (Identical with 45.)

57. Good and bad are the same.

58. (Good and bad are one; at any rate, as Herakleitos says) physicians, who cut and burn and in every way torment the sick, complain that they do not receive any adequate recompense from them.

59. Thou shouldst unite things whole and things not whole, that which tends to unite and that which tends to separate, the harmonious and the discordant; from all things arises the one, and from the one all things.

60. They would not have known the name of justice, were it not for these things.

61. (God, ordering things as they ought to be, perfects all things in the harmony of the whole, as Herakleitos says that) for god all things are fair and good and just, but men suppose that some are unjust and others just.

62. Men should know that war is general and that justice is strife; all things arise and [pass away] through strife.

63. For they are absolutely destined. . . .

64. All the things we see when awake are death, and all the things we see when asleep are sleep.

65. v.19.

66. The name of the bow is life, but its work is death.

67. Gods are mortals, men are immortals, each living in the others' death and dying in the others' life.

68. For to souls it is death to become water, and for water it is death to become earth; but water is formed from earth, and from water, soul.

69. Upward, downward, the way is one and the same.

70. Beginning and end are common (to both ways).

71. The limits of the soul you could not discover, though traversing every path.

72. It is a delight to souls to become wet.

73. Whenever a man gets drunk, he is led about by a beard-

less boy, stumbling, not knowing whither he goes, for his soul is wet.

74. The dry soul is wisest and best.

75. A dry beam is the wisest and best soul.

76. Where the earth is dry, the soul is wisest and best.

77. Man, like a light in the night, is kindled and put out.

78. Life and death, and waking and sleeping, and youth and old age, are the same; for the latter change and are the former, and the former change back to the latter.

79. Lifetime is a child playing draughts; the kingdom is a child's.

80. I inquired of myself.

81. In the same rivers we step and we do not step; we are and we are not.

82. It is weariness to toil at the same things, and to be subject to them.

83. Changing it finds rest.

84. Even a potion separates into its ingredients when it is not stirred.

85. Corpses are more fit to be thrown away than dung.

86. Being born they wish to live and to meet death, [or rather to find rest,] and they leave behind children to die.

87. Thirty years make a generation, according to Herakleitos.

88. Not without reason does Herakleitos call a month a generation.

89. A man may become a grandfather in thirty years.

90. The sleeping are workmen (and fellow-workers) in what happens in the world.

91. Understanding is common to all. It is necessary for those who speak with intelligence to hold fast to the common element of all, as a city holds fast to law, and much more strongly. For all human laws are nourished by one which is divine, and it has power so much as it will; and it suffices for all things and more than suffices.

92. And though reason is common, most people live as though they had an understanding peculiar to themselves.

93. With what they most constantly associate, with this they are at variance.

94. It is not meet to act and speak like men asleep.

95. They that are awake have one world in common, but of the sleeping each turns aside into a world of his own.
96. For human nature has not wisdom, but divine nature has.
97. Man is called a baby by god, even as a child is by man.
98. And does not Herakleitos, whom you bring forward, say this very thing, that the wisest of men will appear as an ape before God, both in wisdom and in beauty and in all other respects?
99. You are ignorant, sir, of that fine saying of Herakleitos, that the most beautiful of apes is ugly in comparison with beings of another kind, and the most beautiful of earthen pots is ugly in comparison with maidenkind, as Hippias the wise man says.
100. The people ought to fight for their law as for a wall.
101. Greater deaths gain greater portions.
102. Gods and men honour those slain in battle.
103. Wantonness must be quenched more than a conflagration.
104. It is not good for men to have whatever they want. Disease makes health sweet and good; hunger, satiety; toil, rest.
105. It is hard to contend with passion; for whatever it desires to get it buys at the cost of soul.
106. It is the part of all men to know themselves and to be temperate.
107. To be temperate is the greatest virtue; and it is wisdom to speak the truth and to act according to nature with understanding.
108. It is better to conceal stupidity, but it is an effort in time of relaxation and over the wine.
109. It is better to conceal ignorance than to put it forth into the midst.
110. It is law to obey the counsel of one.
111. For what sense or understanding have they? They follow the bards and employ the crowd as their teacher, not knowing that many are bad and few good. For the very best choose one thing before all others, immortal glory among mortals, while the masses eat their fill like cattle.

112. In Priene was born Bias son of Teutamas, who is of more account than the rest.
113. To me one man is ten thousand if he be the best.
114. The Ephesians deserve to be hanged, every one that is a man grown, and the youth to abandon the city, for they cast out Hermodoros the best man among them, saying:—Let no one among us be best, and if one be best, let him be so elsewhere and among others.
115. Dogs also bark at those they do not know.
116. As the result of incredulity (divine things) miss being known.
117. The fool is wont to be in a flutter at every word.
118. The most esteemed of those in estimation knows how to be on his guard; yet truly justice shall overtake forgers of lies and witnesses to them.
119. (He used to say that) Homer deserved to be cast out of the lists and flogged, and Archilochos likewise.
120. One day is equal to every other.
121. Character is a man's guardian divinity.
122. There awaits men at death what they do not expect or think.
123. Then [it is necessary] that God raise them up, and that they become guardians of the living and the dead.
124. Night-walkers, wizards, bacchanals, revellers, sharers in the mysteries.
125. For what are esteemed mysteries among men they celebrate in an unholy way.
126. *vide* 130.
127. For if it were not to Dionysos that they made the procession and sang the song with phallic symbols, their deeds would indeed be most shameful; but Hades and Dionysos are the same, to whomever they go mad and share the revel.
128. I distinguish two kinds of sacrifices; those of men altogether purified, which would occur rarely, as Herakleitos says, in the case of a single individual, or of some very few men easily counted; secondly, those that are material and corporeal and composite through change, such as are in harmony with those who are still restrained by the body.

129. (Herakleitos fittingly called religious rites) cures (for the soul).

130. They purify themselves by defiling themselves with blood, as if one who had stepped into the mud were to wash it off with mud. If any one of men should observe him doing so, he would think he was insane. And to these images they pray, just as if one were to converse with men's houses, for they know not what gods and heroes are.

130a. If they are gods, why do ye lament them? And if ye lament them, no longer consider them gods.

[b] Diogenes Laertius, Bk. 4, 9, 8–12. Coming to his particular tenets, we may state them as follows: fire is the element, all things are exchange for fire and come into being by rarefaction and condensation; but of this he gives no clear explanation. All things come into being by conflict of opposites, and the sum of things flows like a stream. Further, all that is is limited and forms one world. And it is alternately born from fire and again resolved into fire in fixed cycles to all eternity, and this is determined by destiny. Of the opposites that which tends to birth or creation is called war and strife, and that which tends to destruction by fire is called concord and peace.

Change he called a pathway up and down, and this determines the birth of the world. For fire by contracting turns into moisture, and this condensing turns into water; water again when congealed turns into earth. This process he calls the downward path. Then again earth is liquefied, and thus gives rise to water, and from water the rest of the series is derived. He reduces nearly everything to exhalation from the sea. This process is the upward path.

Exhalations arise from earth as well as from sea; those from sea are bright and pure, those from earth dark. Fire is fed by the bright exhalations, the moist element by the others.

He does not make clear the nature of the surrounding element. He says, however, that there are in it bowls with their concavities turned toward us, in which the bright exhalations collect and produce flames. These are the heavenly bodies.

The flame of the sun is the brightest and hottest; and other stars are further from the earth and for that reason give it less light and heat. The moon, which is nearer to the earth, traverses a region which is not pure. The sun, however, moves in a clear and untroubled region, and keeps a proportionate distance from us. That is why it gives us more heat and light. Eclipses of the sun and moon occur when the bowls are turned upwards; the monthly phases of the moon are due to the bowl turning round in its place little by little.

Day and night, months, seasons and years, rains and winds and other similar phenomena are accounted for by the various exhalations. Thus the bright exhalation, set aflame in the hollow orb of the sun, produces day, the opposite exhalation when it has got the mastery causes night; the increase of warmth due to the bright exhalation produces summer, whereas the preponderance of moisture due to the dark exhalation brings about winter. His explanations of other phenomena are in harmony with this.

He gives no account of the nature of the earth, nor even of the bowls.

These, then, were his opinions.

[c] Sextus Empiricus, *adv. Math.* 7.129. The natural philosopher is of the opinion that what surrounds us is rational and endowed with consciousness. According to Heraclitus, we become intelligent when we get this divine reason by breathing it in, and in sleep we are forgetful, but on waking we gain our senses again. For in sleep since the openings of the senses are closed, the mind in us is separated from what is akin to it in what surrounds us, and its connection through openings is only preserved like a sort of root (from which the rest may spring again); and being cut off it loses its former power of memory; but when we wake it looks through the openings of the senses, as through little doors, and entering into connection with what surrounds us it regains (assumes) the power of reason.

THE ELEATIC SCHOOL

Heraclitus derives from the Milesians and proceeds to a conception of the universe and its components in constant motion and flux. This process of change is correctly exemplified in all phenomena in a manner best manifested in the bow, the lyre and the river. Three philosophers,[1] Xenophanes, Parmenides and Zeno, discover assumptions in Milesian philosophy which, if carried to their logical conclusions, would mean the denial of motion, change and flux and a further denial of the reality of the concrete exemplifications of change. These philosophers were called Eleatic, after the Greek colony of Elea, in Italy, in which they were resident. Aristotle summarizes their teaching (Eleatic, *Introductory*) in the words, "(they) expressed the opinion about the universe that it is one in its essential nature."

As Aristotle suggests (*loc. cit.*), the expression of this philosophical position is given in varied form. Xenophanes approaches the problem of the universe as "one" from a theological point of view and in the language of the religious teacher. Parmenides pursues the problem metaphysically and proceeds to the establishment of his conclusions by dialectical method. Zeno attempts the defence of the principle by the negative method of demonstrating the impossibility of supporting the opposing point of view. He proceeds by a further refinement of the dialectical procedure of Parmenides.

[1] The fragments of the philosophy of the fourth member of the school, Melissus, are given in Appendix I, p. 221.

Since their author was a wandering poet and a maker of satires and elegies, Xenophanes' writings are more closely related to religion and to conduct than to philosophy. Two fragments of his writings seem clearly to indicate the reasons for that emphasis. These portions of his writings (Frs. 17 and 24) may be assumed to relate to the conquest of Ionia, the land of which Xenophanes was native, by the Persians under Harpagos. The fragments indicate that Xenophanes was twenty-five years of age at the time of the defeat of the Ionians and his birth would, therefore, have occurred in 565 B.C. After this invasion, Xenophanes wandered sixty-seven years over Hellas but tradition indicates that he lived in Elea, in Italy, a colony to which the Phocaeans emigrated after the Persian conquest. The extent and duration of his wanderings indicate clearly that it is an affinity of spirit rather than an identity of habitat that causes Xenophanes to be allied with Parmenides and Zeno as an Eleatic. It is, however, not too strained an inference to conclude that the Persian conquest caused much of the emphasis placed by Xenophanes upon the maintenance of good morals and upon the eradication of anthropomorphic conceptions of the gods. It may, perhaps, be inferred not only that those driven from Ionia desired to hear of old customs but that Xenophanes, with the fervour of a reformer and religious teacher, attempted to impress upon his auditors the necessity for an abandonment of certain luxurious practices in living, the prevalence of which had weakened the Greeks and aided the Persians in their conquest (Fr. 20). Xenophanes scorns the excesses of perfumery copied from the Lydians. He decries the extravagant interest of the Greeks in athletics and insists that wisdom is preferable to physical strength (Fr. 19). Rules of etiquette are touched upon, with the admonition that too much drinking is to be avoided (Fr. 21).

The most important part of Xenophanes' writings for philosophy is to be found in the attacks upon the traditional views of the gods. In a manner similar to that of Euripides, Xenophanes decries the attribution of all manner of vice and crime to the deities. This is the motive for his criticism of the writings of Homer and Hesiod (Fr. 7). The attribution of depravity to gods follows from the anthropomorphic conception of deity. Men create gods in their own images, just as animals would construct deities with animal characteristics, had they the ability to draw (Frs. 5, 6, 7). It is in the elaboration of an alternative theory of the nature of god that Xenophanes reveals at once the didactic reason for his attack upon anthropomorphism and the Eleatic characteristics of his thought. Mindful, no doubt, of the conquest that had caused the Ionians to leave their native land and mindful, too, perhaps that the vanquished usually attribute their defeat to failures to observe ritual or to evil fortune rather than to their own deficiencies, Xenophanes seems to insist that men must depend upon their own efforts and not upon the assistance of deities who, as he points out, incorporate such contrary characteristics and who vary so greatly among peoples. It is not fitting that god "move from one place to another" (Fr. 4) presumably at the beck and call of any man or any prayer. When Xenophanes has denied motion to god, however, he proceeds to indicate that common opinion has erred not only in the attribution of motion to god but also in the attribution of sensory organs. For Xenophanes, god is remote from toil (Fr. 3), all perceiving, but without sensory organs (Frs. 1 and 2).

The Milesians had insisted that the material substances they selected as explanatory principles maintained their identity despite change and were divine. Xenophanes calls the ruler of the universe god and insists that god is homogeneous and unchanging. Aristotle (*Introductory*) interpreted Xenophanes' system as a pantheism and with this interpretation there is general agreement. It follows, therefore, that the universe is homogeneous and not subject to change or alteration. Movement and change would be illusions similar to those causing an anthropomorphic conception of deity. There is implicit the assumption that if god be homogeneous and identical with the universe, changes in substance will shortly be denied. Substance can undergo no changes, no transformations, since it could not be different in one part than in another, and no alteration could occur. The ease with which Xenophanes postulates a new sun every day (b. Hipp.) and devotes himself to a study of past life in fossilized form (c. Hipp.) indicates clearly, however, how little capable he was of working out the implications of his own theory.

The implications are carried to their conclusions by Parmenides unencumbered as he was by theological or moral mission. Son of Pyres and a native of Elea, Parmenides is characterized in the *Theatetus* (b. Plato) as "a man to be reverenced and at the same time feared." The dates of Parmenides' life have never been satisfactorily established. He is said by Plato to have conversed with Socrates (*loc. cit.*). This statement would fix the date of his visit to Athens *ca.* 451–449 B. C. He is said by Diogenes Laertius to have flourished in the years 504–500 B. C. Other than this, tradition has it that he was brought to philosophy by the Pythagorean, Ameinias; that he erected a statue to Diochartes, another Pythagorean; and that he gave laws to Elea, which the natives of that city swore each year to uphold.

In l. 50, Parmenides writes in opposition to those "who consider being and not-being as the same and not the same; and that all things follow a back-turning course." This is a clear reference to Heraclitus' "upward and downward movement." No concession will be made in Parmenides' system to the appearance of change: "Therefore justice does not slacken her fetters to permit generation or destruction, but holds being firm.—Wherefore all these things will be but a name, all these things which mortals determined in the belief that they were true, *viz.* that things arise and perish, that they are and are not, that they change their position and vary in colour" (l. 70 *et seq.* and ll. 98–100).

The problem from which Parmenides starts in Heraclitus' system is implicit in the philosophy of the Milesians. The attempt to discover the material substance or "world stuff" that maintains its identity despite change carries with it the implication that all objects of our experience are that substance in one or the other of its transformations. For example, water would be, for Anaximenes, air in a particular state of condensation. Despite its further condensation into earth or stones or its rarefaction into fire, these particular forms, presented to us by the senses as various substances, are in reality but one substance, air.

If now we ask why air appears to be stones or earth or fire, Parmenides' answer to our question suggests that such appearance is due to the difference between the senses and thought. Parmenides adopts an hypothesis prevalent among the Greeks that thought is similar to or identical with what is known—"for thought and being are the same thing" (l. 40).

The senses present us with variants. Thought reveals what the stones or what the air is because thought seeks the common, the universal and the invariant. Heraclitus' attempt to solve the problem of reality, an hypothesis that emphasizes the reality of the particular concrete manifestation of change, never solves a primary difficulty. The particular concrete manifestations evidence to the senses qualities contrary to the qualities attributed to the substance of which they are a particular manifestation. Water is cold and wet; fire is hot and dry. The senses take these differences to be real. But these qualitative distinctions of fire and water may only be adequately designated by thought through reference to the common; for example, in Anaximenes' philosophy, to air. In such a reference, it is clear that they are not air. But just in so far as they are not air, it follows, since air is the material of which all is composed, that they are in that sense non-existent.

Parmenides does not select earth, air, fire or water as the material substance of which the universe is composed. *Being* is that concrete substance. Having selected it, Parmenides proceeds to insist that anything that is not *being* is non-existent. Throughout, he argues logically in this form: If x is white and y is brown and x is *being,* then y is either identical with *being* or it is non-existent. *Y* would be identical with *x* only if difference were denied and the common or universal, which is the object of thought, were insisted upon. To put the matter more generally still, suppose that *per impossibile* there existed two different kinds of *being, x* and *y*. Then if *x* is a kind of *being,* not-*x* or *y* would be a kind of *non-being*. For example, if *x* is a chair, then *x* represents many ways of not existing, as for example, in the fashion of a table or a desk. If we try to express the difference between *x* and *y,* therefore, in the form *x* is not-*y,* all we have said is that *x* is a way of not existing and no positive difference has been expressed or is expressible.

With this logical conclusion as a premise, Parmenides proceeds dialectically to destroy the possibility of generation, destruction, change and motion. Since *being* is the common and the invariant, it cannot have come into existence nor could it be destroyed. Parmenides' dialectical method is one of repeated dichotomies: *Being* could not have come into existence, since to do so it must have come either from *not-being* or from *being*. It could not have come from *not-being,* since *not-being* is non-existent. It could not have come from *being,* in any meaningful sense of the term, since *being* itself is the existent and the common, and generation or change must mean transformation from one state into another. Similar dialectical argument denies divisibility (l. 78). Parmenides' argument is not, however, carried on in a purely metaphysical manner, for, as has been remarked, he conceives *being* to be a concrete substance. He proceeds to think pictorially and in concrete images. *Being* is homogeneous throughout and is compared to the mass of a rounded sphere, "perfected on every side,—equally distant from the centre at every point" (ll. 103–105). It is probable that Parmenides chose the example to demonstrate the analogy between *being,* as the limit at which apparent difference disappears, and the sphere, as a limit toward which by a repeated division of surfaces all other regular geometrical figures approach. Since, therefore, *being* is spatially extended and *being* is all that exists, there is no empty space. In Parmenides' world, motion is, therefore, impossible.

Considerable controversy centres around Parmenides' *On Opinion*. Parmenides himself undertakes the second portion of his poem with the avowed purpose of ceasing "trustworthy discourse" (l. 110) and giving the "opinion of mortals" (l. 112). The implication seems to be that Parmenides left the realm of pure philosophy to put his thoughts into language comprehensible to the multitude. Aristotle, (b. *Met.*), however, seeing clearly in *On Truth* that Parmenides has destroyed the possibility of motion and change, urges that *On Opinion* is the author's attempt to account for phenomena. The implication in Aristotle's comment is that no system could be upheld unless empirical data be explained. On the assumption that *On Opinion* is an attempt to "save appearances," Aristotle finds that Parmenides has recourse to two explanatory causal principles, fire and earth. Recent criticism, particularly that of Burnet, attributes *On Opinion* to Parmenides' desire to acquaint his disciples with an opposing Pythagorean doctrine, presumably better to prepare them for the task of confounding the adherents of the opposed doctrine.

To Zeno, son of Teleutagoras and disciple of Parmenides, fell the task of supporting the teachings of the great Eleatic. Since Parmenides' philosophy runs counter to what man believes through sense perception and experience in general to be the nature of the universe, powerful advocacy of the theory of *being* was needed. The repeated attempts in the history of philosophy to demonstrate solutions to Zeno's paradoxes indicate that the advocacy could have fallen into no abler hands. Born *ca.* 495–490 B. C., Zeno was a favourite of Parmenides. According to Strabo, Zeno promoted law and order in Elea. Tradition attaches to his name an heroic effort to avoid giving incriminating evidence against friends. Rather than implicate them, Zeno is said to have bitten off his tongue.

Plato tells us (a. *Parm.*) that Zeno formulated his paradoxes for the avowed purpose of supporting Parmenides' theory of *being*. This support is further indicated in fragment 4, where the Parmenidean argument against the possibility of empty space is maintained by showing that to suppose *being* to be other than a *plenum* involves the further supposition that space has an end or limit, that limited space is in another space, and so on *ad infinitum*. This is perhaps the first historical example of a distrust of an infinite regress. The remaining paradoxes concern themselves with multiplicity, in respect to magnitude and to motion.

Restatements of two or three of Zeno's arguments will suffice to demonstrate his method. The problem of the moving arrow (d. 1. Arist.) may be stated as follows: A body must either be moving in a place where it is or where it is not. It cannot be moving in a place where it is or it would not be there. It cannot be moving in a place where it is not for it is not there. Therefore the flying arrow cannot be moving. Stated in another way, Zeno's argument involves the assumption that the flying arrow is at rest at any point in its trajectory. But this can be said of every point in the trajectory and what is at rest at every point does not move at all. The solution to the paradox is impossible for philosophy until mathematics, by the development of the differential calculus could deal with the general problem of velocity at a point. Once the mathematics is developed, the paradox of the flying arrow may be considered as involving a definite velocity for the arrow at every point of its trajectory.

Concerning magnitude, we may take as an example a restatement of fragment 3. A line xy is either divisible or it is indivisible. It is divisible if a point not corresponding either to x or to y can be inserted between the end points x and y. Zeno's method of argument would be as follows: If the line is indivisible, the argument of Parmenides is admitted, for *being* has no parts. If the line is divisible, it is divisible into a finite number of parts or into an infinite number of parts. Both possibilities must be tested. If the line is divisible into a finite number of parts only, when that number is reached, the parts have no length and the division disappears, since otherwise the division could progress. If the line is divisible into an infinite number of parts, the parts must have either no length or some length. If the parts really have no length, and yet by definition the line has an infinite number of parts, an impossibility results since no number would add up to anything. If the parts have some length and the infinite division has ended, the line can be made to grow and to grow as long as we like by adding part to part since our supply of parts can never be exhausted.

The most famous of Zeno's paradoxes is that of Achilles and the Tortoise. Achilles running swiftly cannot catch the tortoise running slowly, for he will have to come to the end of an infinite series and an infinite series has no end. For example, if the distance be divided according to the law of $\frac{1}{2}, \frac{1}{4}, \frac{1}{8}, \frac{1}{16} \ldots \frac{1}{2^n}$, before he can reach the tortoise he must have passed through the last term. But the series has no last term. Therefore he can never come up to the tortoise.

A solution is offered as follows: Suppose we deny the compulsion of the major premise.[1] If there is no last term, why does Achilles have to pass through the last term in order to come up to the tortoise? This classifies Zeno's problem as a fallacy, as a case of contradiction in definition. It might also be classified as the fallacious use of all in the collective and in the distributive sense.[2] Achilles in order to catch the tortoise has to go through every term of an infinite series in the sense that you can name no term through which he does not have to pass. But he does not have to go through them all collectively because the series, being open at one end, does not constitute a collection. There is no such thing as an infinite collection.

THE ELEATIC SCHOOL

Aristotle, *Metaphysics* 1.5; 986 b 10; b 23. There are some who have expressed the opinion about the universe that it is one in its essential nature, but they have not expressed this

1 The solution offered is that of H. B. Smith in *How the Mind Falls into Error*.

2 The statement of the problem is that of E. A. Singer, Jr.

opinion after the same manner nor in an orderly or natural way.—Xenophanes first taught the unity of these things (Parmenides is said to have been his pupil), but he did not make anything clear, nor did he seem to have grasped either of these two kinds of unity, but looking up into the broad heavens he said: The unity is god. These are to be dismissed, as we have said, from the present investigation, two of them entirely as being rather more crude, Xenophanes and Melissus;[1] but Parmenides seems to speak in some places with more insight.

[A.] Xenophanes

[a] *Fragments of Xenophanes.*

1. God is one, supreme among gods and men, and not like mortals in body or in mind.

2. The whole [of god] sees, the whole perceives, the whole hears.

3. But without effort he sets in motion all things by mind and thought.

4. It [i.e. being] always abides in the same place, not moved at all, nor is it fitting that it should move from one place to another.

5. But mortals suppose that the gods are born (as they themselves are), and that they wear man's clothing and have human voice and body.

6. But if cattle or lions had hands, so as to paint with their hands and produce works of art as men do, they would paint their gods and give them bodies in form like their own—horses like horses, cattle like cattle.

7. Homer and Hesiod attributed to the gods all things which are disreputable and worthy of blame when done by men; and they told of them many lawless deeds, stealing, adultery, and deception of each other.

8. For all things come from earth, and all things end by becoming earth.

9. For we are all sprung from earth and water.

10. All things that come into being and grow are earth and water.

[1] See Appendix I, p. 221 *et seq.*, for Melissus' philosophy.

11. The sea is the source of water and the source of wind; for neither would blasts of wind arise in the clouds and blow out from within them, except for the great sea, nor would the streams of rivers nor the rain-water in the sky exist but for the sea; but the great sea is the begetter of clouds and winds and rivers.
12. This upper limit of earth at our feet is visible and touches the air, but below it reaches to infinity.
13. She whom men call Iris (rainbow), this also is by nature cloud, violet and red and pale green to behold.
14. Accordingly there has not been a man, nor will there be, who knows distinctly what I say about the gods or in regard to all things, for even if one chances for the most part to say what is true, still he would not know; but every one thinks he knows.
15. These things have seemed to me to resemble the truth.
16. In the beginning the gods did not at all reveal all things clearly to mortals, but by searching men in the course of time find them out better.
17. The following are fit topics for conversation for men reclining on a soft couch by the fire in the winter season, when after a meal they are drinking sweet wine and eating a little pulse: Who are you, and what is your family? What is your age, my friend? How old were you when the Medes invaded this land?
18. Now, however, I come to another topic, and I will show the way. . . . They say that once on a time when a hound was badly treated a passer-by pitied him and said, "Stop beating him, for it is the soul of a dear friend; I recognized him on hearing his voice."
19. But if one wins a victory by swiftness of foot, or in the pentathlon, where the grove of Zeus lies by Pisas' stream at Olympia, or as a wrestler, or in painful boxing, or in that severe contest called the pancration, he would be more glorious in the eyes of the citizens, he would win a front seat at assemblies, and would be entertained by the city at the public table, and he would receive a gift which would be a keepsake for him. If he won by means of horses he would get all these things although he did not deserve them, as I de-

serve them, for our wisdom is better than the strength of men or of horses. This is indeed a very wrong custom, nor is it right to prefer strength to excellent wisdom. For if there should be in the city a man good at boxing, or in the pentathlon, or in wrestling, or in swiftness of foot, which is honoured more than strength (among the contests men enter into at the games), the city would not on that account be any better governed. Small joy would it be to any city in this case if a citizen conquers at the games on the banks of the Pisas, for this does not fill with wealth its secret chambers.

20. Having learned profitless luxuries from the Lydians, while as yet they had no experience of hateful tyranny, they proceeded into the market-place, no less than a thousand in number all told, with purple garments completely covering them, boastful, proud of their comely locks, anointed with unguents of rich perfume.

21. For now the floor is clean, the hands of all and the cups are clean; one puts on the woven garlands, another passes around the fragrant ointment in a vase; the mixing bowl stands full of good cheer, and more wine, mild and of delicate bouquet, is at hand in jars, which says it will never fail. In the midst frankincense sends forth its sacred fragrance, and there is water, cold, and sweet, and pure; the yellow loaves are near at hand, and the table of honour is loaded with cheese and rich honey. The altar in the midst is thickly covered with flowers on every side; singing and mirth fill the house. Men making merry should first hymn the god with propitious stanzas and pure words; and when they have poured out libations and prayed for power to do the right (since this lies nearest at hand), then it is no unfitting thing to drink as much as will not prevent your walking home without a slave, if you are not very old. And one ought to praise that man who, when he has drunk, unfolds noble things as his memory and his toil for virtue suggest; but there is nothing praiseworthy in discussing battles of Titans or of Giants or Centaurs, fictions of former ages, nor in plotting violent revolutions. But it is good always to pay careful respect to the gods.

22. For sending the thigh-bone of a goat, thou didst receive the rich leg of a fatted bull, an honourable present to a man, the fame whereof shall come to all Greece, and shall not cease so long as there is a race of Greek bards.
23. Nor would any one first pour the wine into the cup to mix it, but water first and the wine above it.
24. Already now sixty-seven years my thoughts have been tossed restlessly up and down Greece, but then it was twenty and five years from my birth, if I know how to speak the truth about these things.
25. Nor is this (an oath) an equal demand to make of an impious man as compared with a pious man.
26. Much more feeble than an aged man.
27. Bacchic wands of fir stand about the firmly built house.
28. From the beginning, according to Homer, since all have learned them.
29. If the god had not made light-coloured honey, I should have said that a fig was far sweeter.
30. Holy water trickles down in thy grottoes.
31. As many things as they have made plain for mortals to see!

[b] HIPP., *Phil.* 1.14. *Dox.* 565. The sun is formed each day from small fiery particles which are gathered together; the earth is infinite and is not surrounded by air or by sky; an infinite number of suns and moons exist, and all things come from earth.

AET., *Plac.* 2.13. *Dox.* 343. The stars are formed of burning cloud; these are extinguished each day, but they are kindled again at night, like coals; for their risings and settings are really kindlings and extinguishings. 20; 348. The sun is composed of fiery particles collected from the moist exhalation and massed together, or of burning clouds. 24; 354. Eclipses occur by extinction of the sun; and the sun is born anew at its risings. 24; 355. Xenophanes held that there are many suns and moons according to the different regions and sections and zones of the earth; and that at some fitting time the disk of the sun comes into a region of the earth not inhabited by us, and so it suffers eclipse as though it had gone into a hole; he adds that the sun goes on for an infinite distance, but it seems to turn around by reason of the great distance. 25; 356. The moon is a compressed cloud. 28; 358. It shines by its own light. 29; 360. The moon disappears each month because it is extinguished.

Aet., *Plac.* 3.2; 367. Comets are groups or motions of burning clouds. 3; 368. Lightnings take place when clouds shine in motion. 4; 371. The phenomena of the heavens come from the warmth of the sun as the principal cause. For when the moisture is drawn up from the sea, the sweet water separated by reason of its lightness becomes mist and passes into clouds, and falls as rain when compressed, and the winds scatter it; for he writes expressly (Fr. 11): "The sea is the source of water."

[c] Hipp., *Phil. op. cit.* Xenophanes believes that once the earth was mingled with the sea, but in the course of time it became freed from moisture; and his proofs are such as these: that shells are found in the midst of the land and among the mountains, that in the quarries of Syracuse the imprints of a fish and of seals had been found, and in Paros the imprint of an anchovy at some depth in the stone, and in Melite shallow impressions of all sorts of sea products. He says that these imprints were made when everything long ago was covered with mud, and then the imprint dried in the mud. Farther he says that all men will be destroyed when the earth sinks into the sea and becomes mud, and that the race will begin anew from the beginning; and this transformation takes place for all worlds.

[B.] Parmenides

[a] (Prooemium) The horses which bear me conducted me as far as desire may go, when they had
brought me speeding along to the far-famed road
of a divinity who herself bears onward through all
things the man of understanding. Along this road
I was borne, along this the horses, wise indeed, bore
me hastening the chariot on, and maidens guided
my course. The axle in its box, enkindled by the
heat, uttered the sound of a pipe (for it was driven

on by the rolling wheels on either side), when the maiden daughters of Helios hastened to conduct me to the light, leaving the realms of night, pushing aside with the hand the veils from their heads. There is the gate between the ways of day and night; lintel above it, and stone threshold beneath, hold it in place, and high in air it is fitted with great doors; retributive Justice holds the keys that open and shut them. However, the maidens addressed her with mild words, and found means to persuade her to thrust back speedily for them the fastened bolt from the doors; and the gate swinging free made the opening wide, turning in their sockets the bronze hinges, well fastened with bolts and nails; then through this the maidens kept horses and chariot straight on the high-road. The goddess received me with kindness, and, taking my right hand in hers, she addressed me with these words:— Youth joined with drivers immortal, who hast come with the horses that bear thee, to our dwelling, hail! since no evil fate has bid thee come on this road (for it lies far outside the beaten track of men), but right and justice. 'Tis necessary for thee to learn all things, both the abiding essence of persuasive truth, and men's opinions in which rests no true belief. But nevertheless these things also thou shalt learn, since it is necessary to judge accurately the things that rest on opinion, passing all things carefully in review.

Concerning Truth

Come now I will tell thee—and do thou hear my word and heed it—what are the only ways of enquiry that lead to knowledge. The one way, assuming that being is and that it is impossible for it not to be, is the trustworthy path, for truth attends it. The other, that not-being is and that it necessarily is, I call a wholly incredible course, since thou canst not recognize not-being (for this is impossible), nor couldst thou speak of it, for thought and being are the same thing.

It makes no difference to me at what point I begin, for I shall always come back again to this.

It is necessary both to say and to think that being is; for it is possible that being is, and it is impossible that not-being is; this is what I bid thee ponder. I restrain thee from this first course of investigation; and from that course also along which mortals knowing nothing wander aimlessly, since helplessness directs the roaming thought in their bosoms, and they are borne on deaf and likewise blind, amazed, headstrong races, they who consider being and not-being as the same and not the same; and that all things follow a back-turning course.

That things which are not are, shall never prevail, she said, but do thou restrain thy mind from this course of investigation.

And let not long-practised habit compel thee along this path, thine eye careless, thine ear and thy tongue overpowered by noise; but do thou weigh the much contested refutation of their words, which I have uttered.

There is left but this single path to tell thee of: namely, that being is. And on this path there are many proofs that being is without beginning and indestructible; it is universal, existing alone, immovable and without end; nor ever was it nor will it be, since it now *is,* all together, one, and continuous. For what generating of it wilt thou seek out? From what did it grow, and how? I will not permit thee to say or to think that it came from not-being;

for it is impossible to think or to say that not-being is. What thing would then have stirred it into activity that it should arise from not-being later rather than earlier? So it is necessary that being either is absolutely or is not. Nor will the force of the argument permit that anything spring from being except being itself. Therefore justice does not slacken her fetters to permit generation or destruction, but holds being firm.

(The decision as to these things comes in at this point.)

Either being exists or it does not exist. It has been decided in accordance with necessity to leave the unthinkable, unspeakable path, as this is not the true path, but that the other path exists and is true. How then should being suffer destruction? How come into existence? If it came into existence, it is not being, nor will it be if it ever is to come into existence. . . . So its generation is extinguished, and its destruction is proved incredible.

Nor is it subject to division, for it is all alike; nor is anything more in it, so as to prevent its cohesion, nor anything less, but all is full of being; therefore the all is continuous, for being is contiguous to being.

Farther it is unmoved, in the hold of great chains, without beginning or end, since generation and destruction have completely disappeared and true belief has rejected them. It lies the same, abiding in the same state and by itself; accordingly it abides fixed in the same spot. For powerful necessity holds it in confining bonds, which restrain it on all sides. Therefore divine right does not permit being to have any end; but it is lacking in nothing, for if it lacked anything it would lack everything.

Nevertheless, behold steadfastly all absent things as present to thy mind; for thou canst not separate being in one place from contact with being in another place; it is not scattered here and there through the universe, nor is it compounded of parts.

Therefore thinking and that by reason of which thought exists are one and the same thing, for thou wilt not find thinking without the *being* from which it receives its name. Nor is there nor will there be anything apart from being; for fate has linked it together, so that it is a whole and immovable. Wherefore all these things will be but a name, all these things which mortals determined in the belief that they were true, viz. that things arise and perish, that they are and are not, that they change their position and vary in colour.

But since there is a final limit, it is perfected on every side, like the mass of a rounded sphere, equally distant from the centre at every point. For it is necessary that it should neither be greater at all nor less anywhere, since there is no not-being which can prevent it from arriving at equality, nor is being such that there may ever be more than what is in one part and less in another, since the whole is inviolate. For if it is equal on all sides, it abides in equality within its limits.

Concerning Opinions

At this point I cease trustworthy discourse and the thought about truth; from here on, learn the opinions of mortals, hearing of the illusive order of my verses.

Men have determined in their minds to name two principles [*lit.* forms]; but one of these they ought not to name, and in so doing they have erred. They distinguish them as antithetic in character, and give them each character and attributes distinct from those of the other. On the one hand there is the aethereal flame of fire, fine, rarefied, everywhere identical with itself and not identical with its opposite; and on the other hand, opposed to the first, is the second principle, flameless darkness, dense and heavy in character. Of these two principles I declare to thee every arrangement as it appears to men, so that no knowledge among mortals may surpass thine.

But since all things are called light and darkness, and the peculiar properties of these are predicated of one thing and another, everything is at the same time full of light and of obscure darkness, of both equally, since neither has anything in common with the other.

And the smaller circles are filled with unmixed fire, and those next them with darkness into which their portion of light penetrates; in the midst of these is the divinity who directs the course of all. For she controls dreaded birth and coition in every part of the universe, sending female to join with male, and again male to female.

First of all the gods she devised love.

Thou shalt know the nature of the heavens and all signs that are in the sky, the destructive deeds of the pure bright torch of the sun and whence they arose, and thou shalt learn the wandering deeds of the round-eyed moon and its nature. Thou shalt know also the sky surrounding all, whence it arose, and how necessity took it and chained it so as to serve as a limit to the courses of the stars. How earth and sun and moon and common sky and the milky way of the heavens and highest Olympos and the burning (might of the) stars began to be.

It (the moon) wanders about the earth, shining at night with borrowed light. She is always gazing earnestly toward the rays of the sun.

For as at any time is the blending of very complex members in a man, so is the mind in men constituted; for that which thinks is the same in all men and in every man, *viz.* the essence of the members of the body; and the element that is in excess is thought.

On the right hand boys, on the left hand girls.

So, according to men's opinions, did things arise, and so they are now, and from this state when they shall have reached maturity shall they perish. For each of these men has determined a name as a distinguishing mark.

When male and female mingle seed of Venus in the form [the body] of one, the excellence from the two different bloods, if it preserves harmony, fashions a well-formed body; but if when the seed is mingled the excellencies fight against each other and do not unite into one, they will distress the sex that is coming into existence, as the twofold seed is mingled in the body of the unfortunate woman.

With this there are fineness and heat and light and softness and brightness; and with the dense are classed cold and darkness and hardness and weight, for these are separated the ones on one side, the others on the other.

[b] Aristotle, *Metaphysics* 1.5; 986 b 18 *et seq.*—but Parmenides seems to speak in some places with greater care. For believing that not-being does not exist in addition to being, of necessity he thinks that being is one and that there is nothing else,—and being compelled to account for phenomena, and assuming that things are one from the standpoint of reason, plural from the standpoint of sense, he again

asserts that there are two causes and two first principles, heat and cold, or, as he calls them, fire and earth; of these he regards heat as being, its opposite as not-being.

Diogenes Laertius, *Lives* ix. 21, 22. Theophrastus, Fr. 6a *Dox.* 482. Parmenides, son of Pyres, the Eleatic, was a pupil of Xenophanes, yet he did not accept his doctrines— He was the first to declare that the earth is spheroidal and situated in the middle of the universe.

Plato, *Theatetus* 183 E. Parmenides seems to me, in the words of Homer, a man to be reverenced and at the same time feared. For when I was a mere youth and he a very old man, I conversed with him, and he seemed to me to have an exceedingly wonderful depth of mind. *ibid* 180 D. I almost forgot, Theodoros, that there were others who asserted opinions the very opposite of these: "the all is alone, unmoved; to this all names apply," and the other emphatic statements in opposition to those referred to, which the school of Melissus and Parmenides make, to the effect that all things are one, and that the all stands by itself in itself, not having space in which it is moved.

Hipp., *Phil.* 11. *Dox.* 564. Parmenides supposes that the all is one and eternal, and without beginning and spheroidal in form; but even he does not escape the opinion of the many, for he speaks of fire and earth as the first principles of the all, of earth as matter, and of fire as agent and cause, and he says that the earth will come to an end, but in what way he does not say. He says that the all is eternal, and not generated, and spherical, and homogeneous, not having place in itself, and unmoved and limited.

Aristotle, *Physics* i. 3; 186 a 4. To those proceeding after this impossible manner things seem to be one, and it is not difficult to refute them from their own statements. For both of them reason in a fallacious manner, both Parmenides and Melissus; for they make false assumptions, and at the same time their course of reasoning is not logical— And the same sort of arguments are used by Parmenides—and the refutation consists in showing both that he makes mistakes of fact and that he does not draw his conclusions correctly. He makes a mistake in assuming that being is to be spoken of absolutely, speaking of it thus many times; and he draws the false conclusion that, in case only whites are considered, white meaning one thing, none the less there are many whites and not one; since neither in the succession of things nor in the argument will whiteness be one. For what is predicated of white will not be the same as what is predicated of the object which is white, and nothing except white will be separated from the object; since there is no other ground of separation except the fact that the white is different from the object in which the white exists. But Parmenides had not yet arrived at the knowledge of this.

[c] Aet., *Plac.* 2. 7. *Dox.* 335. Parmenides taught that there were crowns encircling one another in close succession, one of rarefied matter, another of dense, and between these other mixed crowns of light and darkness; and that which surrounded all was solid like a wall, and under this was a crown of fire; and the centre of all the crowns was solid, and around it was a circle of fire; and of the mixed crowns the one nearest the centre was the source of motion and generation for all, and this "the goddess who directs the helm and holds the keys," he calls "justice and necessity."

[C.] Zeno

[a] Plato, *Parmenides* 128. In truth, these writings are a kind of support to the doctrine of Parmenides against those who endeavour to ridicule it, (by saying) that if "one" exists, it would follow that such an assertion would suffer many things of a laughable kind, and contrary to itself. This writing therefore contradicts those, who assert that "the many" exists; and it gives in return these and many other reasons; as it intends to show that the hypothesis, which (asserts) the existence of "the many" would suffer things still more laughable than (would) the assumption of "the one," if it is sufficiently worked out.

[b] *Fragments*

Fr. 1. If being did not have magnitude, it would not exist at all.—If anything exists, it is necessary that each thing should have some magnitude and thickness, and that one part of it should be separated from another. The same argument applies to the thing that is in front of it, for that also will have magnitude and will have something in front of it. The same may be said of each thing once for all, for there will be no such thing as last, nor will one thing differ from another. So if there is a multiplicity of things, it is necessary that these should be great and small—small enough not to have any magnitude, and great enough to be infinite.

Fr. 2. For if anything were added to another thing, it could not make it any greater; for since greatness does not exist, it is impossible to increase the greatness of a thing by adding to it. So that which is added would be nothing. If when something is taken away that which is left is no less, and if it becomes no greater by receiving additions, evidently that which has been added or taken away is nothing.

Fr. 3. If there is a multiplicity of things, it is necessary that these should be just as many as exist, and not more nor fewer. If there are just as many as there are, then the number would be finite. If there is a multiplicity at all, the number is infinite, for there are always others between any two, and yet others between each pair of these. So the number of things is infinite.

Fr. 4. If there is such a thing as space, it will be in something, for all being is in something, and that which is in something is in space. So space will be in space, and so on *ad infinitum*. Accordingly, there is no such thing as space.

[c] Aristotle, *Metaphysics* B.4; 1001 b 7. If the absolute unit is indivisible it would, according to Zeno's axiom, be nothing at all. For that which neither makes anything larger by its addition, nor makes anything smaller by its subtraction, is not one of the things that are, since it is clear that what is must be a magnitude, and, if a magnitude, corporeal, for the corporeal has being in all dimensions. Others things, such as the surface and the line, when added in one way make things larger, when added in another way do not; but the point and the unit do not make things larger however added.

[d] Aristotle, *Physics* 6.9; 239 b 5. (*abridged*)

1. If, Zeno says, everything is at rest (or in motion) when it is in a space equal to itself, and the moving body is always in the present moment (in a space equal to itself), then the

moving arrow is still. Therefore the arrow in flight is stationary.

2. Motion does not exist because the moving body must go half the distance before it goes the whole distance. (Compare *Physics* 8.8; 263 a 5 "The same method should also be adopted in replying to those who ask, in the terms of Zeno's argument, whether we admit that before any distance can be traversed half the distance must be traversed, that these half-distances are infinite in number, and that it is impossible to traverse distances infinite in number.")

3. The Achilles problem: The slow runner will never be overtaken by the swiftest, for it is necessary that the pursuer should first reach the point from which the pursued started, so that necessarily the slower is always somewhat in advance. This argument is the same as the preceding, the only difference being that the distance is not divided each time into halves.

4. With reference to equal bodies moving in opposite directions past equal bodies in the stadium with equal speed, some from the end of the stadium, others from the middle, Zeno thinks half the time equal to twice the time. [Burnet's reconstruction of the paradox (Early Greek Philosophy, page 319) is as follows:

Half the time may be equal to double the time. Let us suppose three rows of bodies, one of which (A) is at rest while the other two (B, C) are moving with equal velocity in opposite directions (Fig. 1). By the time they are all in the same part of the course, B will have passed twice as many of the bodies in C as A (Fig. 2).

```
    Fig. 1                    Fig. 2

A      o o o o           A o o o o
B o o o o                B o o o o
C          o o o o       C o o o o
```

Therefore the time which it takes to pass C is twice as long as the time it takes to pass A. But the time which B and C take to reach the position of A is the same. Therefore double the time is equal to the half.]

THE PLURALISTS

THE philosophies of Empedocles, Anaxagoras and the Atomists, Leucippus and Democritus, are attempts to escape from the dilemma which the opposing views of Heraclitus and the Eleatics had produced. Heraclitus, concentrating upon the orderly process of change and its exemplification in concrete phenomena, affords an approach to an explanation of the constant variation and mutability of the world of experience. Primarily, Heraclitus' system, in accounting for the periodicity of the seasons, the recurrence of life and death and the phenomena of generation and corruption, attempts to face the "hard facts" of the world, the "fact" observed that this or that bow releases an arrow and that this or that river flows. Parmenides and Zeno, concentrating upon the identity of being, deny its change. Thought or reason demands fixity and universality, as opposed to change or flux or the concentration upon individual "facts" as explanatory of reality. How Heraclitus' fire transforms itself into other elements is, however, left unanswered. Why appearances seem real and why "facts" and phenomena compel us is dismissed by Parmenides and Zeno with compelling logic but without an attempt to satisfy the mind's craving for the relation of being to becoming or, at least, to the appearance of becoming.

Empedocles, Anaxagoras and the Atomists refuse to accept the absolute dichotomy between being and change.

Logically, their position may be indicated by saying that the Pluralists refused to accept the alternative "*either* being *or* becoming" but subjected previous thought to a further analysis and demonstrated that all of the possibilities had not been exhausted by their predecessors.

Empedocles, son of Meton and a native of Agrigentum, is the first philosopher to attempt the reconciliation of Eleatic and Heraclitean philosophy. Zeller puts the dates of Empedocles' life *ca.* 494–434 B.C. Of an aristocratic family, Empedocles opposed tyranny and refused the crown of his native town. Forced to leave Agrigentum for political reasons, tradition had it that Empedocles leapt, after a feast, into the crater of Mt. Etna. Empedocles was not only a philosopher but a religious teacher and magician. He is said, for example, to have forbidden the winds to enter Agrigentum and to have halted them by stretching asses' skins across the hollows through which the winds ordinarily passed. On his own evidence, he was a healer of the sick, one who recalled the dead to life and a believer in the transmigration of the soul (24, 369 and 383).

As a starting point for his thought, Empedocles adopts the implications of Parmenides' philosophy of being. The coming into existence of being or its destruction cannot be maintained (45 and 48). Nevertheless, while the acceptance of Parmenides' being carries with it the denial of origin and destruction, changes of location, not affecting the nature of substance but merely its distribution, are admissible. Such a mechanical process is accepted by Empedocles in "mixture and separation" (36, 60). By mixture, what gives the appearance of origin, growth or becoming takes place. By separation, decay, destruction and death are accounted for. This, however, necessitates the reinterpretation of being in a most important sense, for if being is homogeneous throughout, the mixture and separation will produce no adequate explanation of change. Empedocles, therefore, seeks the necessary and sufficient "roots" or "elements" to which as being all phenomena will reduce but which are themselves irreducible. These "roots" or "elements" are being—immortal, indestructible and qualitatively unchangeable. The roots are identified by Empedocles with earth, air, fire and water (33). Earth, air, fire and water are to be thought of essentially as the ultimate elements from which the universe is compounded (104) and Empedocles is the first philosopher to introduce them as the four elements. Aristotle indicates, however, that Empedocles following Parmenides' *On Opinion* really has but two elements, the division being fire on one side and earth, air and water on the other (b. Arist. *Met.*). Empedocles pays little attention to an analysis of the characteristics of each element.

It is necessary for Empedocles more specifically to explain change as it is brought about by the mixture and separation of the qualitatively unchangeable "roots" or elements. Since no qualitative change can occur in the element, there can be no such transformation of one element into another as occurred in the theory of Heraclitus. The elements are mixed, always retaining their qualitative differences, through the interpenetration of the protrusions of one element into the pores or interstices of another element: "But these (elements) are the same; and penetrating through each other they become one thing in one place and another in another, while ever they remain alike (i.e. the same)" (87). Separation is the withdrawal of what was intermingled. In what manner such mixture and separation could take place in a world in which empty space is specifically denied and in which the elements are by definition indivisible is not revealed (87). To the question that inevitably arises concerning the relation of the qualitatively changeless elements to the infinity of qualitatively different phenomena of the world, Empedocles offers the analogy of the artist mixing paints (121). Empedocles points out that some mixtures occur more easily than others (284) and this position seems to be based on the generalization that the more closely correspondent the pores of one body are to the protrusions or emanations of another body, the more capable the two are of mixture. This theory is likewise utilized to explain sensation and perception, the assumption being that objects are perceived through the presence of elements in us identical or similar to elements in the things perceived (d. Theophrastus, *de Sensu*).

A factor latent in the Milesian philosophy is made explicit in Empedocles' theory of change. Anaximenes, for example, tacitly assumes changes in temperature for the transformation of air into its varied phenomenal states. Empedocles perceives that the four "roots" cannot, since they constitute being and involve no change or movement within themselves, contain within themselves the force or impulse causing the beginning or continuation of the mixture and separation. An "efficient cause" or "moving force" is essential. Empedocles' solution to the problem is an argument derived from his observation of man. Love is the force that attracts men to men, Strife is the force that repels. Love and Strife are therefore transferred to the universe at large and are the causes of change and motion. Love causes the mixture of the elements, Strife causes their separation (b. Arist. *Met.* and 60, 66, 74, 96 and 110). As a result of the forces of Love and Strife, a process or "immovable circle" (66) occurs in the world. In the first phase of the process, the elements or roots are in a perfect mixture, due to the effects of Love in bringing them together or uniting them. As Strife enters, the elements are separated, causing the second phase of the process. With Strife dominant, the elements are completely separated and the third phase takes place. As Love enters, the uniting or coming together of the mixture takes place. By this process of separation and mixture the physical universe comes into existence (c). Life is possible in the second and fourth phases of the mixture and separation, Love bringing separate parts and organs of men and animals together. But pure chance prevailed and organs united with each other indiscriminately. A theory of the "survival of the fittest" is implied, for those forms survived which were the result of the proper placing and distributing of the organs (244).

THE PLURALISTS

[A.] Empedocles

[a] *Fragments*

Book I

1. And do thou hear me, Pausanias, son of wise Anchites.
2. For scant means of acquiring knowledge are scattered among the members of the body; and many are the evils

that break in to blunt the edge of studious thought. And gazing on a little portion of life that is not life, swift to meet their fate, they rise and are borne away like smoke, persuaded only of that on which each one chances as he is driven this way and that, but the whole he vainly boasts he has found. Thus these things are neither seen nor heard distinctly by men, nor comprehended by the mind. And thou, now that thou hast withdrawn hither, shalt learn no more than what mortal mind has seen.

11. But, ye gods, avert the madness of those men from my tongue, and from lips that are holy cause a pure stream to flow. And thee I pray, much-wooed white-armed maiden Muse, in what things it is right for beings of a day to hear, do thou, and Piety, driving obedient car, conduct me on. Nor yet shall the flowers of honour well esteemed compel me to pluck them from mortal hands, on condition that I speak boldly more than is holy and only then sit on the heights of wisdom.

19. But come, examine by every means each thing how it is clear, neither putting greater faith in anything seen than in what is heard, nor in a thundering sound more than in the clear assertions of the tongue, nor keep from trusting any of the other members in which there lies means of knowledge, but know each thing in the way in which it is clear.

24. Cures for evils whatever there are, and protection against old age shalt thou learn, since for thee alone will I accomplish all these things. Thou shalt break the power of untiring gales which rising against the earth blow down the crops and destroy them; and, again, whenever thou wilt, thou shalt bring their blasts back; and thou shalt bring seasonable drought out of dark storm for men, and out of summer drought thou shalt bring streams pouring down from heaven to nurture the trees; and thou shalt lead out of Hades the spirit of a man that is dead.

33. Hear first the four roots of all things: bright Zeus, life-giving Hera (air), and Aidoneus (earth), and Nestis who moistens the springs of men with her tears.

36. And a second thing I will tell thee: There is no origination of anything that is mortal, nor yet any end in baneful

death; but only mixture and separation of what is mixed, but men call this "origination."

40. But when light is mingled with air in human form, or in form like the race of wild beasts or of plants or of birds, then men say that these things have come into being; and when they are separated, they call them evil fate; this is the established practice, and I myself also call it so in accordance with the custom.

45. Fools! for they have no far-reaching studious thoughts who think that what was not before comes into being or that anything dies and perishes utterly.

48. For from what does not exist at all it is impossible that anything come into being, and it is neither possible nor perceivable that being should perish completely; for things will always stand wherever one in each case shall put them.

51. A man of wise mind could not divine such things as these, that so long as men live what indeed they call life, so long they exist and share what is evil and what is excellent, but before they are formed and after they are dissolved, they are really nothing at all.

55. But for base men it is indeed possible to withhold belief from strong proofs; but do thou learn as the pledges of our Muse bid thee, and lay open her word to the very core.

58. Joining one heading to another in discussion, not completing one path (of discourse) . . . for it is right to say what is excellent twice and even thrice.

60. Twofold is the truth I shall speak; for at one time there grew to be one alone out of many, and at another time, however, it separated so that there were many out of the one. Twofold is the coming into being, twofold the passing away, of perishable things; for the latter (i. e. passing away) the combining of all things both begets and destroys, and the former (i. e. coming into being), which was nurtured again out of parts that were being separated, is itself scattered.

66. And these (elements) never cease changing place continually, now being all united by Love into one, now each borne apart by the hatred engendered of Strife, until they are brought together in the unity of the all, and become subject to it. Thus inasmuch as one has been wont to arise

out of many and again with the separation of the one the many arise, so things are continually coming into being and there is no fixed age for them; and farther inasmuch as they [the elements] never cease changing place continually, so they always exist within an immovable circle.

74. But come, hear my words, for truly learning causes the mind to grow. For as I said before in declaring the ends of my words: Twofold is the truth I shall speak; for at one time there grew to be the one alone out of many, and at another time it separated so that there were many out of the one; fire and water and earth and boundless height of air, and baneful Strife apart from these, balancing each of them, and Love among them, their equal in length and breadth. 81. Upon her do thou gaze with thy mind, nor yet sit dazed in thine eyes; for she is wont to be implanted in men's members, and through her they have thoughts of love and accomplish deeds of union, and call her by the name of Delight, and Aphrodite; no mortal man has discerned her with them (the elements) as she moves on her way. But do thou listen to the undeceiving course of my words. . . .

87. For these (elements) are equal, all of them, and of like ancient race; and one holds one office, another another, and each has his own nature. . . . For nothing is added to them, nor yet does anything pass away from them; for if they were continually perishing they would no longer exist. . . . Neither is any part of this all empty, nor over full. For how should anything cause this all to increase, and whence should it come? And whither should they (the elements) perish, since no place is empty of them? And in their turn they prevail as the cycle comes round, and they disappear before each other, and they increase each in its allotted turn. But these (elements) are the same; and penetrating through each other they become one thing in one place and another in another, while ever they remain alike (i. e. the same).

110. For they two (Love and Strife) were before and shall be, nor yet, I think, will there ever be an unutterably long time without them both.

96. But come, gaze on the things that bear farther witness to my former words, if in what was said before there be

anything defective in form. Behold the sun, warm and bright on all sides, and whatever is immortal and is bathed in its bright ray, and behold the raincloud, dark and cold on all sides; from the earth there proceed the foundations of things and solid bodies. In Strife all things are, endued with form and separate from each other, but they come together in Love and are desired by each other. 104. For from these (elements) come all things that are or have been or shall be; from these there grew up trees and men and women, wild beasts and birds and water-nourished fishes, and the very gods, long-lived, highest in honour.

121. And as when painters are preparing elaborate votive offerings—men well taught by wisdom in their art—they take many-coloured pigments to work with, and blend together harmoniously more of one and less of another till they produce likenesses of all things; so let not error overcome thy mind to make thee think there is any other source of mortal things that have likewise come into distinct existence in unspeakable numbers; but know these (elements), for thou didst hear from a god the account of them.

130. But come, I will tell thee now the first principle of the sun, even the sources of all things now visible, earth and billowy sea and damp mist and Titan aether (i. e. air) binding all things in its embrace.

135. Then neither is the bright orb of the sun greeted, nor yet either the shaggy might of earth or sea; thus, then, in the firm vessel of harmony is fixed God, a sphere, round, rejoicing in complete solitude.

139. But when mighty Strife was nurtured in its members and leaped up to honour at the completion of the time, which has been driven on by them both in turn under a mighty oath. . . .

142. For the limbs of the god were made to tremble, all of them in turn.

143. For all the heavy (he put) by itself, the light by itself.

144. Without affection and not mixed together.

145. Heaped together in greatness.

146. If there were no limit to the depths of the earth and the abundant air, as is poured out in foolish words from

the mouths of many mortals who see but little of the all.
149. Swift-darting sun and kindly moon.
150. But gathered together it advances around the great heavens.
151. It shines back to Olympos with untroubled face.
152. The kindly light has a brief period of shining.
153. As sunlight striking the broad circle of the moon.
154. A borrowed light, circular in form, it revolves about the earth, as if following the track of a chariot.
156. For she beholds opposite to her the sacred circle of her lord.
157. And she scatters his rays into the sky above, and spreads darkness over as much of the earth as the breadth of the gleaming-eyed moon.
160. And night the earth makes by coming in front of the lights.
161. Of night, solitary, blind-eyed.
162. And many fires burn beneath the earth.
163. (The sea) with its stupid race of fertile fishes.
164. Salt is made solid when struck by the rays of the sun.
165. The sea is the sweat of the earth.
166. But air sinks down beneath the earth with its long roots. . . . For thus it happened to be running at that time, but oftentimes otherwise.
168. (Fire darting) swiftly upwards.
169. But now I shall go back over the course of my verses, which I set out in order before, drawing my present discourse from that discourse. When Strife reached the lowest depth of the eddy and Love comes to be in the midst of the whirl, then all these things come together at this point so as to be one alone, yet not immediately, but joining together at their pleasure, one from one place, another from another. And as they were joining together Strife departed to the utmost boundary. But many things remained unmixed, alternating with those that were mixed, even as many as Strife, remaining aloft, still retained; for not yet had it entirely departed to the utmost boundaries of the circle, but some of its members were remaining within, and others had gone outside. 180. But, just as far as it is constantly rushing forth,

just so far there ever kept coming in a gentle immortal stream of perfect Love; and all at once what before I learned were immortal were coming into being as mortal things, what before were unmixed as mixed, changing their courses. And as they (the elements) were mingled together there flowed forth the myriad species of mortal things, patterned in every sort of form, a wonder to behold.

186. For all things are united, themselves with parts of themselves—the beaming sun and earth and sky and sea—whatever things are friendly but have separated in mortal things. And so, in the same way, whatever things are the more adapted for mixing, these are loved by each other and made alike by Aphrodite. But whatever things are hostile are separated as far as possible from each other, both in their origin and in their mixing and in the forms impressed on them, absolutely unwonted to unite and very baneful, at the suggestion of Strife, since it has wrought their birth.

195. In this way, by the good favour of Tyche, all things have power of thought.

196. And in so far as what was least dense came together as they fell.

197. For water is increased by water, primeval fire by fire, and earth causes its own substance to increase, and air, air.

199. And the kindly earth in its broad hollows received two out of the eight parts of bright Nestis, and four of Hephaistos, and they became white bones, fitted together marvellously by the glues of Harmony.

203. And the earth met with these in almost equal amounts, with Hephaistos and Ombros and bright-shining Aether (i. e. air), being anchored in the perfect harbours of Kypris; either a little more earth, or a little less with more of the others. From these arose blood and various kinds of flesh.

208. . . . glueing barley-meal together with water.

209. (Water) tenacious Love.

Book II

210. And if your faith be at all lacking in regard to these (elements), how from water and earth and air and sun

(fire) when they are mixed, arose such colours and forms of mortal things, as many as now have arisen under the uniting power of Aphrodite. . .

214. How both tall trees and fishes of the sea (arose).

215. And thus then Kypris, when she had moistened the earth with water, breathed air on it and gave it to swift fire to be hardened.

217. And all these things which were within were made dense, while those without were made rare, meeting with such moisture in the hands of Kypris.

219. And thus tall trees bear fruit (*lit.* eggs), first of all olives.

220. Wherefore late-born pomegranates and luxuriant apples. . . .

221. Wine is water that has fermented in the wood beneath the bark.

222. For if thou shalt fix them in all thy close-knit mind and watch over them graciously with pure attention, all these things shall surely be thine for ever, and many others shalt thou possess from them. For these themselves shall cause each to grow into its own character, whatever is the nature of each. But if thou shalt reach out for things of another sort, as is the manner of men, there exist countless evils to blunt your studious thoughts; soon these latter shall cease to live as time goes on, desiring as they do to arrive at the longed-for generation of themselves. For know that all things have understanding and their share of intelligence.

232. Favour hates Necessity, hard to endure.

233. This is in the heavy-backed shells found in the sea, of limpets and purple-fish and stone-covered tortoises . . . there shalt thou see earth lying uppermost on the surface.

236. Hair and leaves and thick feathers of birds are the same thing in origin, and reptiles' scales, too, on strong limbs.

238. But on hedgehogs, sharp-pointed hair bristles on their backs.

240. Out of which divine Aphrodite wrought eyes untiring.

241. Aphrodite fashioning them curiously with bonds of love.

242. When they first grew together in the hands of Aphrodite.
243. The liver well supplied with blood.
244. Where many heads grew up without necks, and arms were wandering about naked, bereft of shoulders, and eyes roamed about alone with no foreheads.
247. This is indeed remarkable in the mass of human members; at one time all the limbs which form the body, united into one by Love, grow vigorously in the prime of life; but yet at another time, separated by evil Strife, they wander each in different directions along the breakers of the sea of life. Just so it is with plants and with fishes dwelling in watery halls, and beasts whose lair is in the mountains, and birds borne on wings.
254. But as divinity was mingled yet more with divinity, these things kept coming together in whatever way each might chance, and many others also in addition to these continually came into being.
257. Many creatures arose with double faces and double breasts, offspring of oxen with human faces, and again there sprang up children of men with oxen's heads; creatures, too, in which were mixed some parts from men and some of the nature of women, furnished with sterile members.
261. Cattle of trailing gait, with undivided hoofs.
262. But come now, hear of these things; how fire separating caused the hidden offspring of men and weeping women to arise, for it is no tale apart from our subject, or witless. In the first place there sprang up out of the earth forms grown into one whole, having a share of both, of water and of fire. These in truth fire caused to grow up, desiring to reach its like; but they showed as yet no lovely body formed out of the members, nor voice nor limb such as is natural to men.
270. But the nature of the members (of the child?) is divided, part in the man's, part in the woman's (body).
271. But desire also came upon him, having been united with . . . by sight.
273. It was poured out in the pure parts, and some meeting with cold became females.
275. The separated harbours of Aphrodite.

276. In its warmer parts the womb is productive of the male, and on this account men are dark and more muscular and more hairy.

279. As when fig-juice curdles and binds white milk.

280. On the tenth day of the eighth month came the white discharge.

281. Knowing that there are exhalations from all things which came into existence.

282. Thus sweet was snatching sweet, and bitter darted to bitter, and sharp went to sharp, and hot coupled with hot.

284. Water combines better with wine, but it is unwilling to combine with oil.

286. The bloom of the scarlet dye mingles with shining linen.

287. So all beings breathe in and out; all have bloodless tubes of flesh spread over the outside of the body, and at the openings of these the outer layers of skin are pierced all over with close-set ducts, so that the blood remains within, while a facile opening is cut for the air to pass through. Then whenever the soft blood speeds away from these, the air speeds bubbling in with impetuous wave, and whenever the blood leaps back the air is breathed out; as when a girl, playing with a klepsydra of shining brass, takes in her fair hand the narrow opening of the tube and dips it in the soft mass of silvery water, the water does not at once flow into the vessel, but the body of air within pressing on the close-set holes checks it till she uncovers the compressed stream; but then when the air gives way the determined amount of water enters. (302.) And so in the same way when the water occupies the depths of the bronze vessel, as long as the narrow opening and passage is blocked up by human flesh, the air outside striving eagerly to enter holds back the water inside behind the gates of the resounding tube, keeping control of its end, until she lets go with her hand. (306.) Then, on the other hand, the very opposite takes place to what happened before; the determined amount of water runs off as the air enters. Thus in the same way when the soft blood, surging violently through the members, rushes back into the interior, a swift stream of air comes in with hurrying wave,

and whenever it (the blood) leaps back, the air is breathed out again in equal quantity.

313. With its nostrils seeking out the fragments of animals' limbs, <as many as the delicate exhalation from their feet was leaving behind in the wood>.

314. So, then, all things have obtained their share of breathing and of smelling.

315. (The ear) an offshoot of flesh.

316. And as when one with a journey through a stormy night in prospect provides himself with a lamp and lights it at the bright-shining fire—with lanterns that drive back every sort of wind, for they scatter the breath of the winds as they blow—and the light darting out, inasmuch as it is finer (than the winds), shines across the threshold with untiring rays; so then elemental fire, shut up in membranes, it entraps in fine coverings to be the round pupil, and the coverings protect it against the deep water which flows about it, but the fire darting forth, inasmuch as it is finer. . . .

326. There is one vision coming from both (eyes).

327. (The heart) lies in seas of blood which darts in opposite directions, and there most of all intelligence centres for men; for blood about the heart is intelligence in the case of men.

330. For men's wisdom increases with reference to what lies before them.

331. In so far as they change and become different, to this extent other sorts of things are ever present for them to think about.

333. For it is by earth that we see earth, and by water water, and by air glorious air; so, too, by fire we see destroying fire, and love by love, and strife by baneful strife. For out of these (elements) all things are fitted together and their form is fixed, and by these men think and feel both pleasure and pain.

Book III

338. Would that in behalf of perishable beings thou, immortal Muse, mightest take thought at all for our thought to come by reason of our cares! Hear me now and be present

again by my side, Kalliopeia, as I utter noble discourse about the blessed gods.

342. Blessed is he who has acquired a wealth of divine wisdom, but miserable he in whom there rests a dim opinion concerning the gods.

344. It is not possible to draw near (to god) even with the eyes, or to take hold of him with our hands, which in truth is the best highway of persuasion into the mind of man; for he has no human head fitted to a body, nor do two shoots branch out from the trunk, nor has he feet, nor swift legs, nor hairy parts, but he is sacred and ineffable mind alone, darting through the whole world with swift thoughts.

ON PURIFICATIONS

352. O friends, ye who inhabit the great city of sacred Akragas up to the acropolis, whose care is good deeds, who harbour strangers deserving of respect, who know not how to do baseness, hail! I go about among you an immortal god, no longer a mortal, honoured by all, as is fitting, crowned with fillets and luxuriant garlands. With these on my head, so soon as I come to flourishing cities I am reverenced by men and by women; and they follow after me in countless numbers, inquiring of me what is the way to gain, some in want of oracles, others of help in diseases, long time in truth pierced with grievous pains, they seek to hear from me keen-edged account of all sorts of things.

364. But why do I lay weight on these things, as though I were doing some great thing, if I be superior to mortal, perishing men?

366. Friends, I know indeed when truth lies in the discourses that I utter; but truly the entrance of assurance into the mind of man is difficult and hindered by jealousy.

369. There is an utterance of Necessity, an ancient decree of the gods, eternal, sealed fast with broad oaths: whenever any one defiles his body sinfully with bloody gore or perjures himself in regard to wrong-doing, one of those spirits who are heir to long life, thrice ten thousand seasons shall he wander apart from the blessed, being born meantime in all sorts of mortal forms, changing one bitter path of life for

another. For mighty Air pursues him Seaward, and Sea spews him forth on the threshold of Earth, and Earth casts him into the rays of the unwearying Sun, and Sun into the eddies of Air; one receives him from the other, and all hate him. One of these now am I too, a fugitive from the gods and a wanderer, at the mercy of raging Strife.

383. For before this I was born once a boy, and a maiden, and a plant, and a bird, and a darting fish in the sea. 385. And I wept and shrieked on beholding the unwonted land where are Murder and Wrath, and other species of Fates, and wasting diseases, and putrefaction and fluxes.

388. In darkness they roam over the meadow of Ate.

389. Deprived of life.

390. From what honour and how great a degree of blessedness have I fallen here on the earth to consort with mortal beings!

392. We enter beneath this over-roofed cave.

393. Where were Chthonie and far-seeing Heliope (i. e. Earth and Sun?), bloody Contention and Harmony of sedate face, Beauty and Ugliness, Speed and Loitering, lovely Truth and dark-eyed Obscurity, Birth and Death, and Sleep and Waking, Motion and Stability, many-crowned Greatness and Lowness, and Silence and Voice.

400. Alas, ye wretched, ye unblessed race of mortal beings, of what strifes and of what groans were ye born!

402. She wraps about them a strange garment of flesh.

403. Man-surrounding earth.

404. For from being living he made them assume the form of death by a change. . . .

405. Nor had they any god Ares, nor Kydoimos (Uproar), nor king Zeus, nor Kronos, nor Poseidon, but queen Kypris. Her they worshipped with hallowed offerings, with painted figures, and perfumes of skilfully made odour, and sacrifices of unmixed myrrh and fragrant frankincense, casting on the ground libations from tawny bees. And her altar was not moistened with pure blood of bulls, but it was the greatest defilement among men, to deprive animals of life and to eat their goodly bodies.

415. And there was among them a man of unusual knowledge, and master especially of all sorts of wise deeds, who in truth possessed greatest wealth of mind; for whenever he reached out with all his mind, easily he beheld each one of all the things that are, even for ten and twenty generations of men.

421. For all were gentle and obedient toward men, both animals and birds, and they burned with kindly love; and trees grew with leaves and fruit ever on them, burdened with abundant fruit all the year.

425. This is not lawful for some and unlawful for others, but what is lawful for all extends on continuously through the wide-ruling air and the boundless light.

[b] ARISTOTLE, *de Caelo* iii.2; 302 a 28. Empedocles says that fire and earth and associated elements are elements of bodies, and that all things are composed of these.

ARISTOTLE, *de Gen. et Corr.* i.1; 314 b 7. Wherefore Empedocles speaks after this manner, saying that nothing comes into being, but there is only mixture and separation of the mixed.

ARISTOTLE, *Met.*, i.4; 915 a 21. And Empedokles makes more use of causes than Anaxagoras, but not indeed sufficiently; nor does he find in them what has been agreed upon. At any rate love for him is often a separating cause and strife a uniting cause. For whenever the all is separated into the elements by strife, fire and each of the other elements are collected into one; and again, whenever they all are brought together into one by love, parts are necessarily separated again from each thing. Empedokles moreover differed from those who went before, in that he discriminated this cause and introduced it, not making the cause of motion one, but different and opposite. Further, he first described the four elements spoken of as in the form of matter; but he did not use them as four but only as two, fire by itself, and the rest opposed to fire as being one in nature, earth and air and water.

ARISTOTLE, *Met.*, i.8; 989 a 20. And the same thing is true if one asserts that these are more numerous than one, as

Empedokles says that matter is four substances. For it is necessary that the same peculiar results should hold good with reference to him. For we see the elements arising from each other inasmuch as fire and earth do not continue the same substance (for so it is said of them in the verses on nature); and with reference to the cause of their motion, whether it is necessary to assume one or two, we must think that he certainly did not speak either in a correct or praiseworthy manner.

[c] Aet., *Plac.* ii.6; *Dox.* 334. Empedokles: The aether was first separated, and secondly fire, and then earth, from which, as it was compressed tightly by the force of its rotation, water gushed forth; and from this the air arose as vapour, and the heavens arose from the aether, the sun from the fire, and bodies on the earth were compressed out of the others.

Plut., *Strom.* 10; *Dox.* 582. Empedokles of Agrigentum: The elements are four—fire, water, aether, earth. And the cause of these is Love and Strife. From the first mixture of the elements he says that the air was separated and poured around in a circle; and after the air the fire ran off, and not having any other place to go to, it ran up from under the ice that was around the air. And there are two hemispheres moving in a circle around the earth, the one of pure fire, the other of air and a little fire mixed, which he thinks is night. And motion began as a result of the weight of the fire when it was collected.

[d] Theophrastus, *de sens.* 7; *Dox.* 500. Empedokles speaks in like manner concerning all the senses, and says that we perceive by a fitting into the pores of each sense. So they are not able to discern one another's objects, for the pores of some are too wide and of others too narrow for the object of sensation, so that some things go right through untouched, and others are unable to enter completely. And he attempts to describe what vision is; and he says that what is in the eye is fire and water and what surrounds it is earth and air, through which light being fine enters, as the light in lanterns. Pores of fire and water are set alternately, and the fire-pores recognize white objects, the water-pores black objects; for the

colours harmonize with the pores. And the colours move into vision by means of effluences. And they are not composed alike . . . and some of opposite elements; for some the fire is within and for others it is on the outside, so some animals see better in the daytime and others at night; those that have less fire see better by day, for the light inside them is balanced by the light outside them; and those that have less water see better at night, for what is lacking is made up for them. And in the opposite case the contrary is true; for those that have the more fire are dim-sighted, since the fire increasing plasters up and covers the pores of water in the daytime; and for those that have water in excess, the same thing happens at night; for the fire is covered up by the water. . . . Until in the case of some the water is separated by the outside light, and in the case of others the fire by the air; for the cure of each is its opposite. That which is composed of both in equal parts is the best tempered and most excellent vision. This, approximately, is what he says concerning vision. And hearing is the result of noises coming from outside. For when (the air) is set in motion by a sound, there is an echo within; for the hearing is as it were a bell echoing within, and the ear he calls an "offshoot of flesh": and the air when it is set in motion strikes on something hard and makes an echo. And smell is connected with breathing, so those have the keenest smell whose breath moves most quickly; and the strongest odour arises as an effluence from fine and light bodies. But he makes no careful discrimination with reference to taste and touch separately, either how or by what means they take place, except the general statement that sensation takes place by a fitting into the pores; and pleasure is due to likenesses in the elements and in their mixture, and pain to the opposite. And he speaks similarly concerning thought and ignorance: Thinking is by what is like, and not perceiving is by what is unlike, since thought is the same thing as, or something like, sensation. For recounting how we recognize each thing by each, he said at length: Now out of these (elements) all things are fitted together and their form is fixed, and by these men think and feel pleasure and pain. So it is by blood especially that we think; for in this specially are mingled <all> the elements of things. And those in whom equal and like parts have been mixed, not too far apart, nor yet small parts, nor exceeding great, these have the most intelligence and the most accurate senses; and those who approximate to this come next; and those who have the opposite qualities are the most lacking in intelligence. And those in whom the elements are scattered and rarefied, are torpid and easily fatigued; and those in whom the elements are small and thrown close together, move so rapidly and meet with so many things that they accomplish but little by reason of the swiftness of the motion of the blood. And those in whom there is a well-tempered mixture in some one part, are wise at this point; so some are good orators, others good artisans, according as the mixture is in the hands or in the tongue; and the same is true of the other powers.

[B.] Anaxagoras

Anaxagoras, as does Empedocles, accepts the Eleatic conclusions concerning *being* but attempts to introduce motion and change into the world. Born *ca.* 500 B.C., the son of Hegesiboulos and native of Klazomenae in Thrace, Anaxagoras was the first philosopher to make his home in Athens. There, as a friend of Pericles, Anaxagoras attracted the attention of men of scientific interests. In 434 B.C., the philosopher was tried for impiety, the charge being that he taught that the sun was a hot stone and the moon was earth. It is probable that the suit had political implications and that it was brought to embarrass Anaxagoras' patron, Pericles. Forced to leave Athens, Anaxagoras lived in Lampsakos, where he established a school and where an altar was erected in his memory. He is described by Aristotle as "older in years, younger in works than Empedocles."

Anaxagoras denies "coming into being" and "perishing." With Empedocles, he believes that change is the result of mixture and separation (Fr. 17; cf. Fr. 5 and Fr. 14). Thus far, Empedocles and Anaxagoras are agreed but Empedocles' selection of the four qualitatively unchangeable elements, earth, air, fire and water, as ultimate *being* is not acceptable to Anaxagoras. For Anaxagoras, *being* is an infinity of "seeds" or "germs." It would naturally be regarded as a scientific retrogression to multiply the number of elements, once they had been reduced to four, since science from Milesian times had sought simplicity and unity. There must be, therefore, strong reasons for such a change. Anaxagoras gives us a clue to his reasons in his statement: "Things in one universe are not divided from each other, nor yet are they cut off with an axe, neither hot from cold, nor cold from hot" (Fr. 13). When Empedocles has explained some "new" phenomenon or situation in the world as the result of the mixture of the four qualitatively unchanged elements, the "new" situation or phenomenon must be in itself unreal, since Empedocles in his own words has accepted the Eleatic doctrine: "Fools! for they have no far-reaching studious thoughts who think that what was not before comes into being or anything dies or perishes utterly" (Fr. 45). Since the four qualitatively unchanged elements will not account for the infinite variety and differentiation of the world of experience, the only alternative, if qualitative distinctions in elements are to be maintained, is to assume that qualitative distinctions are ultimate. Since there is an infinity of qualitative distinctions in the world, there must be on this hypothesis ultimate substances, "seeds" or "germs infinite in number, in no way like each other" (Fr. 4).[1]

Since the seeds are infinite and qualitatively distinct, what for Empedocles would be a novel and ultimately inexplicable situation or phenomenon is for Anaxagoras proof that the "new" (i.e. qualitatively differentiated) is the ultimate. To establish this position, Anaxagoras contends that "In all things there is a portion of everything—" (Fr. 5) and "that in all the objects that are compound there existed many things of all sorts, and germs of all objects, having all sorts of forms and colour and tastes." On these grounds, the Eleatic assumption of the indestructibility and uncreatedness of *being* may be accepted, for phenomena may be explained without resort to the addition or subtraction of qualities. This view is maintained in Anaxagoras' statement, "For how could hair come from what is not hair? Or flesh from what is not flesh?" (Fr. 18) The "coming into being" of hair or flesh is explicable on the ground that hair and flesh, as well as eyes, teeth, bone, etc., are contained in food. The names we apply to things are determined by the preponderance of certain seeds in them (cf. c, Arist. *Phys.*).

That all things contain a portion of everything seems a paradoxical position, but Anaxagoras, having learned perhaps from Zeno the possibilities of infinite divisibility, is making an application of his theory of *being* to material

[1] cf. Zeller: "Anaxagoras—supposes all the qualities and differences of derived things already inherent in the primitive matter, and therefore conceives the original substances unlimited in kind as well as in number" (p. 330). "—the substances of which things consist, are in this, their qualitative determinateness, underived and imperishable; and since there are innumerable things, no two of which are perfectly alike, he says there are innumerable seeds, not one of which resembles another" (p. 331).

things in much the same way that the Pythagoreans applied their geometrical hypotheses to physical things. At any rate, one may perhaps clarify Anaxagoras' position by an analogy to the points on a line: If you take away a portion of a straight line, there still remains an infinity of points. Anaxagoras argues, similarly, that if you separate a material fragment of any thing, you have left an infinity of seeds and an infinity of each kind.

Anaxagoras' universe, before separation, was an infinite mass, in which "nothing was clear and distinct" (Fr. 1), "not even was any colour clear and distinct" (Fr. 4). This mass corresponds to Anaximander's infinite, spoken of in terms of undifferentiated *being*. Motion must be introduced into the mass to account for change, since the ultimate substances are not self-moved. To account for motion, Empedocles had introduced Love and Strife. Anaxagoras likewise argues from his observation of man and selects mind or *nous* as the cause of motion. *Nous* is material but it is the purest and most rarefied of things. It is apart from all else for "things mingled with it would prevent it from having power over anything in the same way that it does now that it is alone by itself" (Fr. 6). As an efficient cause, *nous* sets up a rotary motion in the undifferentiated mass of *being* and separation occurs. The separation involves no increase or decrease in the "seeds" (Fr. 14). Air and aether (Fr. 2) are first separated off from the mass by the swiftness of the rotary motion initiated by mind. (Fr. 11). Air, all that is cold, dark and dense, moves to the centre. Aether, all that is warm, light and rare, moves to the periphery (Fr. 8 and d, Hipp. *Phil.*). Condensation produces water, earth and stones (Fr. 9).

Thus far, *nous* has been utilized solely to initiate the rotation necessary for the separation of the mass of *being*. Moreover, it is clear that Anaxagoras is content to explain phenomena by the rotation and by the further method of condensation and rarefaction. It is on this ground that Aristotle and Plato (c, *Met.* and *Phaedo*) criticize the conception of *nous,* Aristotle pointing out that Anaxagoras uses it merely as a *deus ex machina* when other means of explanation fail him. Despite the authority of antiquity, it may be indicated, however, that other hypotheses are implicit in Anaxagoras' *nous.* That it should function as mind and still be material is in the tradition of Anaxagoras' predecessors. It is clear, however, that Anaxagoras differentiates it as much as possible from the other material substances in the universe. It is homogeneous, omniscient, omnipotent and has a specific function in ruling over all that has life. It is important to notice, too, that *nous* arranges all things in order, apparently with reference to ends (Fr. 6) and that it makes distinct the things set in motion. Without giving *nous* personality, it is possible to assume that it makes comprehensible the mass of *being* and this it does by giving order or structure to *being.*

Anaxagoras is not consistent in separating *nous* from all else, for he says "In all things there is a portion of everything except mind; and there are things in which there is mind also" (Fr. 5). It is probable that the presence of *nous* distinguishes the animate from the inanimate.

Anaxagoras assumed that perception is caused by differences between the perceiving substance and the perceived substance (e, Theophrastus).

[B.] Anaxagoras

[a] Aristotle, *Metaphysics* i.3; 984 a 11. Anaxagoras of Klazomenae, who preceded him (Empedocles) in point of age and followed him in his works, says that the first principles are infinite in number; for nearly all things being made up of like parts (homoeomeries), as for instance fire and water, he says, arise and perish only by composition and separation, and there is no other arising and perishing, but they abide eternal.

Aristotle, *de Caelo* iii.3; 302 a 31. Anaxagoras says the opposite to Empedocles, for he calls the homoeomeries elements (I mean such as flesh and bone and each of those things), and air and fire he calls mixtures of these and of all the other "seeds"; for each of these things is made of the invisible homoeomeries all heaped together. Wherefore all things arise out of these things; for he calls fire and aether the same.

[b] *The Fragments*

1. All things were together, infinite both in number and in smallness; for the small also was infinite. And when they were all together, nothing was clear and distinct because of their smallness; for air and aether comprehended all things, both being infinite; for these are present in everything, and are greatest both as to number and as to greatness.

2. For air and aether are separated from the surrounding mass; and the surrounding (mass) is infinite in quantity.

4. But before these were separated, when all things were together, not even was any colour clear and distinct; for the mixture of all things prevented it, the mixture of moist and dry, of the warm and the cold, and of the bright and the dark (since much earth was present), and of germs infinite in number, in no way like each other; for none of the other things at all resembles the one the other.

3. And since these things are so, it is necessary to think that in all the objects that are compound there existed many things of all sorts, and germs of all objects, having all sorts of forms and colours and tastes.

10. And men were constituted, and the other animals, as many as have life. And the men have inhabited cities and works constructed as among us, and they have sun and moon and other things as among us; and the earth brings forth for them many things of all sorts, of which they carry the most serviceable into the house and use them. These things then I have said concerning the separation, that not only among us would the separation take place, but elsewhere too.

11. So these things rotate and are separated by force and swiftness. And the swiftness produces force; and their swiftness is in no way like the swiftness of the things now existing among men, but it is certainly many times as swift.

14. When they are thus distinguished, it is necessary to recognise that they all become no fewer and no more. For it is impossible that more than all should exist, but all are always equal.

5. In all things there is a portion of everything except mind; and there are things in which there is mind also.

6. Other things include a portion of everything, but mind is infinite and self-powerful and mixed with nothing, but it exists alone itself by itself. For if it were not by itself, but were mixed with anything else, it would include parts of all things, if it were mixed with anything; for a portion of everything exists in everything, as has been said by me before, and things mingled with it would prevent it from having power over anything in the same way that it does now that it is alone by itself. For it is the most rarefied of all things and the purest, and it has all knowledge in regard to everything and the greatest power; over all that has life, both greater and less, mind rules. And mind ruled the rotation of the whole, so that it set it in rotation in the beginning. First it began the rotation from a small beginning, then more and more was included in the motion, and yet more will be included. Both the mixed and the separated and distinct, all things mind recognized. And whatever things were to be, and whatever things were, as many as are now, and whatever things shall be, all these mind arranged in order; and it arranged that rotation, according to which now rotate stars

and sun and moon and air and aether, now that they are separated. Rotation itself caused the separation, and the dense is separated from the rare, the warm from the cold, the bright from the dark, the dry from the moist. And there are many portions of many things. Nothing is absolutely separated nor distinct, one thing from another, except mind. All mind is of like character, both the greater and the smaller. But nothing different is like anything else, but in whatever object there are the most, each single object is and was most distinctly these things.

7. And when mind began to set things in motion, there was separation from everything that was in motion, and however much mind set in motion, all this was made distinct. The rotation of the things that were moved and made distinct caused them to be yet more distinct.

8. The dense, the moist, the cold, the dark, collected there where now is the earth; the rare, the warm, the dry, the bright, departed toward the farther part of the aether.

9. Earth is condensed out of these things that are separated. For water is separated from the clouds, and earth from the water; and from the earth stones are condensed by cold; and these are separated farther from water.

12. But mind, as it always has been, especially now also is where all other things are, in the surrounding mass, and in the things that were separated, and in the things that are being separated.

13. Things in the one universe are not divided from each other, nor yet are they cut off with an axe, neither hot from cold, nor cold from hot.

15. For neither is there a least of what is small, but there is always a less. For being is not non-being. But there is always a greater than what is great. And it is equal to the small in number; but with reference to itself each thing is both small and great.

16. And since the portions of the great and the small are equal in number, thus also all things would be in everything. Nor yet is it possible for them to exist apart, but all things include a portion of everything. Since it is not possible for the least to exist, nothing could be separated, nor yet could

it come into being of itself, but as they were in the beginning so they now are, all things together. And there are many things in all things, and of those that are separated there are things equal in number in the greater and the lesser.

17. The Greeks do not rightly use the terms "coming into being" and "perishing." For nothing comes into being nor yet does anything perish, but there is mixture and separation of things that are. So they would do right in calling the coming into being "mixture," and the perishing "separation."

(18.) For how could hair come from what is not hair? Or flesh from what is not flesh?

[c] Plato, *Phaedo* 97 c. I heard a man reading from a book of one Anaxagoras (he said), to the effect that it is mind which arranges all things and is the cause of all things. 98 b. Reading the book, I see that the man does not make any use of mind, nor does he assign any causes for the arrangement of things, but he treats air and aether and water as causes, and many other strange things.

Aristotle, *Metaphysics* i.3; 984 b 8. Besides these and similar causes, inasmuch as they are not such as to generate the nature of things, they (again compelled, as we said, by the truth itself) sought the first principle which lay nearest. For perhaps neither fire nor earth nor any other such things should fittingly be or be thought a cause why some things exist and others arise; nor is it well to assign any such matter to its voluntary motion or to chance. Moreover one who said that as mind exists in animals, so it exists in nature as the cause of the universe and of all order, appeared as a sober man in contrast with those before who spoke rashly.

Aristotle, *Metaphysics* i.4; 985 a 18. Anaxagoras uses mind as a device by which to construct the universe, and when he is at a loss for the cause why anything necessarily is, then he drags this in, but in other cases he assigns any other cause rather than mind for what comes into being.

Aristotle, *Phys.* i.4; 187 a 36. They thought that (what arose) arose necessarily out of things that are and their attributes, and, because the masses were so small, out of what we cannot perceive. Wherefore they say that everything was mixed in everything because they saw everything arising out of everything; and different things appeared and were called different from each other according to what is present in greater number in the mixture of the infinites; for the whole is not purely white or black or sweet or flesh or bone, but the nature of the thing seems to be that of which it has the most.

[d] Hipp., *Phil.* 8. *Dox.* 561. After him came Anaxagoras of Klazomenae, son of Hegesiboulos. He said that the first principle of the all is mind and matter, mind the active first principle, and matter the passive. For when all things were together, mind entered and disposed them. The material first principles are infinite, and the smaller ones of these he calls infinite. And all things partake of motion when they are moved by mind and like things come together. And objects in the heavens have been ordered by their circular motion. The dense and the moist and the dark and the cold and all heavy things come together into the midst, and the earth consists of these when they are solidified; but the opposite to these, the warm, the bright, the dry, and the light move out beyond the aether. The earth is flat in form, and keeps its place in the heavens because of its size and because there is no void; and on this account the air by its strength holds up the earth, which rides on the air. And the sea arose from the moisture on the earth, both of the waters which have fallen after being evaporated, and of the rivers that flow down into it. And the rivers get their substance from the clouds and from the waters that are in the earth. For the earth is hollow and has water in the hollow places. And the Nile increases in summer because waters flow down into it from snows at the north.

Sun and moon and all the stars are fiery stones that are borne about by the revolution of the aether. And sun and moon and certain other bodies moving with them, but invisible to us, are below the stars. Men do not feel the warmth of the stars, because they are so far away from the earth; and they are not warm in the same way that the sun is, because they are in a colder region. The moon is below the sun and nearer us. The sun is larger than the Peloponnesos. The moon does not have its own light, but light from the sun. The revolution of the stars takes them beneath the earth. The moon is eclipsed when the earth goes in front of it, and sometimes when the bodies beneath the moon go in front of it; and the sun is eclipsed when the new moon goes in front of it. And the solstices are occasioned because the sun and the moon are thrust aside by the air. And the moon changes its course frequently because it is not able to master the cold. He first determined the matter of the moon's phases. He said the moon is made of earth and has plains and valleys in it. The milky way is a reflection of the light of the stars which do not get their light from the sun. The stars which move across the heavens, darting down like sparks, are due to the motion of the sphere.

And winds arise when the air is rarefied by the sun, and when objects are set on fire and moving towards the sphere are borne away. Thunders and lightnings arise from heat striking the clouds. Earthquakes arise from the air above striking that which is beneath the earth; for when this is set in motion, the earth which rides on it is tossed about by it. And animals arose in the first place from moisture, and afterwards one from another; and males arise when the seed that is separated from the right side becomes attached to the right side of the womb, and females when the opposite is the case.

[e] Theophr., *de sens.* 27. *Dox.* 507. Anaxagoras held that sensation takes place by opposite qualities; for like is not affected by like. And he attempts to enumerate things one by one. For seeing is a reflection in the pupil, and objects are not reflected in the like, but in the opposite. And for many creatures there is a difference of colour in the daytime, and for others at night, so that at that time they are sharpsighted. But in general the night is more of the same colour as the eyes. And the reflection takes place in the daytime, since light is the cause of reflection; but that colour which prevails the more is reflected in its opposite. In the same manner both touch and taste discern; for what is equally warm or equally cold does not produce warm or cold when it approaches its like, nor yet do men recognize sweet or bitter by these qual-

ities in themselves, but they perceive the cold by the warm, the drinkable water by the salt, the sweet by the bitter, according as each quality is absent; for all things are existing in us. So also smell and hearing take place, the one in connection with breathing, the other by the penetration of sound into the brain; for the surrounding bone against which the sound strikes is hollow. And every sensation is attended with pain, which would seem to follow from the fundamental thesis; for every unlike thing by touching produces distress. And this is evident both in the duration and in the excessive intensity of the sensations. For both bright colours and very loud sounds occasion pain, and men are not able to bear them for any long time. And the larger animals have the more acute sensations, for sensation is simply a matter of size. For animals that have large, pure, and bright eyes see large things afar off, but of those that have small eyes the opposite is true. And the same holds true of hearing. For large ears hear large sounds afar off, smaller ones escape their notice, and small ears hear small sounds near at hand. And the same is true of smell: for the thin air has the stronger odour, since warm and rarefied air has an odour. And when a large animal breathes, it draws in the thick with the rarefied, but the small animal only the rarefied, so that large animals have a better sense of smell. For an odour near at hand is stronger than one far off, because that is thicker, and what is scattered is weakened. It comes about to this, large animals do not perceive the thin air, and small animals do not perceive the thick air.

[C.] The Atomists

The classical hypothesis of a universe explicable in terms of atoms and void exerted an important influence upon later science and philosophy. Greek Atomism is important, however, not alone because of its historical influence but as a philosophical system in which were brought to their culmination many of the motives underlying Greek philosophy from the time of its inception in Miletus. No system followed more rigidly the implicit demand of the Milesians that the explanatory principles be reduced to a minimum and that their adequacy be tested by application to phenomena. In its incorporation of Anaximenes' hypothesis of quantitative differentiations, in its denial of the qualitative differentiations necessary for Anaxagoras' theory, in its reinterpretation of Parmenides' *being,* and in its forcing to their logical conclusions certain suggestions in Empedocles' philosophical poetry, Atomism may be represented as a culmination of a development in the philosophy that was to extend its province in the systems of Plato and Aristotle.

With reference to Leucippus, the founder of Atomism, tradition is vague. There is certainty concerning neither the dates of his life nor his actual contribution to philosophy. He is said to have been born in Abdera, the birthplace, *ca.* 460 B.C., of his disciple Democritus. The development of the Atomists' philosophy is commonly attributed to Democritus, who was reputed to have been the most learned man of his time (for Democritus' life, see text A.1).

The problem for the Atomists is to account for phenomena and "to save appearances," while yet maintaining the validity of Parmenides' postulate of *being*. The Atomists' theories may be clarified by comparison to and contrast with those held by Empedocles and Anaxagoras. In spite of Empedocles' assumption that *being* consists of four qualitatively changeless elements, his explanation of change by mixture through the interpenetration of the elements easily leads to the assumption that such change may take place only if the elements be subdivided into parts or particles. The Atomists accept such a division of *being* as logically necessary. Consequently, *being* is defined in terms of infinite atoms, which may neither be created nor destroyed. Atoms are not subject to change, as they are homogeneous and contain no spaces. They vary infinitely in size below the level at which the individual atom could be observed.

In their assumption that *being* is an infinity of atoms, Leucippus and Democritus propound a theory similar to that of Anaxagoras, who had seen the necessity for infinite seeds or germs to explain the infinite variety of phenomena. However, the seeds or germs of Anaxagoras' philosophy varied infinitely in quality. In contrast, atoms are qualitatively homogeneous. Qualitative differentiations observed in the world are explained by the Atomists on strictly quantitative principles. In their reduction of qualitative differentiations to quantitative principles, the Atomists carry to a logical conclusion the motive underlying Anaximenes' hypothesis of rarefaction and condensation.

To account for the interpenetration of the elements, Empedocles postulated pores or interstices, but denied the existence of empty space. The Atomists, assuming that the atoms varied not only in shape but in order and in position (Democritus, A.45, A.37, A.38), insist that void or *non-being* is as real as the *plenum* or *being* (Democritus, A.38). Since atoms have an inherent velocity, their movement in empty space results in collision, union, separation, variation in position and change in order. Upon the combination and separation of atoms in space depend the observable characteristics of the world. Since such combinations and separations of atoms occur by necessity (Leucippus, Fr. 2), the phenomenal characteristics of the universe at a given time will be due to the spatial distribution of the atoms. Generation or "coming into being" is explicable, on the Atomists' hypothesis, by the union of atoms, destruction or "passing out of being" by the subtraction of atoms (Democritus, A.58). Change, then, is the redistribution of atoms in space (Democritus, A.37).

The economy and explicitness of the Atomists' system may be further illustrated by specific reference to Democritus' philosophy. The weight of composite bodies is in proportion to the density of the atoms of which it is constructed. Larger bodies may, therefore, be lighter than smaller ones if the former contain more void (A.60). Worlds originate as a result of the collision of atoms in the void. "Lighter" atoms are driven "upward." A vortex is produced by the resultant collisions, since like atoms join with like (A.43 and B.164). The inclusiveness of the system and the economy of the principles used are further demonstrated in the Atomists' hypotheses concerning life and death, the relation of the soul to the body, and the nature of "secondary qualities." Like the body, the soul is composed of atoms. The atoms composing the soul are, however, the most mobile (A.101). To the presence of these swiftly moving atoms which alternate with the less mobile somatic atoms (cf. A.108) life is attributable. The dispersion of the "soul" atoms brings death, a constantly impending danger, owing to the fineness and mobility of the "soul-atoms." The dispersion of the soul is prevented by breathing in the surrounding air, which is likewise composed of the mobile atoms (A.106). With reference to tastes, Democritus assigned "a shape to each quality." Sour tastes, for example, are caused by "very large, rough shapes, with many angles and no curves" (*vide* A.129, cf. A.77 and A.49, B.11, 166 for the general theory of perception and secondary qualities).

In its historical development in classical times, Atomism underwent important alterations. The most important consequences arose, perhaps, through the addition of weight to atoms. The doxographical tradition attributes this change to Epicurus (A.47, cf. A.50). The weight of the atoms caused them to fall "downward" in straight lines. Since the atoms move by their inherent velocity, are governed by necessity, and originally are separated one from another, the doxographers assumed that no atom could overtake any other atom. As a result, the collisions essential to the formation of composite bodies, including worlds, could not occur. According to tradition, Epicurus solved the difficulty by introducing into the atoms "an inherent declination" (A.50) to ensure the necessary collision and entanglement. It was in this "declination" of atoms that Lucretius found the solution to the problem of human freedom in a world subject in all else to mechanical law and necessity. Through this one exception, later Atomism destroyed at once the law of nature governing the universe and the adequacy with which all phenomena had been explained. The earlier Atomism of Leucippus and Democritus remains, despite the inadequacies brought out by its later adherents, a model for future science and philosophy in its economy of principles and in its demand that those principles be tested in all phenomena.

The Atomists

[A.] Leucippus

Fr. 2. Nothing occurs at random, but everything for a reason and by necessity.[1]

Diogenes Laertius, *Lives* [2] ix.31. He declared the All to be unlimited, as already stated; but of the All part is full and part empty, and these he calls elements. Out of them arise the worlds unlimited in number and into them they are dissolved. This is how the worlds are formed. In a given section many atoms of all manner of shapes are carried from the unlimited into the vast empty space. These collect together and form a single vortex, in which they jostle against each other and, circling round in every possible way, separate off, by like atoms joining like. And, the atoms being so numerous that they can no longer revolve in equilibrium, the light ones pass into the empty space outside, as if they were being winnowed; the remainder keep together and, becoming entangled, go on their circuit together, and form a primary spherical system. This parts off like a shell, enclosing within it atoms of all kinds; and, as these are whirled round by virtue of the resistance of the centre, the enclosing shell becomes thinner, the adjacent atoms continually combining when they touch the vortex. In this way the earth is formed by portions brought to the centre coalescing. And again, even the outer shell grows larger by the influx of atoms from outside, and, as it is carried round in the vortex, adds to itself whatever atoms it touches. And of these some portions are locked together and form a mass, at first damp and miry, but, when they have dried and revolve with the universal vortex, they afterwards take fire and form the substance of the stars.

The orbit of the sun is the outermost, that of the moon nearest the earth; the orbits of the other heavenly bodies lie between these two. All the stars are set on fire by the speed of their motion; the burning of the sun is also helped by the

[1] *Trans.* Cyril Bailey, *The Greek Atomists and Epicurus,* p. 85.
[2] *Trans.* R. D. Hicks, *Diogenes Laertius,* Loeb Classical Library.

stars; the moon is only slightly kindled. The sun and the moon are eclipsed <when . . . , but the obliquity of the zodiacal circle is due> to the inclination of the earth to the south; the regions of the north are always shrouded in mist, and are extremely cold and frozen. Eclipses of the sun are rare; eclipses of the moon constantly occur, and this because their orbits are unequal. As the world is born, so, too, it grows, decays and perishes, in virtue of some necessity, the nature of which he does <not> specify.

ARISTOTLE, *de Gen. et Corr.*[1] A 8 325 a 23. . . . Leucippus thought he had a theory, which should be consistent with sense-perception and not do away with coming into being or destruction or motion or the multiplicity of things. He agreed so far with appearances, but to those who hold the theory of the One, on the ground that there could be no motion without empty space, he admitted that empty space is not real, and that nothing of what is real is not real: for the real in the strict sense is an absolute *plenum*. But the *plenum* is not one, but there is an infinite number of them, and they are invisible owing to the smallness of their bulk. These move in empty space (for there is empty space), and by the coming together produce coming into being and by their separation destruction.

[B.] DEMOCRITUS [2]

A. Life and Teaching

LIFE

1. DIOG. ix, 34 ff.[3]

Democritus was the son of Hegesistratus, though some say of Athenocritus, and others again of Damasippus. He was a native of Abdera or, according to some, of Miletus. He was a pupil of certain Magians and Chaldaeans. For when King Xerxes was entertained by the father of Democritus he left

1 *Trans.*, Cyril Bailey, *The Greek Atomists and Epicurus*, p. 70.

2 The translation of Democritus, except where otherwise noted, is the work of Dr. Gordon H. Clark. Professor Isaac Husik graciously revised a large number of the paragraphs.

3 The translation of R. D. Hicks in the Loeb Classical Library.

men in charge, as, in fact, is stated by Herodotus; and from these men, while still a boy, he learned theology and astronomy. Afterwards he met Leucippus and, according to some, Anaxagoras, being forty years younger than the latter. But Favorinus in his *Miscellaneous History* tells us that Democritus, speaking of Anaxagoras, declared that his views on the sun and the moon were not original but of great antiquity, and that he had simply stolen them. (35) Democritus also pulled to pieces the views of Anaxagoras on cosmogony and on mind, having a spite against him, because Anaxagoras did not take to him. If this be so, how could he have been his pupil, as some suggest?

According to Demetrius in his book on *Men of the Same Name* and Antisthenes in his *Successions of Philosophers,* he travelled into Egypt to learn geometry from the priests, and he also went into Persia to visit the Chaldaeans as well as to the Red Sea. Some say that he associated with the Gymnosophists in India and went to Aethiopia. Also that, being the third son, he divided the family property. Most authorities will have it that he chose the smaller portion, which was in money, because he had need of this to pay the cost of travel; besides, his brothers were crafty enough to foresee that this would be his choice. (36) Demetrius estimates his share at over 100 talents, the whole of which he spent. His industry, says the same author, was so great that he cut off a little room in the garden round the house and shut himself up there. One day his father brought an ox to sacrifice and tied it there, and he was not aware of it for a considerable time, until his father roused him to attend the sacrifice and told him about the ox. Demetrius goes on: "It would seem that he also went to Athens and was not anxious to be recognized, because he despised fame, and that while he knew of Socrates, he was not known to Socrates, his words being, 'I came to Athens and no one knew me.' "

(37) "If the *Rivals* be the work of Plato," says Thrasylus, "Democritus will be the unnamed character, different from Oenopides and Anaxagoras, who makes his appearance when conversation is going on with Socrates about philosophy, and to whom Socrates says that the philosopher is like the all-round

athlete. And truly Democritus was versed in every department of philosophy, for he had trained himself both in physics and in ethics, nay more, in mathematics and the routine subjects of education, and he was quite an expert in the arts." From him we have the saying, "Speech is the shadow of action." Demetrius of Phalerum in his *Defence of Socrates* affirms that he did not even visit Athens. This is to make the larger claim, namely, that he thought that great city beneath his notice, because he did not care to win fame from a place, but preferred himself to make a place famous.

(38) His character can also be seen from his writings. "He would seem," says Thrasylus, "to have been an admirer of the Pythagoreans. Moreover, he mentions Pythagoras himself, praising him in a work of his own entitled *Pythagoras*. He seems to have taken all his ideas from him and, if chronology did not stand in the way, he might have been thought his pupil." Glaucus of Rhegium certainly says that he was taught by one of the Pythagoreans, and Glaucus was his contemporary. Apollodorus of Cyzicus, again, will have it that he lived with Philolaus.

He would train himself, says Antisthenes, by a variety of means to test his sense-impressions by going at times into solitude and frequenting tombs. (39) The same authority states that, when he returned from his travels, he was reduced to a humble mode of life because he had exhausted his means; and, because of his poverty, he was supported by his brother Damasus. But his reputation rose owing to his having foretold certain future events; and after that the public deemed him worthy of the honour paid to a god. There was a law, says Antisthenes, that no one who had squandered his patrimony should be buried in his native city. Democritus, understanding this, and fearing lest he should be at the mercy of any envious or unscrupulous prosecutors, read aloud to the people his treatise, the *Great Diacosmos,* the best of all his works; and then he was rewarded with 500 talents; and, more than that, with bronze statues as well; and when he died, he received a public funeral after a lifetime of more than a century. (40) Demetrius, however, says that it was not Democritus himself but his relatives who read the *Great Dia-*

cosmos, and that the sum awarded was 100 talents only; with this account Hippobotus agrees.

Aristoxenus in his *Historical Notes* affirms that Plato wished to burn all the writings of Democritus that he could collect, but that Amyclas and Clinias the Pythagoreans prevented him, saying that there was no advantage in doing so, for already the books were widely circulated. And there is clear evidence for this in the fact that Plato, who mentions almost all the early philosophers, never once alludes to Democritus, not even where it would be necessary to controvert him, obviously because he knew that he would have to match himself against the prince of philosophers, for whom, to be sure, Timon has this meed of praise:

> Such is the wise Democritus, the guardian of discourse, keen-witted disputant, among the best I ever read.

(41) As regards chronology, he was, as he says himself in the *Lesser Diacosmos,* a young man when Anaxagoras was old, being forty years his junior. He says that the *Lesser Diacosmos* was compiled 730 years after the capture of Troy. According to Apollodorus in his *Chronology* he would thus have been born in the 80th Olympiad, but according to Thrasylus in his pamphlet entitled *Prolegomena to the Reading of the Works of Democritus,* in the third year of the 77th Olympiad, which makes him, adds Thrasylus, one year older than Socrates. He would then be a contemporary of Archelaus, the pupil of Anaxagoras, and of the school of Oenopides; indeed he mentions Oenopides. (42) Again, he alludes to the doctrine of the One held by Parmenides and Zeno, they being evidently the persons most talked about in his day; he also mentions Protagoras of Abdera, who, it is admitted, was a contemporary of Socrates.

Athenodorus in the eighth book of his *Walks* related that, when Hippocrates came to see him, he ordered milk to be brought, and, having inspected it, pronounced it to be the milk of a black she-goat which had produced her first kid; which made Hippocrates marvel at the accuracy of his observation. Moreover, Hippocrates being accompanied by a maidservant, on the first day Democritus greeted her with "Good morning, maiden," but the next day with "Good morning, woman." As a matter of fact the girl had been seduced in the night.

(43) Of the death of Democritus the account given by Hermippus is as follows. When he was now very old and near his end, his sister was vexed that he seemed likely to die during the festival of Thesmophoria and she would be prevented from paying the fitting worship to the goddess. He bade her be of good cheer and ordered hot loaves to be brought to him every day. By applying these to his nostrils he contrived to outlive the festival; and as soon as the three festival days were passed he let his life go from him without pain, having then, according to Hipparchus, attained his one hundred and ninth year.

In my *Pammetros* I have a piece on him as follows:

> Pray who was so wise, who wrought so vast a work as the omniscient Democritus achieved? When Death was near, for three days he kept him in his house and regaled him with the steam of hot loaves.

Such was the life of our philosopher.

(44) His opinions are these. The first principles of the universe are atoms and empty space; everything else is merely thought to exist. The worlds are unlimited; they come into being and perish. Nothing can come into being from that which is not nor pass away into that which is not. Further, the atoms are unlimited in size and number, and they are borne along in the whole universe in a vortex, and thereby generate all composite things—fire, water, air, earth; for even these are conglomerations of given atoms. And it is because of their solidity that these atoms are impassive and unalterable. The sun and the moon have been composed by such smooth and spherical masses [i. e. atoms], and so also the soul, which is identical with reason. We see by virtue of the impact of images upon our eyes.

(45) All things happen by virtue of necessity, the vortex being the cause of the creation of all things, and this he calls necessity. The end of action is tranquillity, which is not identical with pleasure, as some by a false interpretation

have understood, but a state in which the soul continues calm and strong, undisturbed by any fear or superstition or any other emotion. This he calls well-being and many other names. The qualities of things exist merely by convention; in nature there is nothing but atoms and void space. These, then, are his opinions.

Of his works Thrasylus has made an ordered catalogue, arranging them in fours, as he also arranged Plato's works. (46) The ethical works are the following:

I. Pythagoras.
Of the Disposition of the Wise Man.
Of those in Hades.
Tritogeneia (so called because three things, on which all mortal life depends, come from her).

II. Of Manly Excellence, or Of Virtue.
Amalthea's Horn (the Horn of Plenty).
Of Tranquillity.
Ethical Commentaries: the work on Well-being is not to be found.

So much for the ethical works.

The physical works are these:

III. The Great Diacosmos (which the school of Theophrastus attribute to Leucippus).
The Lesser Diacosmos.
Description of the World.
On the Planets.

IV. Of Nature, one book.
Of the Nature of Man, or Of Flesh, a second book on Nature.
Of Reason.
Of the Senses (some editors combine these two under the title Of the Soul).

V. Of Flavours.
Of Colours.
(47) Of the Different Shapes (of Atoms).
Of Changes of Shape.

VI. Confirmations (summaries of the aforesaid works).

On Images, or On Foreknowledge of the Future.

On Logic, or Criterion of Thought, three books.

Problems.

So much for the physical works.

The following fall under no head:

Causes of Celestial Phenomena.

Causes of Phenomena in the Air.

Causes on the Earth's Surface.

Causes concerned with Fire and Things in Fire.

Causes concerned with Sounds.

Causes concerned with Seeds, Plants and Fruits.

Causes concerned with Animals, three books.

Miscellaneous Causes.

Concerning the Magnet.

These works have not been arranged.

The mathematical works are these:

VII. On a Difference in an Angle, or On Contact with the Circle or the Sphere.

On Geometry.

Geometrica.

Numbers.

VIII. On Irrational Lines and Solids, two books.

Extensions (Projections).

(48) The Great Year, or Astronomy, Calendar.

Contention of the Water-clock <and the Heaven.>

IX. Description of the Heaven.

Geography.

Description of the Pole.

Description of Rays of Light.

These are the mathematical works.

The literary and musical works are these:

X. On Rhythms and Harmony.

On Poetry.

On Beauty of Verses.

On Euphonious and Cacophonous Letters.

XI. Concerning Homer, or On Correct Epic Diction, and On Glosses.

Of Song.
On Words.
A Vocabulary.

So much for the works on literature and music.

The works on the arts are these:

XII. Prognostication.
Of Diet, or Diaetetics.
Medical Regimen.
Causes concerned with Things Seasonable and Unseasonable.

XIII. Of Agriculture, or Concerning Land Measurements.
Of Painting.
Treatise on Tactics, and
On Fighting in Armour.

So much for these works.

(49) Some include as separate items in the list the following works taken from his notes:

Of the Sacred Writings in Babylon.
Of those in Meroë.
A Voyage round the Ocean.
Of <the Right Use of> History.
A Chaldaean Treatise.
A Phrygian Treatise.
Concerning Fever and those whose Malady makes them Cough.
Legal Causes and Effects.
Problems wrought by Hand.

The other works which some attribute to Democritus are either compilations from his writings or admittedly not genuine. So much for the books that he wrote and their number.

The name of Democritus has been borne by six persons: (1) our philosopher; (2) a contemporary of his, a musician of Chios; (3) a sculptor, mentioned by Antigonus; (4) an author who wrote on the temple at Ephesus and the state of Samothrace; (5) an epigrammatist whose style is lucid and ornate; (6) a native of Pergamum who made his mark by rhetorical speeches.

TEACHING

35. Arist. *de gen. et corr.* A 2. 315 a 34. On the whole, no one gave more than superficial attention to any [of these] problems, except Democritus; and he seems to have thought deeply on them all and is particularly superior in respect to method.

36. ——— *de partt. anim.* A 1. 642 a 24. The reason our predecessors did not arrive at this method is that they could not define reality or conceptual being; Democritus was the first to grasp it, not however as necessary to physical investigation, but he was led up to it by the subject matter. In the time of Socrates this method flourished, but the investigation of nature declined, for the philosophers turned to politics and utilitarianism. *Metaph.* M. 4. 1078 b 19. In natural science Democritus grasped the method only slightly, and after a fashion defined hot and cold.

37. Simplic. *de caelo* p. 293, 33 Heib. A few notes from Aristotle's *On Democritus* will clarify the thought of these men. "Democritus considers the eternal objects to be small substances infinite in number. For these he posits a place infinite in magnitude, and he calls place by such names as void, nothing, and infinite, but each of the substances he calls, something, solid, and existent. He thinks the substances are so small that we cannot perceive them, yet they have all sorts of forms and shapes, and differences in size. Accordingly from these as from elements he generates and combines visible objects and perceptible masses. And they are disturbed and move in the void because of their dissimilarity and the other differences mentioned, and as they move they collide and become entangled in such a fashion as to be near to and touch each other. However this does not in truth give rise to any one single nature, for it is altogether silly that two or more things may ever become one. The coherence up to a certain point of substances he explains by the gripping and intermingling of the bodies, for some of them are scalene in shape, some are barbed, some concave, some convex and others have countless other differences. Accordingly he thinks

they cling to each other and cohere until some stronger necessity from the surroundings approaches, shakes and scatters them." And he speaks of genesis and its contrary, separation, not only with reference to animals, but to plants, and worlds, and, in general, all sensible bodies. If, therefore, genesis is the commingling of atoms, and destruction is their separation, then according to Democritus genesis is also the same as qualitative change.

38. SIMPL. *Phys.* 28, 15. And likewise his friend, Democritus the Abderite, posited as principles the full and the void, of which he called the first Being and the second Non-being. For positing the atoms as the material of things, they [Democritus and Leucippus] produce the other things by their differences. And these are three, proportion, impulsion, and arrangement, which is the same as saying shape, position, and order. For the like is naturally set in motion by the like, and the homogeneous is drawn together, and each of the shapes when it is arranged into a different combination produces another design. Consequently, since the elements are infinite, they could reasonably promise to render an account of all qualities and things, an account both of the cause and the process of anything's generation. Therefore they also claim that only if we assume the elements to be infinite will all things happen according to reason. And they say the number of shapes among the atoms is infinite because there is no more reason for an atom to be of one shape than another. And this is the cause they themselves assign for the infinity of the atoms.

39. PLUTARCH. *Strom.* 7 (D 581). Democritus the Abderite supposed the universe to be infinite because it had not been fashioned by any Maker. And again he says it is unchangeable, and in general he states in express terms the kind of universe it is: The causes of what now exists have no beginning, but from infinitely preceding time absolutely everything which was, is, and shall be, has been held down by necessity. But he says the sun and the moon came into existence. They had their own motion without having any heat or light but having, on the contrary, a nature similar to earth. Each of them first came into being by a peculiar change

of the cosmos, and later when the circle of the sun was enlarged fire was included in it.

40. Hippolyt. *Refut.* I 13 (D 565). Democritus was an acquaintance of Leucippus. Democritus, son of Damasippus an Abderite, consulted with the Gymnosophists in India and with the priests in Egypt and with the astrologers and wise men in Babylon. Now like Leucippus he says of the elements, solid and void, that the solid really exists and the void does not. And he would say that the realities were always moving in the void; and there are an infinite number of worlds differing in size; in some there is neither sun nor moon, in others they are larger than ours, and in others there are many suns and moons. The distances between the worlds is unequal and in some quarters there are more worlds, in others fewer, and some are growing and others have reached their full size, and others are disintegrating, and in some quarters worlds are coming into being and in others they are ceasing to exist. They are destroyed by colliding with each other. And some worlds are devoid of living beings and all moisture. In our system the earth came into being before the stars, and the moon is nearest the earth, and then the sun, and then the fixed stars. The planets are not equally distant from the earth. The world remains at its maturity until it can no longer receive any [nourishment] from outside. This man ridiculed everything as if all human interests were ridiculous.

41. Arist. *Phys.* Γ 4. 203 a 33. Democritus affirms that no element arises from any other. However, their common property, body, differing in its parts by size and shape, is the principle of all things.

42. Arist. *Metaph.* Z 13. 1039 a 9. For it is impossible, he says, for one thing to come from two or two from one. For the magnitudes or atoms constitute reality.

43. Dionys. from Eus. *P.E.* XIV. 23, 2.3. Those who spoke of atoms, i. e. certain infinitely numerous, indestructible, and extremely small bodies, and who assumed a void space of unbounded size, say that these atoms move at random in the void and collide with each other by chance because of an irregular momentum, and they catch hold of each other and are entangled because of the variety of shapes. Thus they

produce the world and its contents, or rather, an infinite number of worlds. Epicurus and Democritus accepted this view, but they differed in that the former held all atoms to be minute and imperceptible, while Democritus believed that some atoms were large. But both assert the existence of atoms, so called because of their indestructible hardness. Cf. Epicur. *Ep.* I 55 [p. 15, 12 Us.]. But, for appearances not to contradict us, we ought not to attribute every size to the atoms, though we should admit certain differences in size.

44. HERM. *Irris.* 13. (D. 654). Democritus . . . makes the principles Being and Non-being. Being is the full and Non-being the void. And the full produces all things by its impulsion and proportion in the void.

45. ARIST. *Phys.* A 5. 188 a 22. Democritus asserts the solid and the void exist, of which the former is like Being and the latter like Non-being. Then again [there are differences] in position, shape, and order. The following are their generic contraries: of position, up and down, backwards and forwards; of shape, angular, straight, and round.

46. AET. I 3, 16. (D. 285). The well-kneaded [solid] and the void [are principles.] Galen VIII 931 K. What the word "well-kneaded" may mean I do not rightly know because it is not customary with the Greeks to use this word in such a context. For they call a kind of bread well-kneaded but I do not know that they call any thing else by that name. Archigenes himself . . . seems to use the word well-kneaded for the full.

47. AET. I 3, 18. (D. 285). For Democritus ascribed two qualities [to the atoms], size and shape. But Epicurus added to these a third, weight; for, he says, the atoms require the impact of weight to move. 12, 6. (D. 311). Democritus says the primary bodies (these, as we have seen, are the solids) do not have weight, but are moved in the infinite by striking each other. And there can be an atom the size of a whole world. Cic. *de fat.* 20, 46. [Epicurus] said the atom has a declination. First, why? Because they have a certain force of motion which Democritus calls impact, but which you, Epicurus, refer to gravity and weight. Simpl. *Phys.* 42, 10.

Democritus says the atoms, naturally immobile, are set in motion by an impact. Aet. I 23, 3. (D. 319). Democritus declared that there is but one kind of motion, namely through striking.

48. ——— I 16, 2. (D. 315). Those who believe in atoms say that division stops at the indivisible substances and does not continue to infinity.

49. GALEN *de elem. sec. Hipp.* I 2. [I 417 K]. "For by convention colour exists, by convention bitter, by convention sweet, but in reality atoms and void," [Fr. 125] says Democritus, believing that from the conjunction of atoms all sensible qualities come into being for us who perceive them, but by nature nothing is white, black, yellow, red, bitter, or sweet; for the phrase "by convention" means the same thing as "by custom," and "for us," not according to the nature of the things themselves, which he calls "in reality" coining the term from "real" which means true. And the complete sense of his argument would be as follows: Men think that there is such a thing as white, black, sweet, or bitter; but in truth the universe is composed of "thing" and "nothing." [cf. Fr. 156] For this is what he himself says, referring to the atoms by the word "thing," to the void by the word "nothing." Since all the atoms are minute bodies, they have no qualities, and the void is a kind of place in which all these bodies, as they move up and down through all time, either become somehow entangled with each other, or collide and rebound, and they separate and mix again with each other by reason of such contacts, and in this way produce all other combinations including our own bodies with their affections and sensations. But the primary bodies he holds to be without qualities, (and some persons, like the disciples of Epicurus, say they are unbreakable because of their hardness, but others make them indivisible because of their smallness, as do the colleagues of Leucippus,) nor can they in any respect undergo those qualitative changes which all men have believed to exist because they are taught by their senses. For example they deny that any of those bodies can grow warm or cold, and in the same way they can neither become moist nor dry, and still more is it impossible for them to become white or black

or in general to assume any other quality by any change whatever.

50. Diogen. of Oinoanda, Fr. 80.81 col. 3, 3. If any one should use the argument of Democritus, saying that the atoms have no freedom in their motion because they collide with each other, and all things below apparently move by necessity, we shall reply to him: Then you do not know who you are, and there is a certain freedom in the motion of the atoms, which Democritus did not discover, but Epicurus brought to light, namely an inherent declination as is proved by the phenomena.

51. Cic. *de nat. deor.* I 26, 73. [s 62 A 5]. What is there in Epicurus' physics which does not come from Democritus? For although he changed some things, as the declination of the atoms which I have just mentioned, none the less for the most part he says the same things, atoms, void, images, infinity of space, and innumerable worlds, their generation and destruction, practically everything on which the explanation of nature depends.

53. Plut. *adv. Colot* 3 p. 1108 e. And indeed Epicurus for a long time called himself a Democritean, as many assert including Leonteus, one of Epicurus' chief disciples, who wrote to Lycophron that Democritus was honored by Epicurus because he was the first to grasp a right knowledge of things, and that the treatise as a whole is called Democritean because Democritus was the first to hit upon the principles of nature. And Metrodorus [in his work] *On Philosophy* has said plainly that if Democritus had not led the way, Epicurus could never have attained to wisdom.

56. Cic. *de fin.* I 6, 17. He believes in what he calls atoms, that is in bodies indivisible because of their solidity which move in an infinite void which has neither highest, lowest, middle, farthest, nor limit. They collide and stick together and thus all things we see come into being. This motion of the atoms never had a beginning but should be understood to be eternal.

57. Plut. *adv. Colot.* 8 p. 1110 f. For what does Democritus say? Substances infinite in number, indivisible, and different from each other, without qualities and unchanging, are scat-

tered about and move in the void. When they approach each other or collide or become entangled, some of these aggregations form water, some fire, some plants, and some men. But all things are really atoms or forms as he calls them, and besides these nothing exists. For there is no generation from non-being nor can there be any generation from things which exist because the atoms on account of their solidity neither change nor suffer any impression. Therefore color does not arise from the uncolored, nor nature or soul from that which is without quality and impassible. Arist. *Metaph.* I. 1069 b 22. And as Democritus says, all things were together potentially, but not actually.

58. ARIST. *Phys.* Θ 9. 265 b 24. And they say motion exists because of the void; for these men also say that nature moves in space. Simpl. *in loc.* 1318, 33. That is, the natural, primary and atomic bodies, for these they would call nature and used to say that by their weight they move through space because the void gives way and offers no resistance; for they said that they are tossed about. And these men explain that this is not only the primary motion of the elements but the only motion; the other motions belong to compounds. For they say that growth and decay, qualitative change, generation and corruption occur by the combining and separating of the primary bodies.

59. SEXT. VIII 6. The disciples both of Plato and Democritus held that only intelligible objects are real. Democritus thought so because there is no sensible substratum in nature, for the atoms which give rise to things by combining have a nature devoid of all sensible quality; Plato held this view because the sensibles are always in process of becoming, but never really are.

60. ARIST. *de gen. et inter.* A 8. 326 a 9. And Democritus says that each of the indivisibles is heavier according to its excess. *de caelo* Δ 2. 309 a 1. [In opposition to Plato, those who call the primary objects] solids are better able to say that the greater is the heavier. But since this does not always appear true, and we see many heavier compounds with less bulk, for example bronze has less bulk than the same weight of wool, some adopt and assert another explanation. For they

say the void enveloped in the bodies makes them light and makes it possible for the larger bodies sometimes to be lighter than smaller ones, for they have more void. . . . And this is the way they explain it. But to those who so define matters, we must add, not merely that there be more void if a thing is to be lighter, but that there also be less solid, for if a certain ratio be exceeded, the body will not be lighter. For this reason also they say fire is the lightest of all bodies because it has most void. It will follow, then, that a great deal of gold which has more void than a little fire is lighter, unless it also have many times the amount of solid. b 34. [And if matter has] a contrary, (310 a) as the proponents of the void and the full maintain, bodies intermediate between the absolutely heavy and light will have no explanation for their being heavier or lighter than each other, or than the bodies absolutely heavy or light. To make this distinction depend on size and smallness seems more artificial than the previous views . . . and there is nothing absolutely light nor anything which ascends except what is left behind [in falling] or is squeezed up, and many small things are heavier than a few large things.

61. Simpl. *de caelo* 569, 5. Democritus' followers and later Epicurus assert that all the atoms are homogeneous and have weight, but because some are heavier, the lighter ones are thrust aside by the others as they fall and are carried upwards, and thus it is they say, that some things are considered light and some heavy. 712, 27. The Democritean group thinks that all things have weight, but since fire has less weight and is squeezed out by the things ahead of it, it is carried upward, and for this reason it appears light. And they consider that only what is heavy exists, and it is always in motion toward the centre. *Contra Democritum,* Epicurus *Ep.* I 61. [p. 18, 15 Us.] The atoms necessarily have equal speeds when they move through the void which offers no resistance. For neither will the [large and] heavy atoms move more quickly than the small and light, when nothing obstructs them, nor will the small atoms, all of which have commensurate passageways, move more slowly than the large ones when nothing resists them either.

62. Arist. *de caelo* Δ 6. 313 a 21. The impression that all these phenomena [the floating of metal discs etc. on water] are explained by Democritus' theory is erroneous. For he says that the warm particles which move upwards through the water support broad bodies even though they are heavy, but the narrow bodies fall through, for all the resisting particles are too sparse for them. But this ought to occur still more in air, as he himself objects. And his solution of the objection is poor; for he says the rush does not start in one direction, where by "rush" he means the motion of the rising particles.
63. ——— *de gen. et int.* A 7. 323 b 10. Democritus in opposition to other philosophers had a peculiar theory of his own. For, he says, agent and patient must be the same and similar. For things that are other and different cannot be affected by each other, but even if several different things actually affect one another, it is not in so far as they are other that this happens but in so far as they are the same.
64. Alex. *de mixt.* 2. [II 214, 18 Bruns.] Democritus, therefore, considering that [chemical] "mixture" so-called occurs by the juxtaposition of bodies, which are divided into minute particles and produce the mixture by the positions of the particles alongside of each other, asserts that in truth things are not mixed even in the beginning, but the apparent mixture is a juxtaposition of bodies in minute particles, preserving the proper nature of each, which they had before the mixing. They seem to be mixed because on account of the smallness of the juxtaposed particles our senses cannot perceive any one of them by itself [cf. Anaxagoras A 54.]
65. Arist. *Phys.* Θ 1. 252 a 32. But in general, to think that, because something always is or always happens in a given fashion, we have sufficiently explained it, is not to understand the matter aright. By such a principle Democritus reduces the explanation of nature to the statement that, thus it happened formerly also, and there is no sense in looking for an explanation of what always happens.
66. Cic. *de fato*. 17, 39. All things so happen by fate that fate produces the force of necessity: of which opinion were Democritus, Heraclitus, Empedocles and [Anaxagoras]. Arist. *de gen. animal.* E 8. 789 b 2. Democritus denies purpose

by saying, everything which nature uses reduces to necessity. Aet. I 26, 2 (D. 321; concerning the nature of necessity) Democritus calls it the resistance, motion, and impulsion of the material. [cf. A 83.]

67. Simpl. *Phys.* 327, 24. Democritus also, where he says "A vortex of all sorts of forms was separated from the universe," (how and through what cause he does not say) seems to produce the world by chance and luck.

68. Arist. *Phys.* B 4. 195 b 36. For some doubt whether [luck] exists or not; for they say nothing comes by luck, but all things which we say come by chance or luck, have some definite cause. Simpl. p. 330, 14. The phrase, "the old theory which eliminates luck," seems to refer to Democritus. For even though he seems to have used luck in the formation of the world, yet in the parts of the world, he says, luck is the cause of nothing, but refers phenomena to other causes, for example, the cause of discovering the treasure was digging, or planting the olive tree, and the reason why the baldheaded man's skull was cracked was that the eagle dropped a tortoise so that the shell might break. For this is how Eudemus tells the story.

69. ——— ——— B 4. 196 a 24. And there are some who explain our system and all worlds by chance; for chance gave rise to the vortex or motion which separates and fixes the universe in its present arrangement. . . . For they affirm that neither animals nor plants exist or come into being by luck, but that nature, or intelligence, or some other such thing is their cause (for it is not any chance thing which grows from a given seed, but from one sort of seed we get olives, from another kind, human beings) but the heavens and the most divine of visible things arose by chance without a cause such as plants and animals have.

70. ——— ——— B 4. 196 b 5. There are some to whom chance seems to be a cause, but a cause obscured from human understanding as something divine and mysterious. Aet. I 29, 7. (D. 326 n). Anaxagoras, Democritus, and the Stoics [make luck] a cause hidden from human understanding.

71. ARIST. *Phys.* Θ 1. 251 b 16. Democritus proves it impossible for all things to have come into being, for time never came into being. Simpl. *Phys.* 1153, 22. Democritus, however, was so persuaded that time is eternal that when he wished to prove that not everything has come into being, he used the fact that time has not come into being as something self-evident.

72. SEXT. X. 181. Such a notion of time as "time is an appearance under the forms of day and night" seems to refer to the schools of Epicurus as well as Democritus.

73. THEOPHR. *d. sign.* 52. One may ask why the form of fire is pyramidal. And Democritus says that as its extremities are cooled it is contracted to a small size and finally becomes pointed.

77. PLUT. *Quaest conv.* viii. 10, 2. p. 734 f. And Favorinus, . . . taking down an old saying of Democritus, obscured as it were by the smoke of centuries, was able to dust it off and polish it up, assuming that common principle of Democritus, viz: images pass through the pores into the body and, rising [to the head,] cause dreams. These images go to and fro in every direction, springing off implements, clothes, plants, and especially living beings because of their motion and warmth, and they not only have impressed on them the same shape as the bodies (as Epicurus thinks, agreeing with Democritus thus far, but abandoning the argument at this point), but they also assume the appearances of the changes, thoughts, habits, and emotions of each person's soul and so are drawn together. And if with these qualities they strike a person, then like living beings they announce and declare to those who receive them the opinions, arguments, and impulses of those who released them, provided they retain the likenesses articulate and unconfused for impingement. The best results are obtained in calm air, since their motion is then unimpeded and swift. But the air of autumn when the trees shed their leaves is irregular and blustery. Therefore it twists and distorts the images in various ways dimming and weakening their clearness which is obscured by the slowness of their progress, while on the

other hand those which dart forth from things warm and fertile and are quickly conveyed, deliver fresh and significant impressions.

80. CIC. *Ac. pr.* II, 38, 121. [note: Diels has quoted material Cicero attributes to Strato, not Democritus. A line or two above we find the following reported of Democritus.] The world is composed of rough and smooth and hooked and bent bodies with void all around.

81. ——— ——— 17, 55. Then you have recourse to those scientists who are most ridiculed in the Academy, from whom you will not even now abstain, and you say Democritus holds innumerable worlds to exist and that some of them are not only similar to each other, but so absolutely and perfectly correspondent in every particular that there is no difference at all between them [and they are innumerable] and so also are men.

82. SIMPL. *de cael.* p 310, 5. "For," says Alexander, "the dissolution and destruction of the world did not result in a cosmic matter which had the potentiality of becoming a world, but it results in another world; and since there is an infinite number of them succeeding one another, it does not follow that the process necessarily leads back to the same world as before." Thus it seemed to the followers of Leucippus and Democritus . . . but the worlds of Democritus, since they change into other worlds which are composed of the same atoms, are the same in kind even if not in number.

83. SEXT. IX 113. Consequently the world could not be set in motion by necessity and the vortex, as the school of Democritus asserts.

84. AET. II 4, 9. (D. 331). According to Democritus the world is destroyed when the greater conquers the smaller.

85. ——— ——— 13. [The stars are] stones.

86. ——— ——— 15. The fixed stars come first, and after them the planets among which are the sun, the morning star, and the moon.

87. ——— ——— 20, 7. According to Democritus [the sun is] a red hot mass or a fiery stone.

88. LUCR. V 621 ff. First, it is possible, one would suppose,

for things to happen as the divine wisdom of the great Democritus teaches. If so, the nearer the stars are to the earth, the slower do they revolve in the celestial vortex. For its speed diminishes and loses its force as it descends. Therefore the sun little by little falls behind the signs that accompany it; for it is much lower than the fiery stars, and the moon still more so. Since its path is still farther beneath the sky and is near the earth, all the less can it keep pace with the signs. For the weaker the vortex which propels it in its position below the sun, the more can the signs overtake and pass beyond it. Therefore, it seems to return more quickly to the signs because the signs overtake it again.

89. Aet. II 23, 7. (D. 353). According to Democritus, [the solstices result from] the vortex' making the sun revolve.

89a. Plut. *de fac. in orb. lun.* 16, p. 929 c. Democritus says when [the moon] stands in a straight line with the illuminating body, it receives and takes in the sun. Consequently it was probable that the moon itself was visible and made the sun visible also.

90. Aet. II 25, 9. (D. 356; on the Moon) 30, 3 (D. 361; why the moon appears earth-like). According to Democritus, a kind of shadow cast by the high parts on it, for it has hollows and glens.

91. Arist. *Meteorol.* A 8. 345 a 25. (on the Milky Way) Alex, *in loc.* p. 37, 23. Anaxagoras and Democritus say the Milky Way is the light of certain stars. For the sun at night goes under the earth. Hence those stars above the earth which the sun illumines cannot make their own light visible because it is obscured by the rays of the sun; but those which the shadow of the earth darkens so that they are not illumined by the light of the sun, do show their own light and this is the Milky Way. Aet., III 1. (D. 365). [The Milky Way is] the combined brilliance of many small stars in juxtaposition uniting their light because they are so closely packed.

92. Alex. *in Arist. Meteor.* p. 26, 11. With respect to comets Anaxagoras and Democritus say that the comet is a "conjunction" of the planetary stars, Saturn, Jupiter, Venus, Mars, and Mercury. For these when they come near each other produce an appearance of merging together into one star,

the so-called comet. For "conjunction" means their appearance as one which happens when they come together. Sen. *Nat. quaest.* VII 3, 2. Democritus also, the most acute of all the ancients, said he suspected that there are more planetary stars [than five], but he did not indicate either their number or their names, since they did not then understand the orbits of the five [known] planets. [Note: Alexander, seems to have misunderstood Democritus who guessed that there exist other "planets," i. e. wandering particles, whose conjunction produces comets.]

93. Aet. III 3, 11. (D. 369). Democritus held that thunder is produced by an unstable mixture forcing the cloud enclosing it to move downward. Lightning is a clashing together of clouds by which the fire-producing atoms rubbing against each other are assembled through the porous mass into one place and pass out. And the thunderbolt occurs when the motion is forced by the very pure, very fine, very uniform and "closely-packed" fire-producing atoms, as he himself calls them. But heat lightning occurs when very porous mixtures of fire, which are enclosed in porous places and are made into single bodies each with its own surrounding membrane, start downward because of their heterogeneous composition.

94. ——— ——— 10. (D. 377). [The earth] is like a disc in breadth, but hollow in the middle. Eustath. H. 446 p. 690. Posidonius the Stoic and Dionysius say the inhabited earth is shaped like a sling, but Democritus asserts it is oblong.

95. Aet. III 13, 4. (D. 378). Democritus believed that originally the earth roamed about because of its smallness [rarity?] and lightness, but in time when it became dense and heavy, its position was fixed.

96. ——— ——— 12, 2. (D. 337). Since the south is weaker than the surrounding points, the earth increases in size and leans in that direction; for the northern sections are untempered, whereas the southern are tempered. Hence the world is weighted down in this direction where it abounds in fruits and growth.

97. Arist. *Meteor.* B 7. 365 b 1. Democritus says the earth is full of water, and when it receives an added quantity of rain-water, the water causes it to move. For when there is

too much for the bowels of the earth to contain, the water is forced off and produces earthquakes. And when the earth is drained dry and pulls water to the empty places from the fuller sections, the falling water shakes the earth.

98. Sen. *Nat. qu.* VI 20. [from Posidonius] Democritus thinks that there are many [causes of earthquakes]. For, he says, the motion is sometimes produced by air, sometimes by water, and sometimes by both. And this takes place as follows: A certain part of the earth is concave and in this place a great mass of water collects. Some of this water is lighter and more fluid than the rest. When this is thrust aside by a weight coming upon it, it is dashed against the earth and causes it to quake. For the water cannot surge without moving that which it hits. . . . When the water is crowded into one place and cannot be contained in it, it presses against something and forces a way through first by its weight and then by its impetus. For, after being impounded for so long a time, it cannot escape except by a downward motion, nor can it fall straight with moderate force or without shaking the things through which or into which it falls. And if, when it begins to be carried off, it is stopped somewhere, and the force of the stream turns on itself, it is forced back against the earth which contains it, and sets it in motion where it is least stable. And further, the earth, at length almost saturated by the fluid, settles deeper and the foundation itself is weakened. Then that part sinks down, against which the weight of the moving waters presses hardest. And the wind sometimes drives the waves; and if it blows them vehemently, it moves the part of the earth against which it hurls the water. And at other times thrown together in the subterranean passageways and seeking an exit, the wind puts everything in motion. For the wind penetrates the earth and is both too subtile to be excluded and too powerful to be resisted when rapid and violent.

99. Aet. IV 1, 4. (D. 385). As the snow in the north melts under the summer sun and flows away, clouds are formed from the vapour. When these are driven south toward Egypt by the monsoons, violent storms arise and fill the lakes, and the Nile.

99a. Hibeh. Papyr. 16 p. 62. Grenfell and Hunt, [reconstructed]. There has been the greatest disagreement on the source of salt in the sea. Some say it is the deposit of the first moisture after the waters have mostly evaporated. Others say it is the sweat of the earth. Democritus thinks it is produced in the same way as salt things in the earth, [rock] salt and potassium for example. [Lacuna.] After putrefaction [has ceased,] he says, similars [are gathered] to similars in the fluid as is the case in the universe as a whole, and in this manner the sea came into being and all the briny pools when the things of the same kind were brought together. That the sea is composed of things of the same kind is also clear from other considerations. For neither frankincense, nor sulphur, nor silphium, nor alum, nor bitumen, nor whatever is great and marvellous is produced in many places in the earth. For this reason, then, even if for no other, it is worthwhile to examine why, after making the sea a part of the world, he said, "in the same manner the wonders and rarities of nature occur" on the ground that in earth there are not many distinctions. For him, at any rate, who explains flavours by shapes and derives salt from large and angular atoms, it is not unreasonable that the salinity in the earth should occur in the same manner as in the sea.

100. Arist. *Meteor.* B 3. 356 b 4. In discussing the saltness (of the sea) we must also say whether it has always been the same or whether it once did not exist and will in the future cease to exist; for some people think so. Now everyone admits that the sea came into being if the world as a whole did too, for they make the processes simultaneous. Consequently it is clear that if the universe is eternal, we must hold the same opinion regarding the sea. But the notion that the size of the sea is decreasing, as Democritus says, and will finally disappear, is on a par with Aesop's fables. For he propounded the myth that Charybdis had twice gulped down [some of the sea]. The first time it made the mountains appear, the second time, the islands; and on the final gulp it will make everything dry land. Now it was fitting for Aesop when irritated at the boatman to tell such

a myth, but not so appropriate for those who seek the truth. For the cause of the sea's continuing at first, weight as some of them say, . . . will clearly be the cause of its persistence for the rest of time.

101. Arist. *de anima* A 2. 404 a 27. But not entirely like Democritus. For he held that soul and mind are absolutely the same and that appearance is truth. Therefore Homer did well in making "Hector prostrate thinking other thoughts." So he does not use mind as a potentiality for truth, but affirms that soul and mind are the same. 405 a 5. To some it seemed to be fire, for this is the finest and least corporeal of the elements, and further it excels in being moved and in causing motion. And Democritus has spoken very elegantly in explaining each of these phenomena; for soul and mind are the same. And this is that group of the primary, indivisible bodies which produce motion by their minute parts and shape. Now the most mobile of shapes is the sphere, he says; and such is mind and fire. Philop. *in loc.* p. 83, 27 H. He said fire was incorporeal, not strictly incorporeal (for none of them said this), but corporeally incorporeal on account of the fineness of its parts.

104. Arist. *de anima* A 3. 406 b 15. Some say the soul moves the body in which it is as it itself is moved, for example when Democritus uses the same idea as Philippus the comic poet who said, Daedalus made the wooden Aphrodite move by pouring in mercury. Democritus speaks in a similar vein when he says, the indivisible spheres are in motion because by nature they can never be still, and so they draw along and set in motion the whole body.

104a. ——— ——— A 5. 409 a 32. He says [the body] is moved by the soul. . . . If, then, there is a soul in the sentient body as a whole, there will of necessity be two bodies in the same place, since the soul is a body.

105. Aet. IV 4, 6. (D. 390). Democritus and Epicurus held that the soul has two parts, the rational part seated in the chest, and the non-rational part diffused throughout the whole body. 5, 1. (D. 391 n. Theodoret.) For Hippocrates, Democritus, and Plato locate the [Ruler of the soul] in the

brain. Philop. *de anima* p. 35, 12 Hayd. Democritus asserts [the soul] is neither divisible nor multi-functional, for he believes that thinking is the same as perceiving and that these two functions proceed from a single faculty.

106. ARIST. *de resp.* 4. 471 b 30. In animals who breathe, says Democritus, breathing prevents the soul's being squeezed out of the body. He said nothing at all, however, to indicate that this was nature's purpose in the arrangement; for like the other scientists he too fails to grasp this type of explanation. Instead, he says the soul is the same as the hot, the primary forms of the spherical atoms. As they are being mixed together by the atmosphere which squeezes them out, breathing comes to the rescue. For in the air there are numerous atoms of the type he calls mind and soul; accordingly by breathing in the air, these enter too, and ward off the expulsion by preventing the dispersion of the soul which is within the living being. Therefore, to live and to die is to inhale and to exhale; for when the pressure of the atmosphere dominates and the atoms can no longer enter to ward off expulsion because breath has ceased, then the animal dies; for death is the loss of such shaped particles from the body because of the atmospheric pressure. But the reason why everyone must die sometime—for death is not just a chance event, but is either natural owing to old age or unnatural because of violence—he has not made clear at all.

108. LUCRET. III 370. On this point, do not accept the theory of the revered Democritus that the body atoms and soul atoms alternate and so bind our members together.

109. AET. IV 7, 4. (D. 393). Democritus and Epicurus hold [the soul] to be destructible, for it is destroyed along with the body.

112. ARIST. *Metaph.* Γ 5. 1009 b 7. Furthermore, appearances to many of the other animals contradict the appearances of the same things to us, and even in the case of each individual a thing does not always seem the same in sensation. Which, then, are true or false is not clear; for one appearance is no more true than another, they are equally true. For this reason Democritus says, either nothing is true or at any rate we cannot distinguish what is. In general, then, they say the

sensible appearance is necessarily true because they consider that knowledge is sensation and sensation is a [chemical] alteration.

113. Philopon. *de anima* p. 71, 19. (in Ar. A2, 404 a 25 sqq.) If they said mind moves the universe, how could they say that motion is a proper attribute of soul? Yes, he says, for they assumed mind and soul to be the same, just as Democritus did. True we have it nowhere expressly stated by them that mind and soul are the same, but he arrives at this conclusion by a syllogism. For Democritus, he says, evidently had this opinion, for he said plainly that truth and appearance are the same and there is no distinction between truth and the sensible phenomenon; for that which appears and seems to anyone is also true, just as Protagoras said, though if we judge by correct reason, they are different, sensation and imagination dealing with appearance, while mind deals with truth. [cf. Fr. 11.] If, therefore, mind deals with truth and soul with appearance, and truth and opinion are identical, as Democritus teaches, then mind also is identical with soul. For as mind is related to truth so is soul related to appearance; hence also by alternation, as appearance is to truth so is soul to mind. If then, appearance and truth are the same, so are mind and soul the same.

115. Aet. IV 10, 5. (D. 399). How many senses are there? Democritus says that the senses are more numerous than the sensibles, but since the sensibles do not correspond [?] to the number [of senses] we are not aware of the fact. [cf. Lucr. IV 800.] Because they are so fine, the mind cannot perceive them clearly, unless it makes a decided effort.

116. Aet. IV 10, 4. (D. 399). Brutes, sages, and gods have more [than five] senses.

117. Aet. IV 4, 7. (D. 390). Democritus says all things possess a soul of some sort, even corpses, because they clearly always share in a certain warmth and power of sensation, though the greater part disperses in air. Alex. *Top.* 21, 21. Dead bodies perceive, as Democritus thought.

118. Cic. *Epist.* XV 16, 1. (To Cassius). For I do not know how it happens that when I write something to you you seem to be present before me, and not in the sense of

"phantoms of the imagination" as your new friends say who think that even "rational imagination" is produced by the spectres of Catius. For, lest you forget, the Epicurean, Catius, an Insubrian, who died recently, called those things spectres which Epicurus, and, still more remotely, Democritus called "phantoms." But even if these spectres can strike the eye because they collide with it without your permission, how they can strike the mind I cannot understand. You will have to teach me, when you arrive here safely, whether I can make your spectre strike me whenever I wish to think of you, and not only of you who dwell in my heart of hearts, but whether if I begin to think of the island of Britain, its phantom will fly to my soul.

119. Arist. *de sens.* 4. 442 a 29. Democritus and most of the scientists who treat of sensation make a most absurd blunder, for they make all sensible qualities tangible. Now if this were so it is clear that each of the other senses would be a kind of touch.

121. Arist. *de sens.* 2. 438 a 5. When Democritus says that it is water [by which we see] he speaks well, but when he thinks that sight is the reflection, not so well. . . . However, in general, it seems nothing much was made clear on the subjects of refraction and reflections. And it is strange that he did not think of asking why the eye alone can see, but not other things in which the reflections appears.

122. ——— *de anima* B 7. 419 a 15. Democritus was not correct in thinking that if the space between should become void, it would be possible to see accurately whether there were an ant in the sky.

123. ——— *de gen. et inter.* A 2. 316 a 1. Color also does not exist, he says, for a thing becomes coloured by position.

124. Aet. I 15, 11. (D. 314). Those who say no atom ever has any colour, declare that all sensible qualities arise from things which have no qualities but which are apprehended by reason.

125. ——— ——— 15, 8. (D. 314). Colour does not exist by nature. For the elements have no qualities, neither the solids nor the void. What is composed of these, however, is coloured by arrangement, proportion, and impulsion, that is, order,

shape, and position; for appearances arise from these. Of these colours which are due to appearance, there are four types, white, black, red, and yellow.

126. ARIST. *de sens.* 4. 442 b 11. For white is smooth, he says, and black is rough. But flavours he reduces to shapes.

127. SCHOL. DIONYS. THRAC. p. 482, 13 Hildeg. Epicurus, Democritus, and the Stoics assert that sound is a body.

128. AET. IV 19, 3. (D. 408; on sound, presumably from Posidonius). Democritus says that the air, too, is broken into bodies of similar shapes and rolls about with the fragments of the sound. For "birds of a feather flock together" and "God always treats similars alike." [p. 218] For even on the seashore the similar pebbles are seen in the same places, here the spherical pebbles, there the long ones. In sifting also, the same shapes collect in the same places so that the beans and the pulse fall apart from each other. But someone might ask the advocates of this view, how a few fragments of wind completely fill a theatre containing ten thousand men?

129. THEOPHR. *de caus. plant.* VI 1, 6. Democritus in assigning a shape to each quality made sweet to consist of fairly large, spherical atoms. To the quality sour he assigned very large, rough shapes with many angles and no curves. The sharp [in taste], as its name implies, he regarded as consisting of atoms sharp in mass, angular, crooked, thin, and unrounded. The pungent needs atoms which are thin, angular, and bent, but rounded also. Salt is angular, fairly large, twisted, although symmetrical. Bitter is rounded and smooth, unsymmetrical, and small in size. [cf. A 135, 67].

132. ——— ——— VI 7, 2. Against Democritus one might raise the objection how a thing's taste could change. It must be in one of three ways: Either the shapes are remodeled so that what was crooked and angular becomes rounded, or, if all the shapes of sour and sharp and sweet are there together, some must be separated out (that is, the eternal realities which are prior to any specific taste as well as those peculiar to a given taste) while others remain, or, in the third place, some must go out and new ones come in. Since they cannot be remodeled (for an atom undergoes no modification), the second and third possibilities remain. But both

are irrational, for it is necessary to explain further what causes these effects.

133. ——— *de odor.* 64. Why indeed does Democritus explain flavours by a reference to taste, but does not similarly explain odours and colours by referring to their underlying senses? For he ought to derive them from the shapes.

135. Theophr. *de sens.* 49 ff. (D. 513).[1] Democritus in his account of sense perception does not make it entirely clear whether it is due to contrast or to similarity. For in so far as he ascribes the action of the senses to an alteration, it would seem to depend on contrast; for the like is never altered by the like. On the other hand, sense perception would seem to depend on similarity in so far as he ascribes the perceptive process and, in a word, alteration to the fact that something is acted upon. For things that are not the same cannot be acted upon, he says; but even when things that are different do act, <their action is> not due to their difference but to the presence in them of something identical. Upon such matters as these he may consequently be understood either way. He now undertakes to discuss the <senses> each in turn.

(50) Vision he explains by the reflection <in the eye>, of which he gives a unique account. For the reflection does not arise immediately in the pupil. On the contrary, the air between the eye and the object of sight is compressed by the object and the visual organ, and thus becomes imprinted; since there is always an effluence of some kind arising from everything. Thereupon this imprinted air, because it is solid and is of a hue contrasting <with the pupil>, is reflected in the eyes, which are moist. A dense substance does not receive <this reflection>, but what is moist gives it admission. Moist eyes accordingly have a better power of vision than have hard eyes; provided their outer tunic be exceedingly fine and close-knit, and the inner <tissues> be to the last degree spongy and free from dense and stubborn flesh, and free too, from thick oily moisture; and provided, also, the ducts connected with the eyes be straight and dry that they

[1] The translation of G. M. Stratton in *Greek Physiological Psychology.*

may "perfectly conform" to the entering imprints. For each knows best its kindred.

(51) Now in the first place this imprint upon the air is an absurdity. For the substance receiving such an imprint must have a certain consistence and not be "fragile"; even as Democritus himself, in illustrating the character of the "impression", says that "it is as if one were to take a mould in wax". In the second place, an object could make a better imprint upon water <than upon air>, since water is denser. While the theory would require us to see more distinctly <an object in water>, we actually see it less so. In general, why should Democritus assume this *imprint,* when in his discussion of forms he has supposed an *emanation* that conveys the object's form? For these images <due to emanation> would be reflected.

(52) But if such an imprint actually occurs and the air is moulded like wax that is squeezed and pressed, how does the reflection <in the eye> come into existence, and what is its character? For the imprint here as in other cases will evidently face the object seen. But since this is so, it is impossible for a reflection facing us to arise unless this imprint is turned around. What would cause this reversal, and what the manner of its operation, ought, however, to be shown; for in no other way could vision come to pass. Moreover when several objects are seen in one and the same place, how can so many imprints be made upon the self-same air? And again, how could we possibly see each other? For the imprints would inevitably clash, since each of them would be facing <the person> from whom it sprung. All of which gives us pause.

(53) Furthermore, why does not each person see himself? For the imprints <from ourselves> would be reflected in our own eyes quite as they are in the eyes of our companions, especially if these imprints directly face us and if the effect here is the same as with an echo,—since Democritus says that <in the case of the echo> the vocal sound is reflected back to him who utters it. Indeed the whole idea of imprints made on the air is extravagant. For we should be forced to believe, from what he says, that all bodies are

producing imprints <in the air>, and that great numbers of them are sending <their impressions> across one another's path,—a state of things at once embarrassing to sight and improbable on other grounds. If the impression moreover endures, we ought to see bodies that are out of sight and remote,—if not by night, at all events by day. And yet it would be but fair to assume that these imprints would persist at night, since then the air is so much cooler.

(54) Possibly, however, the reflection in the eye is caused by the sun, in sending light in upon the visual sense in the form of rays,—as Democritus seems to mean. For the idea that the sun "drives the air from itself and, in thus repelling, condenses it", as he says,—this is indefensible; since the sun by its very nature disperses the air. He is unfortunate, too, in regarding visual perception as a function not only of the eyes but of the rest of the body as well; for he says that the eye must contain emptiness and moisture, in order that it may the more readily receive <impressions> and transmit <them> to the rest of the body. Farther, it is unreasonable to declare that what is "kindred" to the organ of sight is preëminently the object of vision, and yet to explain the reflection <in the eye> by colour-contrast, on the ground that colours of the eyes' own hue are not reflected in them. And though he tries to explain how magnitudes and distances are reflected, he does not succeed. Thus Democritus in his endeavour to say something unique with regard to vision has bequeathed us the problem even farther from solution.

(55) His explanation of hearing is very much like others'. For the air, he holds, burst into the <aural> cavity and sets up a commotion. And while it gains entrance to the body in this same manner at every point, yet it enters more fully and freely through the ears because there it traverses the largest empty space, where least it "tarries". In consequence no part of the body perceives <sounds> save this <sensory region>. But once the commotion has been started within, it is "sent broadcast" by reason of its velocity; for sound, he holds, arises as the air is being condensed and is making forcible entry <into the body>. So he explains sensation

within the body, just as he explains perception external to it, by contact.

(56) Hearing is keenest, he maintains, when the outer tunic is tough and the ducts are empty and unusually free from moisture and are well-bored in the rest of the body as well as in the head and ears; when, too, the bones are dense and the brain is well-tempered and that which surrounds it is exceedingly dry. For the sound thus enters compact, since it traverses a cavity large and dry and with good orifices, and swiftly the sound is "sent broadcast" impartially through the body and does not again escape.

(57) Such hazy definition is found in other writers as well. Yet it is absurd, while original, to say that sound permeates the entire body, and that when it has entered by the organ of hearing it is spread to every nook and cranny, as though perception here were due not to the ears but to the body entire. For if <the rest of the body> is somehow affected conjointly with the organ of hearing, it by no means follows that the perception depends upon the <body as a whole>. For the <entire body> acts thus in the case of every sense; and not of the senses only, but of the soul as well.

Thus he accounts for sight and hearing. As for our other senses, his treatment hardly differs from that of the mass of writers.

(58) Concerning thought, Democritus says merely that "it arises when the soul's composition is duly proportioned". But if one becomes excessively hot or cold, he says, thinking is transformed; and it was for some such reason, the ancients well believed, that the mind became "deranged". Thus it is clear that he explains thought by the composition of the body, —a view perhaps not unreasonable in one who regards the soul itself as corporeal.

In sum and substance, then, these are the conclusions with regard to perception and thinking, which have come down to us from the earlier investigators.

[*Part II. THE OBJECTS OF SENSE*]

(59) What may be the intrinsic character and quality of

each of the senses' *objects,* the writers other <than Democritus and Plato> fail to state. Of the objects perceived by touch, they discuss the heavy and the light, the warm and the cold, saying that the rare and fine is hot; the dense and thick, cold,—which is the distinction Anaxagoras makes between air and aether. And in general <they explain> weight and lightness by the same <causes>—that is to say, by "tendencies" respectively upward and downward; and they further agree that sound is a movement of the air, and that odour is an emanation. Empedocles discusses the colours also, and holds that white is composed of fire, and black of water. The other investigators confine themselves to the statement that white and black are the fundamental colours and that the rest are derived from these by mixture. For even Anaxagoras treats of the <colours> in only a loose and general way.

(60) Democritus and Plato, however, are the investigators who go into the question most fully, for they define the object of each sense; although <Plato> never robs these objects of their external reality, whereas Democritus reduces them one and all to effects in our sensuous faculty. Where the truth itself lies, is not the question we are now discussing. Let our aim be rather to report the range of each author's treatment and the precise definitions he gives, stating by way of preface his general method.

Democritus has no uniform account of all <the sensory objects>: some he distinguishes by the size <of their atoms>, others by the shape, and a few by the <atomic> order and position. Plato, on the other hand, refers nearly all of them to effects in us, and to our perceptive faculty. Consequently each of these authors would seem to speak directly counter to his own postulate. (61) For the one of them, who would have sensory objects to be but effects in our perceptive faculty, actually describes a reality resident in the objects themselves; while the other, who attributes the objects' character to their own intrinsic being, ends by ascribing it to the passive change of our perceptive faculty.

Heaviness and lightness, to begin with, Democritus distinguishes in terms of size. For if we were to divide each substance into its <atomic> units, then even though these were to differ in shape, he contends, their reality would have as its standard <of weight> their size. In the case of compounds, on the contrary, a substance that contains more of void is lighter; one that contains less is heavier. This at least is what he says in certain passages. (62) In others, he holds that it is simply its fineness that makes a substance light.

And he speaks in almost the same terms of the hard and of the soft. For him anything is hard that is compact; it is soft if loose; while the different degrees, and so on, <of such qualities are also explained> in accord with this idea. Yet the position and grouping of the void spaces that make substances hard or soft differ in some respects from those that make them heavy or light. Consequently though iron is harder than lead, lead is heavier. For iron is of uneven composition, and its void spaces are many and of large extent, although here and there iron is condensed; but speaking generally it contains more void spaces <than does lead>. But lead, though it had less of the void, is of even and uniform composition throughout; and so, while heavier than iron, lead is softer. (63) Such is his account of the heavy, the light, the hard, and the soft.

As for the other sensory objects, he holds that none has an objective reality, but that one and all are effects in our sensuous faculty as it undergoes alteration,—and that from this faculty arises the inner presentation. For not even of heat or cold is there for him an objective reality; but configuration, in "undergoing a change", effects a qualitative alteration in us also; since what is massed together in anything prevails in it, and what is widely diffused is imperceptible.

Proof that <these sensory qualities> are not objectively real is found in the fact that they do not appear the same to all creatures: what is sweet to us is bitter to others, and to still others it is sour or pungent or astringent; and similarly of the other <sensory qualities>.

(64) Moreover Democritus holds that "men vary in composition" according to their condition and age; whence it is evident that a man's physical state accounts for his inner presentation. So we must in general, according to him, hold

this view regarding sensory objects. Nevertheless here too, as elsewhere, he falls back upon <atomic> figures; yet he does not recount the shapes <of the atoms> of all <the sensory objects>, but centres his attention upon those of the tastes and of colours; and even of these, he describes with greater precision the <figures> connected with taste, although he refers the presentation itself to <the sentience of> man.

(65) What is "sour", he holds, is at once "angular" in its <atomic> figure and is "twisted", minute, and thin. By its keenness it swiftly slips in and penetrates everywhere, and by its roughness and "angularity" it draws the parts together and binds them. It also heats the body, in consequence, since it produces emptiness within; for whatever has most of empty space <amongst its atoms> is most heated.

"Sweet" consists of <atomic> figures that are rounded and not too small; wherefore it quite softens the body by its gentle action, and unhastening makes its way throughout. Yet it disturbs the other <savours>, for it slips in among the other <atomic figures>and "leads them from their accustomed ways" and moistens them. And the <atomic figures> thus moistened and disturbed in their arrangement flow into the belly, which is most accessible, since empty space is there in greatest measure.

(66) The "astringent" taste, according to Democritus, is derived from <atomic> figures that are large and of many angles and are least rounded. For when these enter our bodies, they clog and occlude the ducts and prevent <their contents> from intermingling, and consequently stay the action of the bowels.

"Bitter" is composed of small, smooth, round <atomic figures> whose surfaces moreover are furnished with hooks; as a consequence bitter is sticky and viscous.

The taste derived from large <atoms> that are unrounded, —some of them are "crooked", yet for the most part they are regular—this taste is "saline"; <its atoms> therefore are not provided with "many hooks"; (by "crooked" <atoms> he means such as overlap and become entangled in one another). <The saline quality is derived> from large

<atoms> because salt comes to the surface of bodies; while if <its atoms> were small and were battered against the surrounding <particles>, they would mingle with the whole; from unrounded <atoms>, because what is saline is rough while the rounded is smooth; from <atoms> that are not "crooked", because these do not "stick to one another", and in consequence they "crumble apart".

(67) The "pungent" savour according to him is small, round, and angular, but not irregular. Having many angles, this taste heats and melts by reason of its roughness, because it is small, round, and angular; for the angular too has this character.

In a like manner he accounts for all the other effects of each <savour> by referring them to figures. But no one of all these figures is present, he holds, pure and without admixture of the others; on the contrary, there is a multitude of them in each savour, and the self-same taste includes figures that are smooth, rough, round, sharp, and so on. The preponderant figure, however, exerts the most influence upon the faculty of sense and determines the <savour's> effect; and, moreover, the condition in which it finds <us influences the result>. For it makes a great difference <what our condition is>, inasmuch as the same substance at times causes opposite feeling, and opposite substances cause the same feeling. (68) Such is Democritus's account of tastes.

In the first place, it might seem odd not to assign causes to all <sensory qualities> according to a uniform principle, but to explain heaviness and lightness, softness and hardness, by the fact that <the atoms> are large or small, and rare or dense, while heat and cold and the rest are explained by the figures <of the atoms>. In the second place, <it seems strange> to ascribe a resident and objective reality to the qualities heavy, light, hard, and soft (for the properties large and small, dense and rare are not relative to something other than <the substance itself>), and then to make heat, cold, and the rest entirely relative to sense, and this though he repeatedly says that the figure of heat is spherical.

(69) But the one glaring inconsistency running through the whole account is, that he no sooner declares <savours>

to be subjective effects in sense than he distinguishes them by their figures; and he points out that the same substance appears bitter to some persons and sweet to others and has still a third quality for some other group. For the figure cannot possibly be a subjective effect, nor can one and the same figure be spherical for certain persons and of another shape for others (although such an assumption were perhaps inevitable if what is sweet for some is bitter for others), nor can the shapes <of atoms> change according to differences of state in us. And, in general, the <atomic> figure has an absolute existence, while sweetness and the sensuous object generally, as he says, is relative and existent in something beyond itself.

It is strange, furthermore, to insist that to all those who perceive the same things there comes the same subjective appearance, and to examine the true character of these things, when he has already said that to persons in different conditions there come different subjective appearances, and again that no one attains the truth of things better than does another. (70) For it is probable that <in the attainment of truth> the better surpasses the worse, and the well the sick; since the <better and healthier> are more in accord with the reality of things.

But if there be no objective reality in sensory objects because they do not appear the same to all, there is manifestly none in animals or other bodies; for men disagree about these things, too. And yet even if the cause of sweet and bitter is not the same for us all, at least the bitterness and sweetness appear the same for all. Democritus himself seems a witness to this; for how could that which is bitter for us be sweet or astringent for others, unless these very qualities had a definite nature? (71) This he makes even more explicit in those passages where he says that the being of anything and the process by which it originated are real; and particularly when he says of bitter, that "<here we> have a portion of understanding." Upon such a showing, consequently, there would seem to be a general contradiction in his refusal to ascribe any objective reality to sensory objects. But there is, besides, the special contradiction indicated above, when he assigns a figure to the bitter, as he does to the other <savours>, and yet says that <the bitter> has no objective reality. For either no <sensory object> has external reality, or else these tastes have such reality, since a common cause underlies them.

Moreover both heat and cold, which are supposed to be the primal source of things, probably have some objective reality; but if these, then the others also. He does, however, ascribe a certain substantive being to the qualities hard and soft, and heavy and light;—although in spite of this they seem to be counted <among the qualities> relative to us;—but he does not ascribe such substantive being to heat, and cold, and the rest. And yet, as he distinguishes the heavy and the light by the size <of their atoms>, he ought to hold that all simple <bodies> have an impulse to move in the same direction; and consequently they would be of one and the same "matter" and would have a common nature. (72) Yet upon such questions he seems to have followed those who make thought entirely a matter of change, a doctrine from hoary antiquity; since all the ancients, whether poets or sages, represented thought as dependent upon <bodily> disposition.

But in assigning an <atomic> figure to each of the savours, Democritus has made this figure correspond to the effect which the savour produces in our feelings. The <figure therefore should be deduced>, not from the <external savours> merely, but from our sense organs as well; above all, if these savours themselves are but subjective effects in these sense-organs. A spherical figure does not have the same "power" in every case, nor does any other figure; <a savour> must consequently be characterized with reference to the substrate affected, by stating whether it is composed of what is like or unlike <the substance of the sense organ>, and how the change in the sensuous faculty comes to pass. And furthermore there should be offered an explanation applicable alike to all the sensory qualities that arise by touch, and not merely to those involved in taste. And yet these qualities <arising by touch> either show some difference when compared with savours—a difference which he should make clear

—or else he has neglected to tell us what is the common explanation that here is possible.

(73) The simple colours, he says, are four. What is smooth is white; since what neither is rough nor casts shadows nor is hard to penetrate,—all such substances are brilliant. But brilliant substances must also have open passages and be translucent. Now white substances that are hard have the structure just described,—for instance, the inner surface of cockle shells; for the substance here would be shadowless, "gleaming", and with straight passages. But the white substances that are loose and friable are composed of round particles, yet with these placed oblique to one another and oblique in their conjunction by pairs, while the arrangement as a whole is uniform in the extreme. With such a structure these substances are loose because <their particles are> in contact only over a small <portion of their surface>; friable, because their composition is so uniform; shadowless, because they are smooth and flat. But those substances are whiter, compared with one another, in which the figures are more exactly as described above and are freer from admixture with other figures and whose order and position more nearly conform to the given description. From such figures, then, is white derived.

(74) Black is composed of figures the very opposite <to those of white>,—figures rough, irregular, and differing from one another. For these cast shadows, and the passages amongst them are not straight nor easy to thread. Their effluences, too, are sluggish and confused; for the character of the effluence also makes a difference in the inner presentation, as this emanation is changed by its retention of air.

(75) Red is composed of figures such as enter into heat, save that those of red are larger. For if the aggregations be larger although the figures are the same, they produce the quality of redness rather <than of heat>. Evidence that redness is derived from such <figures> is found in the fact that we redden as we become heated, as do other things placed in the fire until they have a fiery colour. Those substances are redder that are composed of large figures—for example, the flame and coals of green wood <are redder>

than those of dry. And iron, too, and other things placed in fire <become redder>. Those are most luminous, however, that contain the most fire and the subtilest, while those are redder that have coarser <fire> and less of it. Redder things, accordingly, are not so hot; for what is subtile is hot.

Green is composed of both the solid and the void,—the hue varying with the position and order of these constituents.

(76) Such are the figures which the simple colours possess; and each of these colours is the purer the less the admixture of other figures. The other colours are derived from these by mixture.

Golden and copper-colour and all such tones, for instance, come from white and red, their brilliance being derived from the white, their ruddiness from the red component; for in combination the red sinks into the empty spaces of the white. Now if green be added to white and red, there results the most beautiful colour; but the green component must be small, for any large admixture would not comport with the union of white with red. The tint will vary according to the amount <of green> that is introduced.

(77) Crimson comes from white, black, and red,—the largest "portion" being red, that of black small, and of white midway; for thus it makes an appearance delightful to the sense. That black and red are present in it is patent to the eye: its brilliance and lustre testify to the presence of white; for white produces such effects.

Woad hue is composed of deep black and golden green, but with the major "portion" black. Leek green is of crimson and woad, or of golden green and purplish. . . . For sulphur colour is of this character, with a dash of brilliance. Indigo is a mixture of woad and fiery red, with round figures and figures needle-shaped to give a gleam to the colour's darkness.

(78) Brown is derived from golden green and deep blue; but if more of the golden green be mixed, flame-colour is the result; for the blackness is expelled because the <golden green> is shadowless. And red, too, when mixed with white, gives almost a "pure" golden green, and not a black; which accounts for the fact that plants at first are of such a green before there is a heating and dispersion.

This completes the tale of colours he recounts; although he holds that the colours, like the savours, are endless in number according to their combinations,—according as we remove some and add others and "combine" them in varying proportion. For no one of these colours would be the same as another.

(79) But first of all, his increase of the number of primaries presents a difficulty; for the other investigators propose white and black as the only simple colours. And in the second place, there is a difficulty when he fails to assign one and the same shape to all kinds of white, but attributes a different shape to the "hard" whites from that which he ascribes to the whites of "loose texture." For it is improbable that <the whiteness> would have a different cause in substances differing merely in their tactile character. And, too, the cause of the difference <between white and black> would not lie in the figure <of the constituent particles>, but in their position. For round figures, and indeed every kind of figure whatever, can cast shadows upon one another. And this is evident, for Democritus himself gives this reason for the smooth things that look black; for they appear thus, he holds, because they have the internal combination and arrangement characteristic of black. And again, <in giving his reason> for the white things that are rough; these are of large particles, he holds, and their junctions are not rounded off but are "battlemented", and the shapes of the figures are broken, like the earthworks in the approach to a city's wall. For such an arrangement, he says, throws no shadow, and brilliance is not hindered.

(80) Moreover, how can he say that the whiteness of certain creatures becomes black if they be so placed that shadows are cast? He seems really to be talking about the nature of transparency and brilliance, rather than of whiteness. For to be easily seen through and to have passages that do not run zig-zag are features of transparency; but how many transparent substances are white? And further, to assume straight passages in substances that are white, and passages zig-zag in those that are black, implies that the very structure of the object enters <our sense organ>. Vision, he says is due to

an emanatition and to the reflection in the organ of sight. But if this be so, what difference does it make whether the passages <in the object> lie end to end or zig-zag? Nor is it easy to believe that an emanation can by any possibility arise from the void. The cause of this, therefore, should be stated. For he seems to derive whiteness from light or something else; and accordingly offers the grossness of the air as also a reason why things seem dark.

(81) His explanation of black, farther, is not easy to comprehend; for a shadow is (in his theory) something black, and at the same time it is an obscuration of what is white; white is therefore essentially prior <to black>. Yet with this, he attributes <black> not only to shading but to the grossness of the air and of the entering emanation, as well as to disturbance of the eye. But whether these arise from mere opacity, or from some other source, and if so, what the character <of this farther source may be>, he does not reveal.

(82) It is singular, also, to assign no shape to green but to constitute it merely of the solid and the void. For these are present in all things, of whatsoever figures they are composed. He should have given some distinctive <figure> to green, as he has to the other colours. And if he holds <green> to be the opposite of red, as black is of white, it ought to have an opposite shape; but if in his view it is not the opposite, this itself would surprise us that he does not regard his first principles as opposites, for that is the universally accepted doctrine. Most of all, though, he should have determined with accuracy which colours are simple, and why some colours are compounded and others not; for there is the gravest difficulty with regard to the first principles. Yet this would doubtless prove a difficult task. For if one could say, of tastes for example, which of them are simple, there would be more in what one said <than is found in Democritus upon them>. As for smell, he says nothing definite except that something subtile emanating from heavy substances is the cause of odour. But what its character is, and by what this process is effected—which is perhaps the most important point of all,—on this we have never a word. There are some

things of this kind, then, that Democritus has neglected.

137. Cic. *de div.* II 58, 120. Do we, therefore, believe that during sleep our minds move themselves, or as Democritus thought, that they are agitated by external and adventitious appearances?

138. ——— ——— I 3, 5. (D. 224). Although . . . that weighty authority Democritus had in many passages approved of premonitions of future events, Dicaiarchus the Peripatetic held to premonitions in dreams and frenzies but rejected other types. 57, 131. [from Posidonius] Democritus, however, considered that the ancients wisely arranged for the inspection of sacrifices, whose condition and colour give evidence of health or sickness and sometimes even of the future sterility or fertility of the fields.

139. Censor. 4, 9. Democritus the Abderite believed the first men were begotten of water and slime. Aet. V 19, 6. Democritus held that animals were first produced by the conjunction of jointless members, and moisture gave them life. Lact. *Inst. div.* VII 7, 9. The Stoics say that the world and all it contains were made for man's sake; and our Holy Scriptures teach the same thing. Democritus, therefore, erred when he thought that they emerged from the ground like worms, without a Maker, and without any reason.

140. Aet. V 4, 3. (D. 417 / 8). Strato and Democritus say the power also [not merely the matter of the seed] is a body, for it is wind-like.

141. ——— ——— 3, 6. (D. 417). According to Democritus, [seed originates] from bodies as a whole and especially from the most important parts, such as the bones, the flesh, and the sinews.

143. Arist. *de gen. animal.* Δ1. 764 a 6. Democritus of Abdera holds that the distinction between male and female takes place in the womb, not however as the result of heat and cold, but it depends on which parent furnishes the dominant seed, or more exactly that "chromosome" which originates in the organs which differentiate male from female. Censor. 6, 5. Whichever parent's principle first occupies the spot, that one's nature, Democritus reports, is reproduced. Aet. V 7, 6. (D. 420) The common parts arise from either one as it

may happen, but the particularizing characteristics come from the dominant strain.

144. Arist. *de gen. animal.* B 4. 740 a 33. The veins join on to the womb like roots through which the foetus receives nourishment. For this reason, the living thing remains in the womb, but not as Democritus says, so the parts may be moulded to the parts of the womb. 7. 746 a 19. Those who say children are nourished in the womb by sucking bits of flesh are in error. Aet. V 16, 1. (D. 426) Democritus and Epicurus say the foetus is nourished in the womb through its mouth. And so immediately when it is born, its mouth is put to the breast; for there are in the womb nipples and mouths by which it is nourished.

145. Arist. *de gen. anim.* B 4. 740 a 13. All who like Democritus assert, the external parts of living beings are first developed, and the internal later, are in error. Cen. 6, 1. Democritus says the belly and the head [come first], which have more of the void in them [than any other part].

146. Arist. *de gen. anim.* Δ 4. 769 b 30. Democritus said monstrosities occur because a prior fertilization mixes with a later. And when the later emission enters the womb the parts grow confusedly together. In the case of birds, since the fertilization occurs quickly, he says the eggs are always confused in their colour, [text possibly corrupt].

147. ——— ——— E 8. 788 b 9. Democritus also has treated of these problems [teeth] . . . for he says the first set fall out because they grow too soon; for they grow according to nature when they are in their prime so to speak. And he explains their too early arrival as due to suckling.

148. Arist. *de partt. anim.* Γ 4. 665 a 30. Bloodless animals have no viscera. And Democritus seems to have been mistaken in this respect, if indeed he thought they were indiscernible because the bloodless animals are so small.

149. ——— *de gen. animal.* B 8. 747 a 29. For Democritus says the [genital] passages in mules are destroyed in the embryo because the process does not begin with animals of the same species.

150. [Arist.] *Hist. anim.* I 39. 623 a 30. Spiders as soon as they are hatched can spin a web, not from within as if it were

an excrement as Democritus says, but from the body like bark [of trees] or like animals which shed their hair or bristles, such as porcupines.

151. AEL. *H. N.* XII 16. Democritus says that pigs and dogs have large litters and gives the explanation that they have several wombs or receptacles for semen. The semen of one emission does not fill them all, but these animals repeat coitus two or three times so that the series fills the receptacles. The mule, he says, does not bear, for its womb, unlike that of other animals and so differently shaped, cannot receive seed; for the mule is not a product of nature, but rather the stratagem and contrivance of human forethought and adulterous daring, so to speak. "It seems to me—he said—an ass by chance forcibly impregnated a horse, and when men learned of it they made this form of fertilization customary." And those who know about these unions say that the very large Libyan asses cover the mare when shorn of her hair, for she who has the glory of her hair would not submit to such a mate.

152. ——— ——— XII 17. Miscarriages, says Democritus, are more likely in southern climates than in the north. This is plausible because the bodies of pregnant animals become flabby on account of the warmth and are distended. And when the body loosens up and does not fit well, the embryo also shifts its position, and as its temperature rises it slips from side to side and a miscarriage is easy. But if there are cold winds and icy weather, the embryo becomes solid, hard to move, and is not tossed about as by the waves of the sea. Such embryos, undisturbed as in a calm, become strong and healthy and await the natural time of birth. And so the Abderite concludes, "In cold weather it holds together but in hot there is often an abortion." And he says the veins and joints necessarily distend when there is too much heat.

160. CIC. *Tusc.* I 34, 82. For assume that the soul is destroyed like the body. Is there, then, any pain or any sensation at all in the body after death? No one says there is, although Epicurus charges it against Democritus. Democritus' disciples, however, deny it. Tertull. *de an.* 51. Plato in the *Republic,* however, cites against this view the fact of the corpse of someone unburied for a long time, preserved without any

deterioration in consequence of the inseparability of the soul. To this Democritus adds the growth of nails and hair a long time after burial. Celsus II 6. Moreover the justly famed Democritus has maintained that even when life has ceased there are no certain symptoms of death in which physicians put their trust. Therefore he did not admit that there are any certain signs of future death.

162. THEOPHR. *de caus.* pl. II 11, 7 sqq. When Democritus explains that straight plants bloom and die sooner than crooked ones because of the same necessary processes (for the nourishment on which the blossom and fruit depend is more quickly diffused through the straight plant, while in the other case more slowly because its [tracheal] tubes are constricted, and the roots themselves get the benefit, for the roots of these plants are both long and thick) he does not seem to be correct. (8) For he says that the roots of the straight plants are weak and for a double reason they break and the plant is destroyed; for both cold and heat descend quickly from the top to the roots because of the easy progress, and since the roots are weak they cannot withstand the shock. In general many plants of this type begin to age from the bottom on account of the weakness of their roots. And further, the aerial parts because they are so slim are twisted by the winds and so disturb the roots. This results in harm and breakage and so decay attacks the whole tree. This, at any rate, is his account of the matter.

165. ALEX. *Quaest.* II 23. (Why the lodestone attracts iron) [II 72, 82 Bruns] Democritus himself asserts that emanations arise and that like moves toward like, although everything moves toward the void also. On this basis he holds that the magnet and the iron are composed of similar atoms, the magnet however of finer atoms, more widely spaced, and inclosing more void than the iron. Therefore, since [its atoms] are more easily moved, they move faster to the iron (for motion proceeds toward the like), and entering the pores of the iron they set its component bodies in motion by slipping through them on account of their fineness. The bodies so set in motion leave the iron as an efflux and move toward the magnet, both because of the similarity in particles and be-

cause the magnet has more void. Then by reason of the wholesale egress of the bodies and their motion, the iron itself follows them and is also carried to the magnet. But the magnet does not move toward the iron because the iron does not have as many void spaces as the magnet. But granted that iron and lodestone are composed of like particles, how about amber and chaff? When anyone offers the same explanation for this case also, it must be recalled that amber attracts many things. Now if amber is composed of the same particles as all these, then the latter also are composed of similar particles and should attract each other.

169. [4N] CIC. *de fin.* V 8, 23. But the security of Democritus which is a sort of tranquillity of mind, which he has named Cheerfulness, should have been barred from this discussion because that very tranquillity of mind is itself the blessed life. 29, 87. Democritus—whether it is true or false we shall not inquire—is said to have put out his own eyes, presumably in order that his mind should be least distracted from contemplation. He neglected his inheritance, left his fields uncultivated, and what else could he have been seeking than the blessed life? And even if he placed that life in knowing things, none the less from his investigations of nature he wished a good mind to result. For he called Cheerfulness, and often Confidence, that is a mind devoid of fear, the highest good. But though this is clear enough, it is not yet complete; for he said little about virtue, and that little was not so clear.

170. CLEM. *Strom.* II 138 p. 503 P. [170 N.] Democritus begs to be excused from marriage and from the procreation of children because of their many annoyances and their distractions from more necessary matters. Epicurus also agrees with him.

B. The Fragments.[1]

3. PLUT. *de tranqu. an.* 2. Stob. IV 103, 25. He that would be cheerful should not do too many things, either as a private individual or as a citizen, nor should the things which he

[1] Words enclosed in parentheses are context; words not so enclosed are quotation.

chooses to do lie beyond his power and capacity, but he should take such care that even when luck goes his way and to all appearances is leading him on to more, he will disregard her and not attempt more than he is able. For sufficiency is safer than superfluity.

6. SEXT. VII 137. (In the book *On Ideas* he says:) Man must know by this rule, that he is far removed from truth.

7. (And again:) And this argument too makes it clear that we really know nothing about anything, but each one's opinion is the flow toward him [of sense images.]

8. (And again:) Although it will be clear that we are at a loss how to know what each thing really is.

9. SEXT. *adv. math.* VII 135. (But Democritus at times abolishes the things which appear to the senses and says that none of them appear really, but only seem to do so, and the only things which really exist are the atoms and the void. For he says,) By convention there is sweet; by convention, bitter; by convention, hot; by convention, cold; by convention, colour; but in truth there exist atoms and void,

[Fr. 125 has the same quotation and adds] (He pictures the sensations speaking to reason as follows:) Miserable mind, will you reject us after receiving the grounds of belief from us? That rejection is ruin for you.

[Continuing Fr. 9.] (which means: Though Sense objects are thought to exist, they do not exist in truth, but only atoms and void. And in his *Verifications,* while professing to entrust the senses with the power of establishing belief, none the less we find that he condemns them. For he says:) We really perceive nothing strictly true, but only what changes with the condition of our body and the influences coming toward it or resisting it.

10. (And again he says:) It has now been truly shown in many ways that we do not perceive what each thing is or is not.

11. SEXT. VII 138. [following B 8.] (In *The Canons* he says there are two forms of knowledge, one through sensations, and one through reason. The one through reason he calls legitimate, testifying to its credibility in the discrimination of truth, but the one through sensations he names obscure,

depriving it of inerrancy in the determination of truth. And he says verbatim:) There are two forms of knowledge, one legitimate, one obscure; the following all belong to the obscure form, sight, hearing, smell, taste, and touch. The other is legitimate, and is quite different from this. (Then, preferring the legitimate to the obscure he adds:) When the obscure can no longer see anything smaller, or hear or smell or taste or perceive by touch, and when into the more delicate [one is required to investigate, then there follows legitimate knowledge, which has a more delicate instrument for knowing.]

[Note: Nothing verbatim in 12, 14, 15, 26, 34.]

12. CENSOR. 18, 8. The [world] year of Philolaus . . . and Democritus comprises eighty-two years with twenty-eight intercalary [months.]

14.1. VITRUV. IX 6, 3. Concerning natural phenomena Thales of Miletus, Anaxagoras of Clazomenae, Pythagoras of Samos, Xenophon of Colophon, and Democritus of Abdera, left [carefully] thought-out explanations according to which these phenomena are governed by nature whatever effects they may have. Following their discoveries Eudoxus, Euctemon, Callippus, Meto, Philippus, Hipparchus, Aratus, and others, discovered through the technique of astronomical tables the rising and setting of the stars and the signs of the seasons and handed down the explanations to posterity. IX 5, 4. I have explained in accordance with the views of the scientist Democritus the shapes and figures of the constellations designed by nature and the divine mind, or rather only those whose rising and setting we can observe and watch with our own eyes.

14.2. EUDOX. *Ars. astron.* col. 22, 21 [p. 25 Blass] For Eudoxus and Democritus the winter solstice occurs sometimes on the twentieth, sometimes on the nineteenth of Athyr. 23, 3. From the autumnal equinox to the winter solstice is by Eudoxus' calculation 92 days; Democritus makes it 91. From the winter solstice to the spring equinox, both Eudoxus and Democritus count 91 days, Euctemon 92.

14.3. [GEMIN] *Isag.* (Calendar perhaps from second century B.C.) p. 218, 14 Mainit. (Scorpio) On the fourth day, says

Democritus, the Pleiades set at daybreak; winter winds for the most part are wont to blow and cold and frost; and the trees begin to shed their leaves in abundance.

p. 220, 5. On the thirteenth, says Democritus, Lyra rises with the sun; and the air is usually cold.

p. 222, 9. (Sagittarius) On the sixteenth, says Democritus, Aquila rises with the sun, and is generally indicative of thunder and storms and water or winds or usually both.

p. 226, 4. On the sixteenth, says Democritus, the northwest winds begin to blow and continue. On the forty-third day from the solstice.

p. 226, 15. (Pisces) On the fourth, says Democritus, there commence the beautiful [unstable] days called halcyon.

p. 226, 23. On the fourteenth, says Democritus, the cold winds blow, the so-called "bird-winds" for nine days at most.

p. 228, 23. (Aries) Democritus says the Pleiades disappear at sunrise, and remain invisible for forty nights.

15. Agathem. I 1, 2. . . . The ancients believed the earth to be round and placed Greece as its centre and Delphi at the centre of Greece; for it was its navel. Democritus, a man of wide experience, first perceived that the earth is oblong in a ratio of three to two. With him Dicaiarchus the Peripatetic also agrees.

26. Procl. *in Crat.* 16 p. 6 Boiss. Pythagoras and Epicurus were of the opinion of Cratylus while Democritus and Aristotle held with Hermogenes.

. . . p. 7. In the expression "the Giver of names" [Pythagoras] hinted at the soul, which derives from mind. Things themselves are not primary realities as is the mind, and [the soul] has likenesses of them and essential, comprehensive notions like images of the realities, such as names which are imitations of the intellectual forms, the numbers. Accordingly, the being of everything derives from the self-conscious and wise mind, but names derive from soul, which imitates mind. Therefore, says Pythagoras, it is not any chance person who can give names to things, but only he who sees mind and the nature of things. Names, therefore, exist by nature. But Democritus by four lines of argument develops the conclusion that names are conventional. First, equivocation, where different things are called by the same name, hence the name is not by nature. Second synonymy. For if different names apply to one and the same thing, they would also apply to each other which is impossible. Third, the exchange of names; for if names were by nature, why did we call Aristocles Plato and Tyrtamus Theophrastus? Fourth, missing derivatives; for why is it that the verb "to think" comes from the noun "thought," while from the noun "justice" no verb is derived? Hence names exist by chance and not by nature. Democritus himself calls the first argument, ambiloquy; the second, equipollence; [the third, metonymy;] the fourth, nonymy.

31. CLEM. *Paed.* I 6 p. 100 P. Medicine heals the diseases of the body, according to Democritus, but wisdom frees the soul of passions.

34. DAVID *Prol.* 38, 14 Busse. (As in the universe we see that one class, the deities, only rules, another class, mankind, both rules and is ruled—for men are ruled by the gods and rule the irrational animals—and another class, the irrational animals, is only ruled, so in the same manner these levels, according to Democritus, are found in) man who is a microcosm. (There is his reason which only rules, his passion which both rules and is ruled, and his appetites which are ruled only.) Gal. III. 241. (The ancients who were competent in science say that a living being is like a universe in miniature.)

The Golden Maxims.[1]

35. If anyone pay intelligent attention to these my maxims, many matters worthy of a good man shall he engage in, and many ignoble matters shall he escape.

37. He that chooses the goods of the soul chooses the more divine; he that chooses those of the body, chooses human goods.

38. It is good to prevent the wrongdoer, but at least not to join with him.

[1] The translation of these short fragments was taken from the handwritten notes of the late Professor William Romaine Newbold.

39. One ought to be good, or pretend to be.
40. Neither their bodies nor their wealth make men happy, but rectitude and much contemplation.
41. Not from fear, but from duty abstain from sins.
42. It is a great thing in misfortunes to think as one ought.
43. Repentance for shameful deeds is the salvation of life.
44. Speak true, not much.
45. He who wrongs is more wretched than he who is wronged.
46. Greatness of soul is to bear trouble patiently.
47. To yield to law, to the ruler, and to the wisest is becoming.
48. The good man does not value the fault-finding of the wicked.
49. It is hard to be governed by a worse man.
50. He that always yields to money could never be just.
51. Speech [or reason] often proves more persuasive than gold.
52. With one that fancies he has understanding, admonition is wasted toil.
53. Many that have learned no reason live reasonably; but many who act most disgracefully give the best of reasons.
54. Fools learn by misfortune.
65. One should cultivate much understanding, not much knowing.
66. To deliberate before one's acts, is better than to repent.
67. Do not trust all men, but those approved; the former is silly, the latter sensible.
69. For all men the good and the true are the same, but the pleasant varies.
70. Immoderate desire marks the child, not the man.
71. Untimely pleasures beget disgust.
72. Excessive desires for anything blind the soul to aught else.
73. Excessively to pursue the beautiful is righteous love.
74. Accept no pleasure that profits not.
75. It is better for the foolish to be ruled than to rule.
77. Glory and wealth without wisdom are not safe possessions.

78. To accumulate wealth is not useless, but nothing is worse than to do so by injustice.
83. The cause of sin is ignorance of the better.
84. Whoever commits disgraceful deeds should be ashamed first before himself.
85. He that contradicts and keeps on talking is unfitted to learn what he should.
86. To do all the talking and not to be willing to hear anything is greediness.
87. One should watch the bad man lest he seize his opportunity.
88. The envious man inflicts pain on himself as though he were an enemy.
89. The enemy is, not he that injures, but he that wants to.
90. The enmity of one's kinfolk is far worse than that of strangers.
91. Be not suspicious of everyone, but careful and wary.
92. One should accept favors with the expectation of returning them many fold.
93. When conferring a favour, keep your eye on the recipient lest he be a cheat who will requite good with evil.
96. Benevolent is, not he that looks to the return, but he that wills to do good.
102. In everything the fair is right; excess and deficiency please me not.
109. Censorius people are not adapted to friendship.
112. It is characteristic of a divine mind always to think on something beautiful.
118. Dionysius, Bishop of Alexandria, quoted by Eus. *P.E.* XIV 27, 4. (Democritus himself, so they tell us, said) I would rather discover one single demonstration than rule over the Persians. (And that too though his demonstrations are vain and are no demonstrations at all because he starts from an empty principle and an erroneous hypothesis, and does not see the root of the matter and the common necessity of the nature of reality, but considers the observation of vain and random occurrences to be the highest wisdom; so he enthrones Luck as queen of divine things and of

things in general, declaring that all things occur by her command; but he denies that she governs the lives of men, and charges those who worship her with ignorance.) [The fifth paragraph continues:]

119. ——— ——— 5. (He commences his advice by saying) Men have devised the idol Luck as a cloak for their want of understanding. (For Luck naturally contends against counsel, and they say it rules over wisdom with great enmity, or rather they wholly suppress and annihilate wisdom and substitute luck, for wisdom, they say, is not lucky, but they celebrate luck as most wise.) Stob. II 8, 16. Men have devised the idol Luck as a cloak for their lack of counsel. For luck opposes wisdom very little; most of life's tangles a keen and intelligent penetration straightens out.

125. cf. B. 9.

142. Olympiod. *in Plat. Phileb.* 2 p. 242 Stallb. (Why does Socrates so greatly reverence the names of the gods? Is it because tradition has consecrated the proper names to the proper persons and it is unreasonable to change the unchangeable, or is it because the names belong to them by nature according to the argument in the *Cratylus,* or because they also are) vocal images of the gods (as Democritus says)? Hierocl. *in Pyth. c. aur.* 25. (The name of Zeus is a symbol and image in sound of the creative reality. For those who first gave names to things did, in the excellence of their wisdom, like great sculptors in their statues, show forth in the names the powers of the things named.)

145. Plut. *de puer. ed.* 14 p. 9. Language is the shadow of action.

146. ——— *de prof. in virt.* 10 p. 81. (Reason is rooted and nourished within oneself and according to Democritus) it habituates itself to derive its pleasures from itself.

149. Plut. *Animine an corp. aff.* 2 p. 500. (Let us say to ourselves that there are many diseases and passions, sir, which your body produces naturally of itself, and there are also many which attack it from without.) But if you will examine yourself from within you will discover a variegated and well stacked storehouse and treasury of evils, (as Democritus says, not flowing in from without, but having its

own inherent, congenital sources produced by a total depravity abundant in passions.)

155. ——— *de commun. not.* 39 p. 1079 e. (Again, therefore, see how he [Chrysippus] replied to Democritus who inquired naturally and wisely:) If a cone is cut by a plane parallel to its base, what must we think of the surfaces of the segments, are they equal or unequal? If they are unequal, the cone will be uneven since it will get step-like incisions or roughnesses. But if they are equal, the segments will be equal and the cone will seem to have the characteristics of a cylinder, for it will be composed of equal, not unequal, circles, which is most absurd.

156. ——— *adv. Colot.* 4 p. 1108 f. ([Colotes] attacks [Democritus] because by saying each thing is no more this than that, he has confused life. But Democritus is so far removed from thinking that each thing is no more this than that, that he has attacked and written many persuasive arguments against the sophist Protagoras who did hold the principle under discussion. Colotes had never become acquainted with these things even in a dream and misunderstood the man's statement in which it is set forth that) Entity exists no more truly than non-entity. (By entity he means body and by non-entity the void, because the void too has a sort of nature and peculiar reality.)

159. ——— *Fragm. de libid. et aegr.* 2. (This seems to be an old law-suit between the body and the soul with respect to the passions. And Democritus putting the blame upon the soul for the misery of the body says:) If the body should bring the soul to trial for all the evils and miseries it has suffered throughout life, and should itself be the judge of the indictment, it would gladly convict the soul because sometimes it destroyed the body through carelessness and broke it by drunkenness, and at other times it shattered and debauched it through lust, just as one might harshly accuse the user of an instrument or vessel which was left in poor condition.

160. Porphyr. *de abst.* IV 21. (The evil, foolish, intemperate, and impious life, Democritus calls) not an evil life but a long extended death.

164. SEXT. *adv. math.* VII 116. (The ancient . . . opinion that like can know like . . . (117) But Democritus states the argument with reference both to living and to inanimate objects:) Animals—he says—herd together with those of the same species, as pigeons with pigeons and cranes with cranes, and so on with the other irrational creatures also. It is the same with inanimate things as well, as can be seen in the case of seeds being sifted and of pebbles on the sea shore; for in the first case the whirling of the sieve separates out and heaps lentils with lentils and barley with barley and wheat with wheat, and in the second case the motion of the waves pushes the long stones into the same place with the long stones and the round with the round, as if the similarity of things in these cases possessed a sort of attractive power. (However, so Democritus says.) cf. A. 128.

165. ——— VII 265. (Democritus whose voice has been compared to the voice of God says) the following things about everything [opening phrase of the *Lesser Cosmology?*] (and attempted to define the concept [of humanity] but could do no more than make the clumsy assertion:) Man is what we all know. Cic. *Ac. pr.* II 23, 73. (Why should I speak of Democritus? Whom can we compare with him not only for greatness of genius, but also of spirit? He who dared to begin) I speak these things about everything. (His statement confesses to no exception, for what can there be in addition to "everything." . . . Moreover, he does not agree with us who do not deny truth exists, although we deny it can be perceived. He flatly denies truth exists and holds that the senses are not dim but "blind," for that is what he calls them.) Arist. *de partt. anim.* A 1. 640 b 29. (If each of the animals and their members exist by shape and colour, Democritus was correct, for so he seems to have believed. At any rate he says it is clear to everyone what sort of shape man is, since he is known by his shape and colour. And yet a corpse has the same shape, but it is not therefore a man.)

166. ——— IX 19. (Democritus asserts that) certain phantoms approach men, (some of which are productive of good, others of evil. Hence he prays) to meet propitious phantoms.

(Although not indestructible these phantoms are hard to destroy and they are great and marvellous for they predict the future experience of men by being both seen and heard. For this reason the ancients seized upon the appearance of these things and considered it a god, as if God whose nature is indestructible were nothing else except these.)

172. Stobaeus [1] From the very things from which our goods come we sometimes get evils, yet we can avoid these evils. For instance, deep water is useful for many things, and again it is evil, for there is danger of drowning. So a means was found—learning to swim.

173. Evils for man spring out of goods when one does not know how to guide and bear them easily. It is not right to reckon these among evils but among goods, and it is possible to use the goods if one will as a defense against the evils.

174. The cheerful man because he is always impelled to just and lawful deeds is happy, vigorous, and free from care, whether waking or dreaming. But whoever thinks naught of right and does not do what he ought, to him all such things are joyless and whatever he remembers brings him fear and self-reproach.

177. Fine talk never covers a mean deed, nor is a good deed marred by slander.

187. It is fitting that men have more regard for the soul than the body, for the soul's perfection corrects the viciousness of the body, but the vigour of the body, without reason, does not make the soul a whit better.

189. It is best for man to pass his life with as much cheerfulness as possible and with as little distress. And this he would do, did he not find his pleasures in mortal affairs.

191. Men attain Cheerfulness through moderation in pleasure and equableness of life. Excess and want are ever alternating and causing great disturbances in the soul. Souls that are shifting from extreme to extreme are neither steadfast nor cheerful. You should, therefore, fix your mind upon what is possible and be content with what you have, giving

[1] The remainder are all from Stobaeus.

little heed to those who are envied and admired, and not allowing your thoughts to dwell upon them. Rather, you should view the lives of the wretched and think of their suffering so that what you now have and possess may seem great and enviable to you, and that it be not your lot, while craving more, to suffer at heart. For he that envies those that have and that are thought happy by other men, and dwells on the thought all the time is compelled to be always trying new ways [of bettering his fortune] and is kept at it by his covetousness, until he does something fatal, forbidden by law. These things you should not seek, but should be content with your lot comparing your own condition with that of them who fare worse. You should take their sufferings to heart and congratulate yourself on faring so much better than they. For if you preserve this frame of mind, you will both live more cheerfully and brush aside not a few of the evils of life—envy, rivalry, and enmity.

194. The great pleasures arise from observing noble deeds.

221. The hope of evil gain is the beginning of ruin.

252. Of all other things, the needs of the city must be considered the most important so that it may be well governed. Unreasonable party strife and personal power must submit to the common good. For a well governed city is the surest regulator. The whole matter is contained in this: When the city is sound everything is sound, but when it is destroyed, everything is destroyed.

THE SOPHISTS

In his inclusion of the theory of "true-born" or objectively valid knowledge in the classical account of a universe explicable in terms of atoms and void, Democritus comes well within the tradition of the science which began in Miletus in "wonder." For if, as Aristotle wrote, (Introductory, p. 53) "for the avoidance of ignorance, men from time to time have been induced to form systems of philosophy . . . . in pursuit of scientific knowledge for the sake of understanding it," these systematic accounts had been enlarged to include man as well as speculation concerning the means by which he knows the cosmos and its processes. But when the great Atomist brings within the scope of the most scientifically formulated philosophy of ancient times an account of "obscure" or "bastard" knowledge, which may be summed up in the proposition, "sweet is by convention," his thought reflects the Sophists' great discovery of subjectivity.[1]

The significance of the emergence in the fifth century B.C. of the problem of subjective experience and its implications transcends the fact of the Sophistic influence upon Democritus and, indeed, goes beyond that of the discovery and its use by the Sophists themselves. The analysis of subjectivity and the consequent tendency of the Sophists to assert the ultimacy of subjective in con-

[1] See below, pp. 226 seq., for earlier suggestions of the problem.

trast to objective judgement in fields as diverse as epistemology, morals and politics marks a turning point in the history of philosophy. The reasons for the redirection of speculation are complex; the central fact, however, which indicates the turning away from the dominant interest in cosmological and physical subjects may be simply put: the most important consequence of Protagoras' theory that "Man is the measure. . . ." (A. A. Protagoras 13, 14, 19, 21a) is precisely the conviction that man, rather than physical or cosmological processes, rightly occupies the center of the speculative stage.

This consequence is evident in the views of the Sophists themselves. For reasons which will shortly be clear, the principal implications of Protagoras' theory, *homo mensura,* are individualism and relativism, and the Sophists, themselves, are understandably implicated in both their teaching and their thought. It is equally evident that to discover, among men who are individualists and who believe in the relativism of knowledge, morality, politics and religion, a factor other than the individuality common to all presents a serious problem. The problem for the student of the Sophists is complicated by the diversity of their interests and the pedagogical role they played in a Greece in which a tremendous increase of interest in all branches of knowledge is an important condition for the origin of Sophism itself. (P. 230) As we shall see, the Sophists are a diverse group. There are "Sophists of Culture," (A) whose object was to stimulate the minds of the young and to examine a variety of fields of knowledge. To this group belong Protagoras and Gorgias, as well as Anonymus Iamblichi. Protagoras was the first man to organize speech and to lay the foundations of grammar, while Gorgias' principal interests lay in art and rhetoric. There are "Encyclopaedists," the systematizers and classifiers of knowledge and information.[1] To this group belong the polymath, Hippias, the most learned and, by repute, the vainest of the Sophists; and Prodicus, who is said to have written a shallow ethics. There are "Sophists of Eristic," (B) who specialized in debate and disputation and who tended to satisfy the contemporary demand for training in the arts of public life and the law-courts. To this latter group belonged Thrasymachus of Chalcedon, Polus, and Critias.

It is small wonder, in the face of such diversity of personality and interests, that there has been serious doubt that the Sophists comprise a "school" of philosophy. For while Plato, especially in *Apology* and *Protagoras,* leaves the impression that the Sophists were closely allied in their teachings and methods, that these men were in close association, and that the adherents to their beliefs esteemed them not only as individuals but as a close-knit group (*Protagoras,* 314 seq.), so distinguished an historian as Grote[2] maintains "It is impossible . . . to predicate anything concerning doctrines, methods, or tendencies, common and peculiar to all Sophists." The situation is further complicated, first, by the fact that the term "Sophist" was used widely and with little discrimination (Introductory, Aristid. 46 and Prot. A. 5. 349A); and secondly, by the diversity of the applications of their cen-

[1] The "Encyclopaedists" are omitted from this book. The remaining fragments of their work, on the whole, are less important for our purposes than are such of Plato's *Dialogues* as the *Hippias Minor* and *Hippias Major,* which are readily available.

[2] *History of Greece,* Part II, Chapter LXVII, p. 175. Cf. H. Sidgwick, "The Sophists," *Journal of Philology,* Vol. 4, No. 8, pp. 288–307, Vol. 5, No. 9. pp. 66–80

tral doctrines. It is doubtful, indeed, that the Sophists were a "school" similar to the Milesian or a "sect" like the Pythagorean. Still, there is no doubt that, with such exceptions as Critias and Callicles who were influenced by them, they were the first professional teachers of Greece (Introductory, *Apology* 19, *Gorgias* 519B and Aristotle, Gorgias, B. 14) and that, as such, they travelled the length and breadth of Greece from 450 to 350 B.C., training the youth in rhetoric and in the art of disputation and dialectic, instructing in subjects far wider in scope than the traditional music and gymnastic, and subjecting knowledge to new modes of classification and to new techniques for public presentation.

To this somewhat external fact of a common profession, significant for other reasons which will shortly be evident, but a fact which suggests that the Sophists had at least an aim in common, should be added their fundamental interest in man. Of the Sophists of Culture, of the Eristics, or of the Encyclopaedists, diverse as they are in personality and unequal as they are in abilities, the Socrates of Plato's *Apology* could have remarked, as he did of himself and with equal accuracy, that they had "nothing to do with physical speculations," nor with the search "into things under the earth and in heaven."[1] Without too great arbitrariness, we may regard the Sophists as a group with a common profession of teaching; with a common interest in the meaning of human rather than physical nature; and with a tendency to inter-

[1] The phrase "with equal accuracy" should be emphasized, both as regards Socrates and men like Gorgias and Antiphon. There is the evidence of the *Clouds* that Socrates in his youth was interested in physics and metaphysics, and evidence in the fragments of Sophistic writing of a similar attitude. But the dominant interest lay elsewhere.

pret this object of common interest in terms of individualism and relativism.

The importance of their professional status is twofold. In the first place, the payment of large sums to the Sophists (Introductory) was at least the ostensible reason for Plato's contemptuous attitude towards them and this, coupled with the reiterated charge that they taught without sound knowledge, whether of the specific subject or of the meaning of true philosophy (Introductory, Plato's *Laws* 889E, and Aristotle, B. Gorgias, 14), brought upon these assiduous gatherers and classifiers of information the suspicion of moral obliquity. Secondly, we discover precisely in the Sophists' fulfillment of their professional duties as pedagogues the most significant reason for the movement's spectacular rise and success. While it is no doubt true, as Plato urged, that certain individual Sophists either offered little or had little to offer of true wisdom in return for the fees collected; and while it is also probably true that the Eristic Sophists tended, as Aristotle intimates, to argue for the sake of argument without concern for the truth or falsity of their premises, it is essential to remember that large fees were forthcoming principally because the Sophistic method and the subjects taught satisfied a profound need. Accompanying the rise of democratic spirit in Greece (see below, p. 229), was a demand for instruction in arts more immediately applicable than music and gymnastic to the training of men for public life. The need was to teach "prudence," to enable a man "to speak and act for the best in the affairs of state." (Protagoras, A. 5. 318D.)

It is a fair inference, moreover, that the Sophists prospered not only because there was need for instruction in the fields of knowledge in which they were interested, as well as training in the arts of rhetoric and disputation in which they were expert, but also because they fulfilled the task set for them. The "measure of the enemy" is not infrequently the defense raised against him. The "measure" of the Sophists as the "enemy" against whom Socrates and Plato waged philosophical combat is patent in the vigor of the arguments, in the basic character of the problems which Sophism forced its adversaries to examine, and in the philosophical techniques perfected for the solution to those problems. Thus, to speak only of Socrates, it is well to remember that in order to combat Sophistic arguments and rhetoric, the great Athenian perfected dialectic and irony; to oppose the theory of the ultimacy of "appearance" and of "sensation," Socrates bought forth the theory of concepts and of functional definition; to counteract "subjectivity," he laid the grounds for demonstrable and "objective" knowledge in the analysis of human nature, the precise field upon which Sophistic interest centered; and to defeat the claims of moral "relativism," he sought objective ethical principles through the examination of virtue and the virtues. It is profitable, also, to recall that in the reaction to Sophism, philosophy was led upon the path to the Platonic and Aristotelian systems of speculation, each sufficiently comprehensive to include the Sophistic interest in man and in subjectivity, as well as to revive Greek philosophy's original concentration upon ontology and cosmology.

The nerve of Sophistic doctrine itself is Protagoras' *homo mensura* (A.1., 14, 15, 21a; B. Fr.1). While it is true, however, that, as Sextus Empiricus states Protagoras' theory, to make man the criterion of all objects is fundamental both to the theory of the greatest of Sophists and to the developments of Sophistic philosophy, it is nonetheless important to remember that the Sophists were not the first thinkers to investigate problems of perception or sensation (Heraclitus, p. 97 [c]; Empedocles, pp. 142–44 [d]; and Anaxagoras, pp. 154–55 [e]). Nor were the Sophists the first to suggest the relativism of knowledge made explicit by their interest in individualism (Heraclitus, p. 97 [c], as well as Frs. 4, 37, 39, 52, 53–54, 57, 69, 78 and 99; see also, Parmenides, lines 54 seq. and p. 119 [b], as well as the systematic distinction between Truth and Opinions). However, in spite of factors present in Sophism which are also discernible in previous and contemporary Greek political and moral relations and in Greek speculation, it is nonetheless true that Protagoras' contribution is unique: he made the subjective experience not only the ultimate and valid ground for experience and judgement; he made the perceiver's experience the only experience, and the sole possible ground for judgement (A. 21a). As Sextus Empiricus correctly inferred, Protagoras "posits only what appears to each individual, and thus he introduces relativity" (A. 14).

The radical character of Protagoras' inference from the Heraclitean doctrine that everything flows and is the combination of contraries is evident once we revert to the contrast between it and Democritus' theory of knowledge with which we began. Sophism influenced the later Atomism [1] (Sextus Empiricus, A. 15) and certainly such Democritean propositions as "sweet is by convention"

[1] The philosophical relations between Protagoras and Democritus have frequently been misinterpreted in consequence of the tradition that the Sophist was a pupil of the Atomist (A. Protagoras, A. 1 [50]).

(pp. 173 seq., pp. 190 seq., especially Fr. 135 [49]) imply not only nominalism in judgements concerning sensation but subjectivity and relativism of all knowledge got by the senses as well. Still, as has been suggested, Democritus maintains also that there is objective knowledge got without the intermediation of sensory organs and to this knowledge the taint of neither nominalism nor relativism attaches (p. 185, Fr. 105, and pp. 209–10, Fr. 11).

The importance of this contrast between Protagoras' and Democritus' theory of knowledge may scarcely be overemphasized. The Sophist, in reducing all possible knowledge to states of subjective experience, avoids the difficulty which confronts Democritus, who fails to explain how tastes can change if atomic structures remain the same (p. 189, Fr. 132). For this advantage, however, Protagoras pays a penalty: in his reduction of what are ordinarily regarded as "judgements of fact" to "judgements of individual taste," there is a consequent and inevitable implication of individualism and relativism which deprives Sophistic philosophy of the strength inherent in the objectivity which is part of previous Greek speculative tradition. To this tradition, especially in Eleatic rationalism (p. 115, ll. 58 and 60; p. 215, Fr. 146; and p. 185, Fr. 105), Democritus returns in order to account for both subjective experience and truly objective knowledge. But Protagoras departs so decisively from the tradition in which the Parmenidean *Being,* the Pythagorean *Limited,* and the Anaxagorean *Nous* played indispensable roles, that his theory of experience denies the presuppositions of law and constancy implicit in the very nature of the Heraclitean philosophy upon which his own epistemology rests (A.1, B. Fr. 1, and Heraclitus, particularly Frs. 10, 14, 16, 18, 37, 46, 81, 105 and p. 97 [c]).

The importance of this radical departure from the rational tradition in philosophy is evident in the historical evaluation of the Sophists. It might justly be thought that the discovery of "inner experience," the investigations of the implications of subjectivity in morality, politics, law, religion, and theory of knowledge, and the direction of speculation into psychology were sufficient contributions to secure for the Sophists an honored place in the history of speculation. Indeed, their studies in grammar, rhetoric, and lexicography might in themselves have warranted such a place and the germ of later theories in their philosophy should have added lustre to their names. In their speculation are anticipations of the Platonic theory of becoming [1] and of opinion, and the modern hypothesis of the social contract, as well as theories of government in the interest of the stronger and of the value of the individual. The magnitude of their contribution has been diminished by history and it is of value to suggest, if possible, some of the historical reasons for this underestimation.

The basic reasons probably lie neither in the fact that the Sophists were paid teachers nor in the discrete philosophical problems they presented to Socrates and Plato. Behind these somewhat superficial facts are discernible the two significant reasons for the virulence of the opposition. The first is that their professional pedagogy is but one aspect of the breaking down of the traditional and

[1] It may profitably be recalled that Plato was influenced by the Heraclitean philosopher, Cratylus, who is treated as a Sophist in the dialogue, *Cratylus*. The Protagorean influence is evident in *Laws* 716 A, where Plato writes that "God ought to be to us the measure of all things, and not man, as men commonly say. . . ."

conservative Greek way of life during the period of the ascendancy, culmination, and decline of democracy. The second is that in Protagoras' proposition, "Man is the measure . . . ," Socrates and Plato are faced with a possible philosophical ground to fortify the individualism and relativism prevalent in nonphilosophical fields in consequence of the difficulties, governmental and commercial, which arose in the democracy. Indeed, in Gorgias' more complete skepticism (A. B. 3) they face the appalling prospect of the Sophistic use of the very dialectical method perfected by Zeno to establish the truth of Permenides' *Being* (pp. 106 and 121 seq.), now employed to assert that nothing exists.

The issue is not, certainly, solely a speculative one, although the epistemological problem presented by Protagoras and the ontological, epistemological, and linguistic problems presented by Gorgias are sufficient to force Plato to employ his greatest philosophic resources in order to invalidate the Sophists' arguments. Plato and Socrates were fundamentally concerned with the fact that Sophism employed philosophical techniques to supply instruments for the skepticism which means the destruction of philosophy itself. There were, however, moral issues in Sophism for Socrates, and moral and political issues for Plato—who, it will be recalled, believed that the ideal state would be one in which the philosopher is king and the king is philosopher—and these arose directly from the conditions of the times. Sophism reflected these conditions and presented philosophical grounds which tended to justify the breakdown of tradition and the breakdown of the distinction between law and custom. In consequence of the defeat of the Persians at Marathon in the times of Darius, and of the final driving out of the invaders a decade later, there came about in Greece an awakening of political sentiment. Greek youth, eager to participate in politics and in public affairs, sought training in arts best fitted to prepare them for their public tasks. The search brought forth the Sophists and, with the breakdown of the old aristocracy, it became clear that power and position—in a word, success—were within the grasp of any man, however humble his origin, provided that he could secure instruction. The Sophists did supply rhetoric and oratory, as well as subjects. They trained men for the law courts in debate all too often leading to Eristic (B. Eristics).

Sophism, then, is a reflection of the times, and of the controversies and political stresses and strains of the times. In Plato's *Dialogues,* it is the Sophist and the political leaders like Thrasymachus and Callicles whom they produced, who expound theories of power, interest, and individualism in politics; it is Protagoras, the Sophist, who expounds his theory of perception, the virtues and the gods; it is Gorgias, the Sophist, who displays his skepticism of knowledge; and it is Hippias, the Sophist, who in parading his extraordinary erudition, also demonstrates his incapacity to distinguish denotation from connotation. But these figures who appear in Plato's writings and elsewhere are but distillations of the forces which Plato feared in the "beast," the people, who had, in his view, killed Socrates. Controversies concerning the value of various forms of government evidence themselves in Herodotus.[1] The dangers inherent for law and politics and morality in Thrasymachus', Callicles', or Critias' con-

[1] *The History of Herodotus,* III, 80–83.

tentions (B. Eristics, A, B, C.) arise as well in the argument put with even greater brutality by the Athenians to the Melians:[1]

> *Athen:* . . . You know as well as we know that what is just is arrived at in human arguments only when the necessity on both sides is equal, and that the powerful exact what they can, while the weak yield what they must. . . . As to pleas of justice, they (our subjects) think that neither the one nor the other lacks them, but that those who preserve their freedom owe it to their power, and that we do not attack them because we are afraid. . . . As to the kindness of the divine favour, neither do we expect to fall short of you therein. . . . For of the gods we hold the belief, and of men we know, that by a necessity of their nature wherever they have power they always rule. And so in our case since we neither enacted this law nor when it was enacted were the first to use it, but found it in existence and expect to leave it in existence for all time, so we make use of it, well aware that both you and others, if clothed with the same power as we are, would do the same thing. And so with regard to the divine favour, we have good reason not to be afraid that we shall be at a disadvantage.

The seeds of Sophistic philosophy fell on fertile soil. The issues at stake were too important for Plato to examine sophistry coolly. He saw in the teachings the reduction of law to custom and human agreement. (Introductory, *Laws* 889E.) He saw this as anarchy, in contrast to law and objectivity, establishing claims by using philosophy's own weapons for the destruction of what he thought philosophy is. It is small wonder that with the strength of a powerful mind and with his superb control over philosophical instruments, Plato could bring it to pass that history underevaluates Sophism's principal contributions to the knowledge of man and of his psychology.

[1] *Thucydides,* Bk. V, lxxxix–cvi.

INTRODUCTORY [1]

ARISTID., 46. They [2] seem to me not to know either how the very name of philosophy stood with the Greeks and what it signified, in fact absolutely nothing at all about this matter. Didn't Herodotus call Solon a Sophist, and Pythagoras too? And hasn't Androtion named the Seven,—I mean of course the Seven Wise Men,—Sophists; and again called the celebrated Socrates himself a Sophist? And then those who concerned themselves with controversy and those self-styled dialecticians, did not Isocrates call them Sophists but call himself a philosopher, along with the orators and those who are occupied with political management? And don't some of his pupils apply these designations in the same way? Doesn't Lysias call Plato a Sophist, and also Aeschines? One might take the view that he is making an allegation. However, the others, while accusing those others, did not attach the same name to them. Moreover, if it were possible for someone who was making an allegation against Plato to do so by calling him a Sophist, what would anyone call those others? But the name Sophist was, I believe, a fairly general designation, and philosophy could thus be a love of the beautiful and a preoccupation with inquiry. And this is not the present way, but education generally. . . . Plato appears somehow always to vilify the Sophist regularly, and Plato, I really believe, was the one who revolted against the designation. And the reason for this is that he despised the majority. But clearly he also applied this appellation with utmost reverence. The god, at any rate, whom he claims is the wisest and with whom the whole of truth resides, he has called somewhere "a perfect Sophist."

[1] The new translations of the philosophy of the Sophists printed in this edition are the work of Professor Alister Cameron. All passages from Plato are in Benjamin Jowett's translation. The sources of other translations are given in footnotes. The enumeration of the fragments follows that in Diels' *Die Fragmente der Vorsokratiker*.

[2] Translated by A. Cameron. Those translations which are not otherwise acknowledged are the work of Professor Cameron.

Plato, *Soph.* 231D. In the first place, he [the Sophist] was discovered to be a paid hunter after wealth and youth. . . . In the second place, he was a merchant in the goods of the soul. . . . In the third place, he has turned out to be a retailer of the same sort of wares. . . . In the fourth place, he himself manufactured the learned wares which he sold. . . . Fifth . . . he belonged to the fighting class, and was further distinguished as a hero of debate, who professed the Eristic art. . . . The sixth point was doubtful, and yet we at last agreed that he was a purger of souls, who cleared away notions obstructive to knowledge.

Plato, *Apology* 19–20. *Socrates:* As little foundation is there for the report that I am a teacher, and take money; this accusation has no more truth in it than the other. Although, if a man were really able to instruct mankind, to receive money for giving instruction would, in my opinion, be an honour to him. There is Gorgias of Leontium, and Prodicus of Ceos, and Hippias of Elis, who go the round of the cities, and are able to persuade the young men to leave their own citizens by whom they might be taught for nothing, and come to them whom they not only pay, but are thankful if they may be allowed to pay them.

Plato, *Laws* 889E. And they say that politics cooperate with nature, but in a less degree, and have more of art; also that legislation is entirely a work of art, and is based on assumptions which are not true. . . . These people would say that the gods exist not by nature, but by art, and by the laws of states, which are different in different places, according to the agreement of those who make them; and that the honourable is one thing by nature and another thing by law, and that the principles of justice have no existence at all in nature, but that mankind are always disputing about them and altering them; and that the alterations which are made by art and by law have no basis in nature, but are of authority for the moment and at the time at which they are made. . . . These, my friends, are the sayings of wise men, poets and prose writers, which find a way into the minds of youth. They are told by them that the highest right is might, and in this way the young fall into impieties, under the idea that the gods are not such as the law bids them imagine; and hence arise factions, these philosophers inviting them to lead a true life according to nature, that is, to live in real dominion over others, and not in legal subjection to them.

THE SOPHISTS

[A.]

The Sophists of Culture

To that group of professional teachers whose primary interest lay in a variety of fields of human knowledge, including poetry, rhetoric, politics, speech and morality, and in the stimulation of the minds of the young in preparation for public life, belong the two most significant philosophical figures among the Sophists, Protagoras and Gorgias. To it, also, belong the writings of an unknown Sophist, referred to as Anonymus Iamblichi, whose work is of especial interest because of the moral theories put forward and of the light it throws upon speculation which affected Plato.

[A.] Protagoras

Protagoras' *homo mensura* (A. 14, 15, 21a; B.1) is, as was pointed out above, central to the meaning and historical development of Sophism. Protagoras was a native of Abdera. Burnet fixes the date of his birth not later than 432 B.C., and of his death early in the Peloponnesian War (A.1, for Protagoras' life). Protagoras, who wrote a book called *The Truth* (probably identical with *The Throwers*) and one entitled *On the Gods,* was the most successful Sophist. His fees for teaching are described as large; "all men praise him. . . . He is reputed to be the most accomplished of speakers." He is described in Plato's *Protagoras* as having been followed to Athens by a "train of listeners," who assembled to hear "the wisest of all living men."

In Plato's *Protagoras* this philosopher from Abdera tells Hippocrates (A.5, 318D) that one who comes to him "will learn that which he comes to learn. And this is prudence in affairs private as well as public; he will learn to order his own house in the best manner, and he will be able to speak and act for the best in the affairs of state." Protagoras' interests, however, lay not alone in this field of "prudence." He is said to have laid the foundations of grammar and to have studied the parts of speech. Significantly, he carried philosophical inference into the realm of religion (A.1. [51]). Tradition, in fact, has it that Protagoras was persecuted as an atheist, that his treatise was burned, and that, driven from Athens, the great Sophist died on his voyage to Sicily.

Some modern scholars have interpreted Protagoras' central theory that man is the measure of all things to mean that "man" is "generic man" or "humanity." Similarly, some interpretations of Protagoras' remark concerning the existence or nonexistence of the gods imply that the Sophist intended to rule this type of speculation, necessarily incomplete in the scope of a lifetime, from the province of philosophy. It is doubtful that either the interpretation of man or of the problem of the existence of the gods would accord with what Protagoras meant and what was the usual interpretation in ancient times (A.21a, B.1, 4). Protagoras, in accepting the Heraclitean theory of the flux of all things, is led by his own interest in epistemology to interpret perception in terms of motions. Since both the perceiver and the object of perception are in constant motion, perception itself will be a form of motion or perceiving which gives "birth to" qualities and sensation. Moreover, since Protagoras reduces all knowing to perceiving, the consequence is that knowledge is not only relative but is relative to each perceiver at the moment of the conjunction of the motions involved (A.14, B.1).

It would appear probable that Protagoras applied to the problem of the existence or nonexistence of the gods the same theory of relativism. The consequent individualism in the epistemological theory would suggest that Plato's presentation of Protagoras' political and moral theory is authentic (*Protagoras*). Plato's account implies that the Sophist held neither that there is a virtue common to all virtues nor that man is by nature or essentially virtuous. Rather, the implication in Protagoras' theory would appear to be that man is virtuous by necessity, with the implication that if external sanctions were removed, he would revert to the state of pre-compact or natural egoism.

Protagoras

A. Life and Teaching

1. Diog., ix (50 seq.) Protagoras,[1] son of Artemon or, according to Apollodorus and Dinon in the fifth book of his *History of Persia,* of Maeandrius, was born at Abdera (so says Heraclides of Pontus in his treatise *On Laws,* and also that he made laws for Thurii) or, according to Eupolis in his *Flatterers,* at Teos; for the latter says:

Inside we've got Protagoras of Teos.

[1] From the Loeb Classical Library. Reprinted by permission of the President and Fellows of Harvard College.

He and Prodicus of Ceos gave public readings for which fees were charged, and Plato in the *Protagoras* calls Prodicus deep-voiced. Protagoras studied under Democritus. The latter was nicknamed "Wisdom," according to Favorinus in his *Miscellaneous History*.

(51) Protagoras was the first to maintain that there are two sides to every question, opposed to each other, and he even argued in this fashion, being the first to do so. Furthermore he began a work thus: "Man . . . are not." He used to say that soul was nothing apart from the senses, as we learn from Plato in the *Theaetetus*, and that everything is true. In another work he began thus: "As to the gods, I have no means of knowing either that they exist . . . human life." (52) For this introduction to his book the Athenians expelled him; and they burnt his works in the market-place, after sending round a herald to collect them from all who had copies in their possession.

He was the first to exact a fee of a hundred minae and the first to distinguish the tenses of verbs, to emphasize the importance of seizing the right moment, to institute contests in debating, and to teach rival pleaders the tricks of their trade. Furthermore, in his dialectic he neglected the meaning in favour of verbal quibbling, and he was the father of the whole tribe of eristical disputants now so much in evidence; insomuch that Timon too speaks of him as

> Protagoras, all mankind's epitome,
> Cunning, I trow, to war with words.

(53) He too first introduced the method of discussion which is called Socratic. Again, as we learn from Plato in the *Euthydemus*, he was the first to use in discussion the argument of Antisthenes which strives to prove that contradiction is impossible, and the first to point out how to attack and refute any proposition laid down: so Artemidorus the dialectician in his treatise *In Reply to Chrysippus*. He too invented the shoulder-pad on which porters carry their burdens, so we are told by Aristotle in his treatise *On Education;* for he himself had been a porter, says Epicurus somewhere. This

was how he was taken up by Democritus, who saw how skilfully his bundles of wood were tied. (54) He was the first to mark off the parts of discourse into four, namely, wish, question, answer, command; others divide into seven parts, narration, question, answer, command, rehearsal, wish, summoning; these he called the basic forms of speech. . . .

The first of his books he read in public was that *On the Gods,* the introduction to which we quoted above; he read it at Athens in Euripides' house, or, as some say, in Megaclides'; others again make the place the Lyceum and the reader his disciple Archagoras, Theodotus's son, who gave him the son of Polyzelus, one of the four hundred; Aristotle, however, says it was Euathlus.

(55) . . . Philochorus says that, when he was on a voyage to Sicily, his ship went down, and that Euripides hints at this in his *Ixion*. (56) According to some his death occurred, when he was on a journey, at nearly ninety years of age, though Apollodorus makes his age seventy, assigns forty years for his career as a Sophist, and puts his *floruit* in the 84th Olympiad [444–441 B. C.]. . . .

5. Plato, *Protag*. 317B. . . . I take an entirely opposite course, and acknowledge myself to be a Sophist and instructor of mankind; . . . 317C. And I have been now many years in the profession—for all my years when added up are many: there is no one here present of whom I might not be the father. . . . 318A. Young man, if you associate with me, on the very first day you will return home a better man than you came, and better on the second day than on the first, and better every day than you were on the day before. . . . 318D. If Hippocrates comes to me he will not experience the sort of drudgery with which other Sophists are in the habit of insulting their pupils; who, when they have just escaped from the arts, are taken and driven back into them by these teachers, and made to learn calculation, and astronomy, and geometry, and music (he gave a look at Hippias as he said this); but if he comes to me, he will learn that which he comes to learn. And this is prudence in affairs private as well as public; he will learn to order his own house in the best manner, and he

will be able to speak and act for the best in the affairs of the state. . . . 319A. Do I understand you, I said; and is your meaning that you teach the art of politics, and that you promise to make men good citizens? That, Socrates, is exactly the profession which I make. . . . 349A. Moreover such confidence have you in yourself, that although other Sophists conceal their profession, you proclaim in the face of Hellas that you are a Sophist or teacher of virtue and education, and are the first who demanded pay in return.

6. PLATO, *Protag.* 328B. And therefore I have introduced the following mode of payment:—When a man has been my pupil, if he likes he pays my price, but there is no compulsion; and if he does not like, he has only to go into a temple and take an oath of the value of the instructions, and he pays no more than he declares to be their value.

14. SEXT., *Pyrrh. h.* I 216 seq. Protagoras [1] also holds that "Man is the measure of all things, of existing things that they exist, and of non-existing things that they exist not"; and by "measure" he means the criterion, and by "things" the objects, so that he is virtually asserting that "Man is the criterion of all objects, of those which exist that they exist, and of those which exist not that they exist not." And consequently he posits only what appears to each individual, and thus he introduces relativity.

(217) What he states then is this—that matter is in flux, and as it flows additions are made continuously in the place of the effluxions, and the senses are transformed and altered according to the times of life and to all the other conditions of the bodies. (218) He says also that the "reasons" of all the appearances subsist in matter, so that matter, so far as depends on itself, is capable of being all those things which appear to all. And men, he says, apprehend different things at different times owing to their differing dispositions; for he who is in a natural state apprehends those things subsisting in matter which are able to appear to those in a natural state, and those who are in a non-natural state the things which can appear

[1] From the Loeb Classical Library. Reprinted by permission of the President and Fellows of Harvard College.

to those in a non-natural state. (219) Moreover, precisely the same account applies to the variations due to age, and to the sleeping or waking state, and to each several kind of condition. Thus, according to him, Man becomes the criterion of real existences; for all things that appear to men also exist, and things that appear to no man have no existence either.

We see, then, that he dogmatizes about the fluidity of matter and also about the subsistence therein of the "reasons" of all appearances, these being non-evident matters about which we suspend judgement.

15. SEXT., *adv. Math.* VII 389. One [1] cannot say that every presentation is true, because this refutes itself, as Democritus and Plato taught in opposing Protagoras; for if every presentation is true, the judgement that not every presentation is true, being based on a presentation, will also be true, and thus the judgement that every presentation is true will become false.

16. HERM., *Irris.* 9. But Protagoras draws me to the other side, where he takes his stand, when he maintains: that man is the criterion and decision of things; that those which come under the observation of the senses *are* things, but those which do not do not exist in the forms of being.

19. . . . ARISTOT., *Metaph.* 4. 1007b 18. Again,[2] if all contradictory statements are true of the same subject at the same time, evidently all things will be one. For the same thing will be a trireme, a wall, and a man, if of everything it is possible either to affirm or to deny anything (and this premiss must be accepted by those who share the views of Protagoras). For if any one thinks that the man is not a trireme, evidently he is not a trireme; so that he also *is* a trireme, if, as they say, contradictory statements are both true. Aristot., *Metaph.* 6. 1062b 13. He [Protagoras] said [2] that man is the measure of all things, meaning simply that that which seems to each man also assuredly is. If this is so, it follows that the same thing both is and is not, and is bad and good, and that the contents of all other opposite statements are true, because often a par-

[1] From the Loeb Classical Library. Reprinted by permission of the President and Fellows of Harvard College.

[2] From *The Works of Aristotle Translated into English.* By permission of the Clarendon Press, Oxford.

ticular thing appears beautiful to some and the contrary of beautiful to others, and that which appears to each man is the measure.

21. Aristot., *Rhet.* B 24. 1402a 23. This [1] sort of argument illustrates what is meant by making the worse argument seem the better. Hence people were right in objecting to the training Protagoras undertook to give them. It was a fraud; the probability it handled was not genuine but spurious, and has a place in no art except Rhetoric and Eristic. Steph. Byz. Eudoxus relates that Protagoras made the worse also the better reason and taught his pupils to blame and praise the same man.

21a. Plato, *Theaet.* 166D seq. [Apology of Protagoras] For I declare that the truth is as I have written, and that each of us is a measure of existence and of non-existence. Yet one man may be a thousand times better than another in proportion as different things are and appear to him. And I am far from saying that wisdom and the wise man have no existence; but I say that the wise man is he who makes the evils which appear and are to a man, into goods which are and appear to him. 167B. But as the inferior habit of mind has thoughts of kindred nature, so I conceive that a good mind causes men to have good thoughts; and these which the inexperienced call true, I maintain to be only better, and not truer than others. And, O my dear Socrates, I do not call wise men tadpoles: far from it; I say that they are the physicians of the human body, and the husbandmen of plants—for the husbandmen also take away the evil and disordered sensations of plants, and infuse into them good and healthy sensations—aye and true ones; and the wise and good rhetoricians make the good instead of the evil to seem just to states; for whatever appears to a state to be just and fair, so long as it is regarded as such, is just and fair to it; but the teacher of wisdom causes the good to take the place of the evil, both in appearance and in reality. And in like manner the Sophist who is able to train his pupils in this spirit is a wise man, and deserves to be well paid by them. And so one man is wiser than another; and no

[1] From *The Works of Aristotle Translated into English.* By permission of the Clarendon Press, Oxford.

one thinks falsely, and you, whether you will or not, must endure to be a measure. On these foundations the argument stands firm.

23. PLATO, *Theaet.* 162D. [Protagoras speaks] Good people, young and old, you meet and harangue, and bring in the gods, whose existence or non-existence I banish from writing and speech.

B. Fragments

1. SEXT., *adv. Math.* VII 60. Some,[1] too, have counted Protagoras of Abdera among the company of those philosophers who abolish the criterion, since he asserts that all sense-impressions and opinions are true and that truth is a relative thing inasmuch as everything that has appeared to someone or been opined by someone is at once real in relation to him. Certainly, at the opening of his book *The Down-Throwers* he has proclaimed that "Of all things the measure is man, of existing things that they exist and of non-existing things that they exist not."

PLATO, *Theaet.* 151E–152A. [Socrates and Theaetetus] [Socrates] Well, you have delivered yourself of a very important doctrine about knowledge; it is indeed the opinion of Protagoras, who has another way of expressing it. Man, he says, is the measure of all things, of the existence of things that are, and of the non-existence of things that are not:—You have read him? —— O yes, again and again. —— Does he not say that things are to you such as they appear to you, and to me such as they appear to me, and that you and I are men? . . . the same wind is blowing, and yet one of us may be cold and the other not, or one may be slightly and the other very cold? —— Quite true. —— Now is the wind, regarded not in relation to us but absolutely, cold or not; or are we to say, with Protagoras, that the wind is cold to him who is cold, and not to him who is not? —— I suppose the last. —— Then it must appear so to each of them? —— Yes. —— And 'ap-

[1] From the Loeb Classical Library. Reprinted by permission of the President and Fellows of Harvard College.

pears to him' means the same as 'he perceives.' —— True. —— Then appearing and perceiving coincide in the case of hot and cold, and in similar instances; for things appear, or may be supposed to be, to each one such as he perceives them? (161C) [Socrates] I am charmed with his doctrine, that what appears is to each one, but I wonder that he did not begin his book on Truth with a declaration that a pig or a dog-faced baboon, or some other yet stranger monster which has sensation, is the measure of all things; then he might have shown a magnificent contempt for our opinion of him by informing us at the outset that while we were reverencing him like a God for his wisdom he was no better than a tadpole, not to speak of his fellow-men.

4. Eus., *P. E.* XIV 3, 7. Protagoras got a reputation for being an unbeliever from having been an associate of Democritus. He is said at least to have used this sort of beginning in his work *Concerning the Gods:* "I do not know about the gods. . . ."

Diog., ix 51. "As to the gods, I have no means of knowing either that they exist or that they do not exist. For many are the obstacles that impede knowledge, both the obscurity of the question and the shortness of human life."

[B.] Gorgias

In Gorgias' philosophy, the epistemological interest of Sophism which had been expressed in Protagoras' theory that man is the measure of all things is shown as it is extended to include ontology and communication (B.3). The skepticism which touches upon the existence or non-existence of *Being* is explicable on fairly simple grounds: both Protagoras and Gorgias had been influenced by the Eleatic philosophy and Gorgias applied the dialectic of Zeno to the *Being,* for the defense of which Zeno had perfected the instrument (Zeno, pp. 106 seq.). Gorgias expresses his skepticism, however, not only in the proposition, "Nothing exists," but also adds that if anything exists, it is unknowable by man. In this, he follows Protagoras' lead. He goes beyond his predecessor, however, in the final proposition, which asserts that if anything does exist and may be known, it is inexpressible and incommunicable to one's neighbor.

This extension of the central doctrine of subjectivity to the problems of *Being* is suggested by the title of Gorgias' book, *Concerning Nature* or *Concerning the Non-Existent.* Its extension to language is probably a natural consequence of Gorgias' principal interest in rhetoric and of the requirements of his diplomatic career. A native of Leontium in Sicily, the dates of his birth and death have been suggested as 483–375 B.C. Gorgias first arrived in Athens in 427 B.C., as head of an embassy, to secure aid against Syracuse. Tradition has it that he starved himself to death in Larisa. Something both of Gorgias' temperament and of his profession as a rhetorician are suggested by his willingness to speak on any subject (A.1a) and by "grand and bold style" with which he equipped his pupils and with which he answered all comers (A.19). Gorgias' description of what Socrates calls the "artificer of persuasion" suggests something of the power which the Sophist judged would be within the grasp of one trained in rhetoric.

Gorgias is principally interesting historically because he showed that the dialectical weapons forged for the defense of the theory of *Being* could be used to support an argument which denies the possibility of predicating anything of anything. It is this view that Plato examines with great care in his later dialogues.

Gorgias

A. Life and Teaching

1. Philostr., *V. S.* 19, (1) Sicily,[1] produced Gorgias of Leontini, and we must consider that the art of the Sophists carries back to him as though he were its father. For if we reflect how many additions Aeschylus made to tragedy when he furnished her with her proper costume and the buskin that gave the actor's height, with the types of heroes, with messengers who tell what has happened at home and abroad, and with the conventions as to what must be done both before and behind the scenes, then we find that this is what Gorgias in his turn did for his fellow-craftsmen. (2) For he set an example to the Sophists with his virile and energetic style, his daring and unusual expressions, his inspired impressiveness, and his use of the grand style for great themes; and also with his habit of breaking off his clauses and making sudden transitions, by which devices a speech gains in sweetness and sublimity; and he also clothed his style with poetic words for the sake of ornament and dignity. (3) That he also improvised with the greatest facility I have stated at the beginning of my narrative; and when, already advanced in years, he delivered discourses at Athens, there is nothing surprising in the fact that he won applause from the crowd; but he also, as is well known, enthralled the most illustrious men, not only Critias and Alcibiades, who were both young men, but also Thucydides and Pericles who were by that time well on in years. Agathon also, the tragic poet, whom Comedy calls a clever poet and "lovely in his speech," often imitates Gorgias in his iambics.

(4) Moreover, he played a distinguished part at the religious festivals of the Greeks, and declaimed his *Pythian Oration* from the altar; and for this his statue was dedicated in gold and was set up in the temple of the Pythian god. His

[1] From the Loeb Classical Library. Reprinted by permission of the President and Fellows of Harvard College.

Olympian Oration dealt with a theme of the highest importance to the state. For, seeing that Greece was divided against itself, he came forward as the advocate of reconciliation, and tried to turn their energies against the barbarians and to persuade them not to regard one another's cities as the prize to be won by their arms, but rather the land of the barbarians. . . .

(6) It is said that though Gorgias attained to the age of 108, his body was not weakened by old age, but to the end of his life he was in sound condition, and his senses were the senses of a young man.

1a. Philostr., *V. S.* I (1). Gorgias of Leontini founded the older type of Sophistic in Thessaly. . . . It was Gorgias who founded the art of extempore oratory. For when he appeared in the theatre at Athens he had the courage to say, "Do you propose a theme"; and he was the first to risk this bold announcement, whereby he as good as advertised that he was omniscient and would speak on any subject whatever, trusting to the inspiration of the moment.

4. Diod., xii 53. (1) At this time the Leontini in Sicily, a colony of Chalcis, but also kin of the Athenians, happened to be under attack from the Syracusans. Harassed by the war and in danger of being overwhelmed by the superiority of the Syracusans, they sent an embassy to the Athenians calling upon the people to come to their aid as quickly as possible and rescue their city from danger. (2) The ranking ambassador was Gorgias the orator, distinguished far beyond his fellows by his skill in speech. He was the first inventor of rhetorical arts and so excelled others in the profession of Sophistry that he received a hundred minae from his pupils. (3) He, then, having reached Athens, was presented to the assembly and talked to the Athenians about the alliance, and astonished the Athenians with the strangeness of his diction, for they were naturally clever and had a taste for eloquence. (4) He was, in fact, first to use figures of speech that were unusual and marked by artistry, antitheses, balanced periods, equal measure, uniform endings and such like, which then, because of the strangeness of the effect, won acceptance but

now seem to be mannered and appear to be composed with a repetition and extravagance that is ridiculous. (5) In the end he did persuade the Athenians to enter an alliance with the Leontini and, much admired for his rhetorical art, he returned to Leontini.

19. PLATO, *Meno* 70A–B. O Meno, there was a time when the Thessalians were famous among the other Hellenes only for their riches and their riding; but now, if I am not mistaken, they are equally famous for their wisdom, especially at Larisa, which is the native city of your friend Aristippus. And this is Gorgias' doing; for when he came there, the flower of the Aleuadae, among them your admirer Aristippus, and the other chiefs of the Thessalians, fell in love with his wisdom. And he has taught you the habit of answering questions in a grand and bold style, which becomes those who know, and is the style in which he himself answers all comers; and any Hellene who likes may ask him anything.

B. Fragments

1. ISOCR., 10, 3. For [1] how could one surpass Gorgias, who dared to assert that nothing exists of the things that are, or Zeno, who ventured to prove the same things as possible and again as impossible. 15, 268. The speculations of the ancient Sophists, who maintain, some of them, that the sum of things is made up of infinite elements . . . Parmenides and Melissus, of one; and Gorgias, of none at all.

3. SEXT., *adv. Math.* VII (65). Gorgias [1] of Leontini belonged to the same party as those who abolish the criterion, although he did not adopt the same line of attack as Protagoras. For in his book entitled *Concerning the Non-existent* or *Concerning Nature* he tries to establish successively three main points—firstly, that nothing exists; secondly, that even if anything exists it is inapprehensible by man; thirdly, that even if anything is apprehensible, yet of a surety it is inexpressible and incommunicable to one's neighbour. (66) Now that nothing exists, he argues in the following fashion: If

[1] From the Loeb Classical Library. Reprinted by permission of the President and Fellows of Harvard College.

anything exists, either it is the existent that exists or the non-existent, or both the existent and the non-existent exist. But neither does the existent exist, as he will establish, nor the non-existent, as he will demonstrate, nor both the existent and the non-existent, as he will also make plain. Nothing, therefore, exists. (67) Now the non-existent does not exist. For if the non-existent exists, it will at one and the same time exist and not exist; for in so far as it is conceived as non-existent it will not exist, but in so far as it is non-existent it will again exist. But it is wholly absurd that a thing should both exist and exist not at one and the same time. Therefore the non-existent does not exist. Moreover, if the non-existent exists, the existent will not exist; for these are contrary the one to the other, and if existence is a property of the non-existent, non-existence will be a property of the existent. But it is not the fact that the existent does not exist; neither, then, will the non-existent exist.

(68) Furthermore, the existent does not exist either. For if the existent exists, it is either eternal or created or at once both eternal and created; but, as we shall prove, it is neither eternal nor created nor both; therefore the existent does not exist. For if the existent is eternal (the hypothesis we must take first), it has no beginning; (69) for everything created has some beginning, but the eternal being uncreated had no beginning. And having no beginning it is infinite. And if it is infinite, it is nowhere. For if it is anywhere, that wherein it is is different from it, and thus the existent, being encompassed by something, will no longer be infinite; for that which encompasses is larger than that which is encompassed, whereas nothing is larger than the infinite; so that the infinite is not anywhere. (70) Nor, again, is it encompassed by itself. For, if so, that wherein it is will be identical with that which is therein, and the existent will become two things, place and body (for that wherein it is is place, and that which is therein is body). But this is absurd; so that the existent is not in itself either. Consequently, if the existent is eternal it is infinite, and if it is infinite it is nowhere, and if it is nowhere it does not

exist. So then, if the existent is eternal, it is not even existent at all.

(71) Nor, again, can the existent be created. For if it has been created, it has been created either out of the existent or out of the non-existent. But it has not been created out of the existent; for if it is existent it has not been created but exists already; nor out of the non-existent; for the non-existent cannot create anything because what is creative of anything must of necessity partake of real existence. Neither, then, is the existent created.

(72) In the same way, it is not both together—at once eternal and created; for these are destructive the one of the other, and if the existent is eternal it has not been created, while if it has been created it is not eternal. So then, if the existent is neither eternal nor created nor both at once, the existent will not exist.

(73) Moreover, if it exists, it is either one or many; but, as we shall show, it is neither one nor many; therefore the existent does not exist. For if it is one, it is either a discrete quantity or a continuum or a magnitude or a body. But whichever of these it be, it is not one; but if it be a discrete quantity it will be divided, and if it be a continuum it will be cut in sections; and similarly, if it be conceived as a magnitude it will not be indivisible, while if it is a body it will be threefold, for it will possess length and breadth and depth. But it is absurd to say that the existent is none of these; therefore the existent is not one. Yet neither is it many. (74) For if it is not one, neither is it many; for the many is a sum of the ones, and hence if the one is destroyed the many also are destroyed with it.

Well, then, it is plain from this that neither does the existent exist nor the non-existent exist; (75) and that they do not both exist—both the existent and the non-existent—is easy to prove. For if the non-existent exists and the existent exists, the non-existent will be identical with the existent so far as regards existing; and for this reason neither of them exists. For it is admitted that the non-existent does not exist; and it has been proved that the existent is identical therewith; therefore it too will not exist. (76) And what is more, if the existent is identical with the non-existent, both of them cannot exist; for if the pair of them both exist, there is no identity, and if there is identity, there is no longer a pair. From which it follows that nothing exists; for if neither the existent exists nor the non-existent nor both, and besides these no other alternative is conceived, nothing exists.

(77) In the next place it must be shown that even if anything exists it is unknowable and inconceivable by man. If, says Gorgias, the things thought are not existent, the existent is not thought. And this is logical; for just as, if it is a property of the things thought to be white it would be a property of white things to be thought—so, if it is a property of things thought not to be existent, it will necessarily be a property of things existent not to be thought. (78) Consequently, this is a sound and consistent syllogism—"If the things thought are not existent, the existent is not thought." But the things thought (for we must take them first) are not existent, as we shall establish; therefore, the existent is not thought. And, in fact, that the things thought are not existent is plain; (79) for if the things thought are existent, all the things thought exist, and in the way, too, in which one has thought them. But this is contrary to sense. For if someone thinks of a man flying or of a chariot running over the sea, it does not follow at once that a man is flying or a chariot running over the sea. So that the things thought are not existent. (80) Furthermore, if the things thought are existent, the non-existent things will not be thought. For opposites are properties of opposites, and the non-existent is the opposite of the existent; and because of this, if "to be thought" is a property of the existent, "not to be thought" will most certainly be a property of the non-existent. But this is absurd; for Scylla and Chimaera and many non-existent things are thought. Therefore the existent is not thought. (81) And just as the things seen are called visible because of the fact that they are seen, and the audible termed audible because of the fact that they are heard, and we do not reject the visible things because they are not heard, nor

dismiss the audible things because they are not seen (for each object ought to be judged by its own special sense and not by another),—so also the things thought will exist, even if they should not be viewed by the sight nor heard by the hearing, because they are perceived by their own proper criterion. (82) If, then, a man thinks that a chariot is running over the sea, even if he does not behold it he ought to believe that there exists a chariot running over the sea. But this is absurd; therefore the existent is not thought and apprehended.

(83) And even if it should be apprehended, it is incommunicable to another person. For if the existent things are objects, externally existing, of vision and of hearing and of the senses in general, and of these the visible things are apprehensible by sight and the audible by hearing, and not conversely,—how, in this case, can these things be indicated to another person? (84) For the means by which we indicate is speech, and speech is not the real and existent things; therefore we do not indicate to our neighbours the existent things but speech, which is other than the existing realities. Thus, just as the visible thing will not become audible, and *vice versa,* so too, since the existent subsists externally, it will not become our speech; and not being speech it will not be made clear to another person.

(85) Speech, moreover, as he asserts, is formed from the impressions caused by external objects, that is to say the sensibles; for from the occurrence of flavour there is produced in us the speech uttered respecting this quality, and by the incidence of colour speech respecting colour. And if this be so, it is not speech that serves to reveal the external object, but the external object that proves to be explanatory of speech. (86) Moreover, it is not possible to assert that speech subsists in the same fashion as the visible and audible things, so that the subsisting and existent things can be indicated by it as by a thing subsisting and existent. For, says he, even if speech subsists, yet it differs from the rest of subsisting things, and the visible bodies differ very greatly from spoken words; for the visible object is perceptible by one sense-organ and speech by another. Therefore speech does not manifest most of the

subsisting things, just as they themselves do not make plain one another's nature.

(87) Such, then, being the difficulties raised by Gorgias, if we go by them the criterion of truth is swept away; for there can be no criterion of that which neither exists nor can be known nor is naturally capable of being explained to another person.

4. PLATO, *Meno* 76A seq. [Meno and Socrates] And now, Socrates, what is colour? —— You are outrageous, Meno, in thus plaguing a poor old man to give you an answer, when you will not take the trouble of remembering what is Gorgias' definition of virtue. —— 76C. Would you like me to answer you after the manner of Gorgias, which is familiar to you? —— I should like nothing better. —— Do not he and you and Empedocles say that there are certain effluences of existence? —— Certainly. —— And passages into which and through which the effluences pass? —— Exactly. —— And some of the effluences fit into the passages, and some of them are too small or too large? —— True. —— And there is such a thing as sight? —— Yes. —— And now, as Pindar says, 'read my meaning':—colour is an effluence of form, commensurate with sight, and palpable to sense. —— That, Socrates, appears to me to be an admirable answer. —— Why, yes, because it happens to be one which you have been in the habit of hearing: and your wit will have discovered, I suspect, that you may explain in the same way the nature of sound and smell, and of many other similar phenomena. —— Quite true. —— The answer, Meno, was in the orthodox solemn vein.

6. PLANUD., *ad Hermog.* V 548. . . . (He [Gorgias] is praising those Athenians who had been distinguished for bravery in battle.)

What did these men not have that men should? And what had they that men should not? May I be empowered to say what I will and will what I should, thus hiding from heaven's retribution and escaping man's ill-will? For these men were possessed of divine virtue but human mortality; in much they preferred gentle fairness to arrogant righteousness, and in much, to the letter of the law, propriety in what is said, believing this to be the most divine and universal law, to speak, to be silent, to do and <to desist> in the right matter at the right moment, and theirs was a twofold training in the necessary things, in mind <and in body> counselling the one, perfecting the other, guardians of those unjustly unfortunate but scourges of those unjustly fortunate, bold towards the common good, agreeable towards the seemly, putting a stop to the unreason <of the body> by the reason of the mind, violent to the violent, restrained to the restrained, without fear to those who have no fear, fearful among the fearful. In witness of this they set up symbols of victory over their enemies, ornaments of Zeus, offerings from themselves, not untried in ingrowing war or lawful loves or armed conflict or gracious peace, reverent towards the gods with justice, pious towards their parents with tendance, just towards their fellow-citizens with equality, righteous towards their friends with fidelity. Thus it is that the longing for them did not die with their death but lives deathless for those not living in bodies which are not deathless.

14. Aristot., *Soph. El.* 34, 183b 36. For the [1] training given by the paid professors of contentious arguments was like the treatment of the matter by Gorgias. For they used to hand out speeches to be learned by heart, some rhetorical, others in the form of question and answer, each side supposing that their arguments on either side generally fall among them. And therefore the teaching they gave their pupils was ready but rough. For they used to suppose that they trained people by imparting to them not the art but its products, as though any one professing that he would impart a form of knowledge to obviate any pain in the feet, were then not to teach a man the art of shoe-making or the sources whence he can acquire anything of the kind, but were to present him with several kinds of shoes of all sorts. . . .

21. Plut., *de Adul. et Am.* 23 p. 64C. For the friend will not, as Gorgias declared, claim service for himself from a

[1] From *The Works of Aristotle Translated into English.* By permission of the Clarendon Press, Oxford.

friend in just matters but himself serve him in many unjust matters as well.

26. PROCL., *in Hes. Opp.* 758. It is not a simple truth which Gorgias said. And he said that being is unknowable if it does not achieve appearance, and appearance is of no consequence if it does not achieve being.

[C.] ANONYMUS IAMBLICHI

In Chapter 20 of Iamblichus' *Protrepticus* appear the writings of an unknown Sophist whose speculations upon the relation of natural virtue to training in virtuous action present clearly the controversy between nature and convention which Eristic Sophistry argued at such length. The theories are referred to "Anonymus Iamblichi" and are generally agreed to date from the end of the fifth century B.C. Not only do they reflect Eristic views, however, but suggest in the author's comments upon the growth of justice, law and society, and upon the relation of specific virtues to good ends, matters which preoccupy Plato and closely parallel the philosophical views enunciated by the great Sophist whose name provides the title to Plato's *Protagoras*.

While the general argument of Anonymus Iamblichi concerns the need for consistent application to and training in virtuous acts to fortify natural capacity, an important section (3.1) raises the fundamental issue of justifying specific virtues only by their relation to "good and useful ends." The writer concludes that the misuse of virtue results in the agent being "utterly bad." The student of moral and political philosophy discovers in these writings equally valuable analyses of the grounds for law and justice. The author denies that obedience to laws is cowardice (6.1) and considers the hypothetical case of a man "tougher than steel in body and soul" who might try to "overreach" all others. He concludes that such a man would not go unscathed (6.2), on the ground that power is consequent to law and justice. Anonymus Iamblichi anticipates Thomas Hobbes' picture of the horrors of "warre," with its lawlessness and fear, and traces to the evils of the lawless state and to "overreaching" the origin of tyranny.

Anonymus Iamblichi

1. (1) Whatever anyone wishes to bring to the highest perfection, whether it be wisdom, courage, eloquence, the whole of virtue or some part of it, can be accomplished from these following: (2) In the first place, there must be the natural capacity, which is a gift of fortune, but in addition a man must become a lover of the things that are beautiful and good, industrious and a precocious learner, passing much time with them. (3) And if even one of these is absent, it is not possible to bring anything to the highest pitch; but when a man has all these, whatever he may cultivate, in this he becomes unsurpassable.

2. (1) In whatever a man wishes to win reputation among men, and to be known for what he is, he must begin this straightaway when young and apply himself consistently throughout, not in different ways at different times. (2) For each of these that has been cultivated for a long time, having been begun early and having grown to completion, wins a secure reputation and renown, because it is then accepted without hesitation and does not incur the ill will of men. . . . (6) Further, if the time given to each action and matter is long, the thing which is being trained also becomes strong in time; but a brief time cannot accomplish this result. (7) And one could learn the art of discourse and having learned it could become no worse than his teacher in a short time; but virtue of any sort is the product of many actions and this it is impossible for any one who has begun late to accomplish

in a short time; but one must be brought up with it and grow up with it, shielded from bad things, both words and habits, but practising and perfecting the other things assiduously and for a long time. . . .

3. (1) Whenever anyone has striven for one of these things and has succeeded in accomplishing and acquiring it, whether it be eloquence, wisdom or strength, he must use it for good and lawful ends. And if anyone shall use the good in his possession for unjust and unlawful ends, this is the worst sort of thing, and it is better for it not to be present at all. (2) And just as he who has any of these things becomes perfectly good by using them for good ends, so he becomes correspondingly utterly bad by using them for wicked ends. (3) Again, he who is reaching for the whole of virtue, must consider from what word or deed he would become best. And the one useful to most would be such. (4) If someone will benefit his neighbors by giving money, he will be compelled to be bad in turn in collecting money. . . . (5) How could anyone, then, not with the distribution of money but indeed in some other way, be a benefactor of men, and this not with evil but with virtue? And still further, how could the recipient retain the gift permanently? (6) This will happen if he defend the laws and justice, for it is this which brings men and cities together and binds them.

4. (1) Moreover, every man must be preeminently master of himself. Such he would certainly be if he should be superior to money—which is the cause of corruption for all—unsparing of his life and soul, being both zealous for just things and pursuing virtue. For in these two things most men are weak. . . .

6. (1) Still further, one must not aim at overreaching others, nor believe that the strength which lies in overreaching is virtue, and obedience to the laws, cowardice. For this is the vilest state of mind and from it arises everything which is opposed to the good things, evil and hurt. . . . (2) If indeed there could be anyone having from the beginning such a nature as this, invulnerable in body, without sickness or suffering, a tremendous man tougher than steel in body and

soul, perhaps one would have believed that the strength which lies in overreaching others would suffice for such a person (on the theory that such a man without knuckling under to the law could remain unscathed). He is, of course, not right in his supposition. (3) For even if there should be such a person (as there could not), if he were an ally of the laws and justices, strengthening them and using his strength for them and the things serviceable to them, in this way such a man would survive, otherwise he could not keep his ground. (4) For, evidently, all men become hostile to a person of this nature because of their own law-abiding, and the mass either by skill or power would be too much for and prevail over such a man. (5) Thus it appears that even power itself, that is to say real power, survives through the law and because of justice.

7. . . . (12) And tyranny, too, so great an evil as it is, comes from nothing but lawlessness. And some men believe—that is, those who reason falsely—that a tyrant is produced by some other cause and that men are deprived of their freedom without their being responsible, but because they have been forced by the tyrant in power. And their reckoning is wrong in this. (13) For whoever thinks a king or a tyrant arises from anything but lawlessness and overreaching, is a fool. For whenever everybody has recourse to evil, then this comes about. For it is impossible for men to live without laws and justice. (14) For whenever these two things pass out from the mass, law and justice, then their guardianship and protection retreats into one. For how otherwise could single rule come round to one unless the law which is of service to the many had been thrust out? (15) For it is necessary for this man, who will put down justice and will appropriate law that is common and serviceable to all, to be tougher than steel, if he, being one among many, means to strip these from the mass of men.

[B.]

The Sophists of Eristic

Plato's condemnation of the Sophists in the *Laws* (*Introductory, Laws* 889E) is principally directed against the masters of dialectical disputation who practised Eristic Sophistry. In the course of satisfying the contemporary demand for training in disputation as a means to success in public life and in the law courts, the efforts of these professional teachers not unnaturally came to appeal primarily to men ambitious for material success. The consequence would appear to have been an increased preference for teaching verbal tricks rather than insistence upon soundly argued philosophical discourse. The resulting emphasis led to an interest in contest or strife for its own sake rather than in the determination of the truth or falsity of the propositions under examination.

Once having derived from Protagoras' proposition, *homo mensura,* the distinction between art or convention and nature, the Eristics proceeded to make explicit its implications in the fields of religion, law and morality. Plato implies that Sophism tended to reduce the grounds for religious belief, moral practice and legal observance to mere convention.

The specific arguments of Eristic Sophistry are adequately displayed in the political and religious theories attributed to Thrasymachus, Callicles and Critias.

[A.] Thrasymachus

Thrasymachus of Chalcedon was a teacher of rhetoric whose very name is used by Aristotle to illustrate the argument that a line of meanings is derived from names: "And Herodicus said of Thrasymachus, 'You are always *bold in battle.*'" The author of a treatise called μεγάλη τέχνη, Thrasymachus appears in Plato's *Republic* as a boisterous and irrepressible but thoroughly honest advocate of the theory that "justice is in the interest of the stronger." (Fr. 6a and *Republic* 336C.) It is noteworthy that, while Thrasymachus in his scorn of Socrates' irony and subtlety impetuously puts forward an argument which he is shown to be unable to defend, Socrates' superior dialectical skill is directed in *Republic* to the refutation of that very argument, reformulated by Glaucon and Adeimantus.

Thrasymachus

B. The Fragments

6a. Plato, *Rep.* 338C. I [Thrasymachus] proclaim that justice is nothing else than the interest of the stronger.

8. Hermias, *d. Plat. Phaedr.* 239. Thrasymachus, in his own speech, said something of this sort, that the gods do not see human matters, for they would not overlook the greatest of all man's goods, justice. For we see that men do not make use of it.

C. Imitation

Plato, *Republic* I. 336B seq. And now I will not have you say that justice is duty or advantage or profit or gain or interest, for this sort of nonsense will not do for me; I must have clearness and accuracy. . . . I proclaim that justice is nothing else than the interest of the stronger. . . . Forms of government differ; there are tyrannies, and there are democracies, and there are aristocracies. . . . And the government is the ruling power in each state. . . . And the different forms of government make laws democratical, aristocratical, tyrannical, with a view to their several interests; and these laws, which are made by them for their own interests, are the justice which they deliver to their subjects, and him who transgresses them they punish as a breaker of the law, and unjust. And that is what I mean when I say that in all states there is the same principle of justice, which is the interest of the government; and as the government must be supposed to have power, the only reasonable conclusion is, that everywhere there is one principle of justice, which is the interest of the stronger.

[B.] Callicles

Callicles of Acharnae presents a subtler form of the Eristic argument concerning law and justice than that attributed to Thrasymachus and, in doing so, emphasizes the distinction drawn by Sophists between convention and nature. Nothing more than may be inferred from Plato's *Gorgias* is known of Callicles and even his argument concerning the methods by which the many weak control the strong individual is better known in its Nietzschean than in its original formulation. Callicles maintains that were the strong individual, shackled by the weak, sufficiently powerful to throw off the conventions of society, his actions would then be "just" according to nature.

Callicles

Plato, *Gorgias* 482E seq. *Callicles:* For the suffering of injustice is not the part of a man, but a slave, who indeed had better die than live; since when he is wronged and trampled upon, he is unable to help himself, or any other about whom he cares. The reason, as I conceive, is that the makers of laws are the majority who are weak; and they make laws and distribute praises and censures with a view to themselves and to their own interests; and they terrify the stronger sort of men, and those who are able to get the better of them, in order that they may not get the better of them; and they say, that dishonesty is shameful and unjust; meaning, by the word injustice, the desire of a man to have more than his neighbours; for knowing their own inferiority, I suspect that they are too glad of equality. And therefore the endeavour to have more than the many, is conventionally said to be shameful and unjust, and is called injustice, whereas nature herself intimates that it is just for the better to have more than the worse, the more powerful than the weaker; and in many ways she shows, among men as well as among animals, and indeed among whole cities and races, that justice consists in the superior ruling over and having more then the inferior. For on what principle of justice did Xerxes invade Hellas, or his father the Scythians? (not to speak of numberless other examples). Nay, but these are the men who act according to nature; yes, by Heaven, and according to the law of nature: not, perhaps, according to that artificial law, which we invent and impose upon our fellows, of whom we take the best and strongest from their youth upwards, and tame them like young lions,—charming them with the sound of the voice, and saying to them, that with equality they must be content, and that the equal is the honourable and the just. But if there were a man who had sufficient force, he would shake off and break through, and escape from all this; he would trample under foot all our formulas and spells and charms, and all our laws which are against nature: the slave would rise in rebellion and be lord over us, and the light of natural justice would shine forth. And this I take to be the sentiment of Pindar, when he says in his poem, that

> 'Law is the king of all, of mortals as well as of immortals;'

this, as he says,

> 'Makes might to be right, doing violence with the highest hand; and as I infer from the deeds of Heracles, for without buying them. . . .'

. . . I do not remember the exact words, but the meaning is, that without buying them, and without their being given to him, he carried off the oxen of Geryon, according to the law of natural right, and that the oxen and other possessions of the weaker and inferior properly belong to the stronger and superior.

[C.] Critias

The subtlety of Callicles' theory of law and justice is paralleled by Critias' attempt to apply the distinction between convention and nature to the field of religion. Protagoras (Protagoras, B.4) had expressed doubt concerning both the existence of the gods and the possibility of securing sound knowledge concerning the problem. Critias' assumptions concerning the origin and nature of religious belief begins with an hypothetical state of war, in which men live without the control of either law or order. The argument proceeds to show that, inasmuch as penal laws for the punishment of discoverable crimes are inadequate to prevent hidden derelictions, a clever man sought to overcome this obstacle by inculcating fear of invisible gods who see all things and who apply divine sanctions. It should be noted that Critias regards this invention as "The truth concealing under words untrue."

Critias' life and career are as interesting to the philosopher as is his theory of religion. He was one of the "Thirty Tyrants" of Athens (and known as the cruelest of the lot), appointed to his office by the Lacedaemonians in 404 B.C., and killed in battle by the returning Democrats. An orator and poet, Critias in his youth had been a pupil of Socrates, and Xenophon, in the *Memorabilia of Socrates,* writes that Socrates' accusers made much of this fact. They asserted that Socrates, in teaching Critias and Alcibiades, had instructed two men unequalled in the evils they had done to the state. It may well be recalled, in estimating Plato's strictures upon the Eristics, that Xenophon remarks of both Critias and Alcibiades that ambition was their very life-blood and that they associated with Socrates not so much to model their lives on his but to perfect themselves in speech and action. Xenophon asserts that Critias and Alcibiades left Socrates when they thought themselves superior to their fellow pupils and concludes that it was solely for political ends that they had associated themselves with him.

Critias

B. The Fragments

9. Stob., III 29, 11. More men are good by training than by nature.

22. Stob., III 37, 15. A worthy character is steadier than the law. For never could an orator pervert it but often he confuses the law this way, that way, and so often brings it to ruin.

25. Sext., *adv. Math.* IX 54 seq. And [1] Critias, one of the Tyrants at Athens, seems to belong to the company of the atheists when he says that the ancient lawgivers invented God as a kind of overseer of the right and wrong actions of men, in order to make sure that nobody injured his neighbours privily through fear of vengeance at the hands of the Gods; and his statement runs thus:—

A time there was when anarchy did rule
The lives of men, which then were like the beasts',
Enslaved to force; nor was there then reward
For good men, nor for wicked punishment.
Next, as I deem, did men establish laws
For punishment, that Justice might be lord
Of all mankind, and Insolence enchain'd;
And whosoe'er did sin was penalized.
Next, as the laws did hold men back from deeds
Of open violence, but still such deeds
Were done in secret,—then, as I maintain,
Some shrewd man first, a man in counsel wise,
Discovered unto men the fear of Gods,
Thereby to frighten sinners should they sin
E'en secretly in deed, or word, or thought.
Hence was it that he brought in Deity,
Telling how God enjoys an endless life,
Hears with his mind and sees, and taketh thought
And heeds things, and his nature is divine,

[1] From the Loeb Classical Library. Reprinted by permission of the President and Fellows of Harvard College.

So that he hearkens to men's every word
And has the power to see men's every act.
E'en if you plan in silence some ill deed,
The Gods will surely mark it; for in them
Wisdom resides. So, speaking words like these,
Most cunning doctrine did he introduce,
The truth concealing under speech untrue.
The place he spoke of as the God's abode
Was that whereby he could affright men most,—
The place from which, he knew, both terrors came
And easements unto men of toilsome life—
To wit the vault above, wherein do dwell
The lightnings, he beheld, and awesome claps
Of thunder, and the starry face of heaven,
Fair-spangled by that cunning craftsman Time,—
Whence, too, the meteor's glowing mass doth speed
And liquid rain descends upon the earth.
Such were the fears wherewith he hedged men round,
And so to God he gave a fitting home,
By this his speech, and in a fitting place,
And thus extinguished lawlessness by laws.

And, after proceeding a little farther, he adds:

Thus first did some man, as I deem, persuade
Men to suppose a race of Gods exists.

49. Pseudodionys, *Ars Rhet.* 6 II 277, 10. For a man, once he is born, nothing but death is sure; while he lives it is certain that he cannot move out of the way of ruin. . . .

Appendix I

Melissus of Samos

The writings of Melissus were directed to the defence and development of the implications of Parmenides' philosophy of *being*. The great Eleatic is said to have been Melissus' teacher. Of Melissus' life little is known except that he was the son of Ithagenes and that his birthplace was Samos. Plutarch, in the *Life of Pericles,* says that Melissus was in command of the Samian fleet which defeated the Athenians.

[a] *The Fragments*

1. If nothing is, how could this be spoken of as though something is? And if anything is, either it has come into being, or else it has always been. If it came into being, it sprung either from being or from not-being; but it is impossible that any such thing should have sprung from not-being (for nothing else that is could have sprung from it, much less pure being).
2. Since then it did not come into being but *is,* it always was and always will be, and has neither beginning nor end, but is infinite. For if it had come into existence it would have had a beginning (for that which once came into existence would have a beginning) and an end (for that which once came into existence would come to an end); if it neither had a beginning nor came to an end, it always was and always will be; it has not beginning or end; but it is impossible that anything which is not the whole should always exist.
3. But as it always exists, so it is necessary also that it be always infinite in magnitude.

4. Nothing which has beginning and end is either eternal or infinite.
5. If it were not one, it would be bounded by something else.
6. And if it is infinite, it is one; for if being were two, both parts could not be infinite, but each would be limited by the other. But being is infinite; there could not be several beings; accordingly being is one.
7. So then the all is eternal and infinite and homogeneous; and it could neither perish nor become greater nor change its arrangement nor suffer pain or distress. If it experienced any of these things it would no longer be one; for if it becomes different, it is necessary that being should not be homogeneous, but that which was before must perish, and that which was not must come into existence. If then the all should become different by a single hair in ten thousand years, it would perish in the whole of time.

And it is impossible for its order to change, for the order existing before does not perish, nor does another which did not exist come into being; and since nothing is added to it or subtracted from it or made different, how could any of the things that are change their order? But if anything became different, its order would already have been changed.

Nor does it suffer pain, for the all could not be pained; it would be impossible for anything suffering pain always to be; nor does it have power equal to the power of what is healthy. It would not be homogeneous if it suffered pain; it would suffer pain whenever anything was added or taken away, and it would no longer be homogeneous. Nor could what is healthy suffer a pang of pain, for both the healthy and *being* would perish, and not-being would come into existence. The same reasoning that applies to pain also applies to distress.

Nor is there any void, for the void is nothing, and that which is nothing could not be.

Nor does it move, for it has nowhere to go to, since it is full; for if there were a void it could go into the void, but since there is no void it has nowhere to go. It could not be rare and dense, for it is not possible for the rare to be as full as the dense, but the rare is already more empty than the dense.

This is the test of what is full and what is not full: if it has room for anything, or admits anything into it, it is not full; if it does not have room for anything, or admit anything into it, it is full.

If no void exists it must be full; if then it is full it does not move.

8. This argument is the strongest proof that being is one only. And the proofs are as follows: For if a multiplicity of things existed it would be necessary that these things should be just such as I say the one is. For if earth exists, and water and air and iron and gold and fire and the living and the dead and black and white, and everything else which men say is real,—if these things exist and we see and hear them correctly, it is necessary that each thing should be such as we first determined, namely, it should not change its character or become different, but should always be each thing what it is. Now we say that we see and hear and understand correctly; but it seems to us that hot becomes cold and cold hot, that hard becomes soft and soft hard, that the living being dies and life comes from what is not living; and that all these things become different, and what they are is not like what they were. It seems to us that iron, being hard to the touch, wastes away because of rust, and so does gold, and rock, and whatever else seems to be strong, so that we conclude that we do not see or know things that are. And earth and rock arise from water. These things then do not harmonise with each other. Though we said that many things are eternal, and have forms and strength, it seems that they all become different and change their character each time they are seen. Evidently we do not see correctly, nor is the appearance of multiplicity correct; for they would not change their character if they were real, but would remain each thing as it seemed, for nothing is nobler than that which is real. But if they change their character, being perishes and not-being comes into existence. So then if a multiplicity of things exist, it is necessary that they should be such as the one is.

9. If being exists it must be one, and being one it is necessary that it should not itself have body; and if it should have thickness, it would have parts and would no longer be a unity.

10. If being is separated it moves; and that which moves could not exist simultaneously.

[b] Aet. *Plac.* i.3; *Dox.* 285. Melissus of Miletus, son of Ithagenes, became his companion, but he did not preserve in its purity the doctrine that was transmitted to him. For he said in regard to the infinite that the world of those things that appear is limited.

Epiph. *adv. Haer.* iii.12; *Dox.* 590. Melissus of Samos, son of Ithagenes, said that the all is one in kind, but that nothing is fixed in its nature, for all things are potentially destructible.

Aristotle, *Physics* i.3; 186 a 6. Both Melissus and Parmenides argue fallaciously, and they make false assumptions and their reasonings are not logical; but the argument of Melissus is the more wearisome, for it sets no problem, but granted one strange thing, others follow; and there is no difficulty in this. The error in the reasoning of Melissus is plain, for he thinks that if everything which has come into being has a beginning, he can assume that that which has not come into being does not have a beginning. This, then, is strange, that he should think that everything has a beginning except time, and this does not, and that simple generation has no beginning but change alone begins, as though change as a whole did not come into being. Even if the all is a unity, why then should it not move? Why should not the whole be moved even as a part of it which is a unity, namely water, is moved in itself? Then why should there not be change? It is not possible that being should be one in form, but only in its source.

Aristotle, *Soph. Elen.* 6; 164 b 35. Or again, as Melissus assumes in his argument that generation and having a beginning are the same thing, or that that which is generated from equals has the same size. The two statements, that what is generated has a beginning, and that what has a beginning is generated, he deems equivalent, so that the generated and the limited are both the same in that they have each a beginning. Because what is generated has a beginning, he postulates that what has a beginning is generated, as though both that which is generated and that which is finite were the same in having a beginning.